MW01067741

Voices of Native American Educators

4 . 160
9 . 80
35 85

Voices of Native American Educators

Integrating History, Culture, and Language to Improve Learning Outcomes for Native American Students

Edited by Sheila T. Gregory

LEXINGTON BOOKS
Lanham • Boulder • New York • Toronto • Plymouth, UK

Published by Lexington Books
A wholly owned subsidiary of The Rowman & Littlefield Publishing Group, Inc.
4501 Forbes Boulevard, Suite 200, Lanham, Maryland 20706
www.rowman.com

10 Thornbury Road, Plymouth PL6 7PP, United Kingdom

Copyright © 2012 by Lexington Books
First paperback edition 2013

All rights reserved. No part of this book may be reproduced in any form or by any electronic or mechanical means, including information storage and retrieval systems, without written permission from the publisher, except by a reviewer who may quote passages in a review.

British Library Cataloguing in Publication Information Available

Library of Congress Cataloging-in-Publication Data

The hardback edition of this book was previously cataloged by the Library of Congress as follows:

Library of Congress Cataloging-in-Publication Data Available

ISBN 978-0-7391-7192-9 (cloth : alk. paper)
ISBN 978-0-7391-8347-2 (pbk. : alk. paper)
ISBN 978-0-7391-7193-6 (electronic)

♾™ The paper used in this publication meets the minimum requirements of American National Standard for Information Sciences—Permanence of Paper for Printed Library Materials, ANSI/NISO Z39.48-1992.

Printed in the United States of America

Contents

Dedication

I dedicate this book to my family. My beloved children, Courtney and Anthony Jones, who make every day a gift to be cherished. You are my strength, my inspiration and my greatest accomplishments. I love you more than words can express. I look forward to sharing your dreams and watching you make a positive difference in this world. Stay strong and always protect your mind and heart. To my Mom and Dad, Tenicia and Karl Gregory, who set the bar high, believed in me, encouraged me, and supported me in all of my endeavors. I hope that I will always make you proud. To my big sister, Karin Gregory, and my baby brother, Kurt Gregory. Thank you for your love, support and wisdom. And for Tony, who reminded me what a strong and powerful child of God I really am, even in the face of great adversity.

And in remembrance of Victor Gregory, Rose Rhodes and Elizabeth French. I love you and miss you.

Acknowledgments

Many people contributed their time, knowledge, research and support for this book. Without their talents, this book would not have been possible, so I would like to acknowledge their contributions.

In my doctoral program at the University of Pennsylvania, George Keller, my chair, mentor, and professor introduced me to scholarship. He encouraged me to apply for grants and became one of my greatest cheerleaders. Although he has transitioned from this life, I still feel his kindred spirit.

I grateful to my entire Fielding Graduate University family, but most especially Judy Witt, Gloria Willingham, Michael Suarez, Yolanda Gayol, Lenneal Henderson, Shawn Ginwright, Jenny Edwards, Joyce Germaine-Watts, and Margie Gonzales.

My long-time Clark Atlanta University faculty colleagues and friends, Trevor Turner and Moses Norman, who have always supported me and my work, and helped to create a nurturing departmental environment. Betty Cooke, who has the answers to my numerous, often obscure, questions.

Alecia Watkins, a brilliant doctoral student makes time to help with last minute work. Rollin Guyden and Wil Johnson have assisted me with my technology issues.

My incredibly talented doctoral students and teachers feed my passion and remind me each day why teaching is the second most important life's work in the world, next to being a mother.

My sister-in-laws, Cynthia Sadler and Burma Jones, who I love dearly, have always encouraged and supported me, even when it was not in their best interests to do so.

I have appreciated the encouraging thoughts and prayers from my prayer partner, Gloria Nobles and to my awesome Pastor, Steve Wood, and his beautiful family who I had the pleasure of spending time with during our St. Lucia mission trip earlier this year. To all of my small church group members, Bible study partners, and to my entire Mt. Pisgah United Methodist Church Family: thank you for your prayers and support.

My dearest friends called to check in on me when I dropped off the face of the earth, cooked me dinner when I did not make time to eat, strong-armed me into going for walks to stretch my legs, increase circulation, and simply clear my head. Senita Birbal, Angelica and Wayne White, and Debra Smith, thank you for helping me stay centered, focused, and mindful of what really matters in life; God, your own health, heart, mind, and your family and friends.

Again, I acknowledge my supportive family, Karl, Tenicia, Karin and Kurt.

To all of our contributors who have graciously shared their work in this book; to Sandy Dixon, who was critical to the development of the books themes and was a key resource, introducing me to those whom I 'needed to know;' and to Tay Goins, who provided essential information, contacts, and important insights; and to Ana Rego, a brilliant young friend who helped me with the index for the book, I give grateful appreciation.

I thank the publishers, Lexington Books, who went above and beyond the call of duty and provided me with an extension when 'life happened.'

And finally, but most importantly, for my children, Courtney now 15 and Anthony 11 years of age, who said way too many times, "I understand mom. Just come when you can." You are my treasures and I promise to keep you at the center of my world where you belong, forever.

Preface

In 1998, while serving as a faculty member in the department of higher education and educational leadership, with the University of Nevada, Las Vegas, I sought out and received two grants. These grants afforded me the opportunity to work in collaboration with the Clark County School District and Las Vegas middle and high schools with the greatest population of Native American Indian students. The first grant I received in 1998 was called the Simulation, Implementation, Transition, and Enhancement (SITE) Grant and the project was entitled, *Styles of Learning and Styles of Teaching: Effective Teaching Strategies for Native American Students.* The second grant I was awarded in 1999 was an Applied Research Initiatives Grant and the project was entitled, *Promoting Academic Achievement among Native American Middle School Students.* Based on the findings of my research, I was able to help non Native teachers understand cultural competence, develop more effective teaching strategies to teach Native students (primarily Paiutes), improve learning outcomes for all students, and reassess the way they require students to demonstrate their learning in the classroom. After leading several teacher in-services and seminars on improving learning outcomes for this group of children, it became clear to me that little research had been written in this area. Most disconcerting to me, however, was that most of the available research on teaching strategies for Native American Indian students were not written by Native scholars. Furthermore, I could not locate any written scholarship by Native scholars which sought to specifically provide tangible teaching strategies to non Native teachers, who teach Native children. With the help Sandy Dixon, Will Moreau Goins, Four Arrows (AKA Don Trent Jacobs), Fielding Graduate University and others, I decided I needed to provide a home for appreciative research written by Native educators for non Native educators who teach Native students.

This edited volume is divided into four sections. The first section, *The Status of Native American Educators and Students*, presents four chapters which combine research studies about the resiliency and self-determination of Native American Indians, voices of women educators, college student's perceptions of retention, and drug use among junior high and high school students. The second section, *Culturally Relevant Pedagogy*, includes three chapters focusing on culturally relevant pedagogy in P-12 education. The third section, *Teaching Models of Cultural Competence and Context*, offers two chapters combining culturally responsive math and building a community of learners. The fourth and final section, *Educational Strategies at the Crossroads*, includes two chapters focusing on the transition from high school to college and closing the mathematics achievement gap.

The first chapter, entitled *American Indian Education: A History of Resilience and Self-Determination*, places a primary focus and concern on the performance of Native students in K-12 school levels, based on the research literature, legislation, and tribal contexts. Vincent Whipple discusses the Indigenous forms of knowledge predating the European presence in the Western Hemisphere, and later, the forced educational practices that were imposed on American Indians through boarding schools and the mission system. He argues that the 20th century brought changed federal dealings with American Indians, leading to enactments of public policies and legislative actions supporting Indian self-determination, which led to tribally-based Native paradigms of teaching and learning as well as formal institutional settings currently under the purview of the *No Child Left Behind Act*. Whipple provides the theoretical approaches which provide explanatory frameworks for understanding American Indian student experiences (Huffman, 2010) and the ongoing effects of colonialism on American Indian communities (Brayboy, 2005). Finally, he discusses the Bureau of Indian Education and public proponent groups, such as the National Indian Education Association who provide an integral system of advocacy, lobbying, and support for developing effective educational policies for Indian students and sound administrative oversight of tribal schools.

Listening to the Voices of Prominent Native American Women: Experiences of Success and Oppression, from Sandra Dixon, investigates the following question: What are the life experiences of prominent Native American women, as related to success and oppression? Her assumption was that prominent Native American women had experiences that included successful and oppressive elements. She interviewed nine prominent Native American women from nine different tribes that were conducted in seven cities and two different states. The prominent Native American women in this study shared stories of life experiences that led to their success and life experiences that they felt were oppressive. While many of these experiences led to success for these prominent Native American women, some experiences were not without perceived oppression. Additionally, the participants offered suggestions to increase Native American women's voices and to encourage self-determination.

In Freda Garnanez's chapter, entitled *The Impact of a College Preparation Training Program and a Student Handbook as a Step toward the Retention of Navajo Students in Higher Education*, she examines the problem of the seeming lack of anticipation about higher education protocol that exists among Navajo college-bound students and its effects on their retention in higher education.

This study was based on the theory that the lack of understanding terminology unique to higher education, affects compliance with higher education protocol that, in turn, affects their retention in higher education. This problem was analyzed from a pre-college perspective using the system dynamics form of systems thinking as approached by Senge, Kleiner, Roberts, Ross, and Smith (1994).

The fourth contribution, *Adolescent Drug Use and its Impact on Learning in Indian Country*, co-authored by Susan Harness, Fred Beauvais, and Kimberly Miller, introduces the Tri-Ethnic Center for Prevention Research (TEC) and its research project that examines illicit drug substance and alcohol use among American Indian youth. It also explores the issues of students' drug and alcohol use and its impacts on the school community, as well as examining the role parents can play in affecting children's decisions with regard to substance use. Funded by the National Institute of Drug Abuse within the National Institutes of Health the study "Drug Use among Young Indians: Epidemiology and Prediction" collected data from over 70,000 American Indian 7th thru 12th graders who attended schools on or near reservations.

The fifth chapter, *Ah neen dush: Harnessing collective wisdom to create culturally relevant science experiences in pre-K classrooms*, was collaborated on by Ann Mogush Mason, Mia Dubosarsky, Gillian Roehrig, Mary Farley, Stephan Carlson, and Barbara Murphy. *Ah neen dush* can roughly be translated as "why?" in Ojibwe and it is a professional development partnership between the White Earth Reservation Head Start program in Northern Minnesota and the University of Minnesota's Department of Curriculum and Instruction. *Ah neen dush* aims to support and mentor teachers as they create engaging environments that weave discovery-based science activities with Ojibwe philosophy and tradition. In this chapter, Mason and her colleagues describes the conceptual framework of the *Ah neen dush* professional development. Building on best practices in early childhood education, they drew on and integrated the theoretical frameworks of culturally relevant pedagogy. The goal was to introduce the processes and concepts of scientific inquiry through a culturally relevant pedagogy that drew from and reflected Ojibwe culture. At the heart of *Ah neen dush* is the goal of enhancing White Earth Head Start students' science experiences through improved teaching practices that are responsive to Ojibwe culture.

In chapter six, *Collapsing the Fear of Mathematics: A Study of the Effects of Navajo Culture on Navajo Student Performance in Mathematics*, Henry Fowler argues that the American schools are in a state of "mediocrity" because of low expectations in math (Nation at Risk Report, 1983, No Child Left Behind Act of 2001, Duncan, 2009). This teacher action research was a quasi-experimental design using qualitative and quantitative data to explore the effects of the Navajo Cultural Component Math Curriculum (NCCMC) on Navajo high school student's math performance and learning experiences. The research was conducted on the Navajo Reservation.

In Carol Rempp's chapter, *Generosity, Fortitude, Respect, Wisdom: Using Popular Culture to Teach Traditional Culture*, she provides an overview of current popular culture texts that can be used to teach both Native and Non-native young adults about traditional culture. The primary goal of this chapter was to demonstrate how to engage students in their learning processes by using content that connects to both Native history and present circumstances of Native people. This chapter will help teachers better understand how they can use the popular culture texts, such as books and movies with Native themes, to engage students while helping them better understand tribal history and culture.

The chapter from Jim Barta and Marilyn Cuch, entitled *When Numbers Dance for Mathematics Students: Culturally Responsive Mathematics Instruction for Our Native Youth,* discusses the systems of education involving Native American children and how they existed long before the forced intervention by outsiders wishing to civilize and improve on native culture. Education from a traditional perspective meant knowing oneself and one's place in the world. This chapter argues that connecting mathematics and the particular cultures of the Native American student can have beneficial effects on their ability to learn mathematics and the way that they value the acquisition of this knowledge (Cajete, 1994). The chapter details efforts to improve mathematics instruction for Native American teachers and their students by infusing relevant cultural and cognitive perspectives in the pedagogy.

In the Kay Fukuda and ku'ualoha ho'omanawanui chapter entitled, *'Olu'olu i ka pä a ke Kaiäulu: Community and Place as a Textbook for Learning,* they explore a place-based cultural project curricular framework that is based on the multiple cultural ecologies of children. This framework guides the work of an after-school program for children and describes the impact the program has upon children's identity development, school engagement, academic achievement, and environmental stewardship. The multiple cultural ecologies approach to culture taken up by PALS (Program for Afterschool Literacy Support) demonstrated the ability to more fully account for children's various strengths and needs, than attention to any one of these approaches alone.

How to Prepare American Indian Youth for the Transition from High School to College, from Jean Ness and Dennis Olson, examines the period of transition from high school to life after high school. They argue that this period of time can be very difficult for American Indian youth and their families, because it can be an uncharted course, full of challenges and changes (Ness & Huisken, 2002). They contend that focusing on the transition years (grades 9-12) is critical in keeping American Indian students engaged in school and motivated to complete high school.

In the final chapter from Judith Hankes, Stacey Skoning, Gerald Fast, Loretta Mason-Williams, John Beam, William Mickelson, and Colleen Merrill, they share recent findings from *Closing the Math Achievement Gap of Native American Students Identified as Learning Disabled Project* (CMAG). CMAG was motivated by the fact that a disproportionate number of Wisconsin Native American children and youth were identified as learning disabled, and received instruction in pull-out special education programs because they underachieved in mathematics. The CMAG Project addressed this problem by preparing special education teachers and regular education inclusion teachers to implement Cognitively Guided Mathematics Instruction and employ culturally responsive teaching methods

In summary, the chapters that are included in this edited volume focus more broadly on Native K-16 students and Native educators. It provides a vivid portrait of best practices for Native American Indian students, as experienced by Native American Indian educators. This book is based primarily on research studies, both quantitative and qualitative, that offers new, practical strategies for teachers to improve the academic performance of Native American students. This Native perspective is important because some research findings have shown that content knowledge of a teacher is not correlated with academic success of Native American students, unless the teacher is able to bridge the gap and make a connection between content and pedagogy in the context of the student's culture. In this edited volume, 'culture' is considered to be constantly evolving, so people who share the same culture, may not always be expected to behave in the same ways. *Voices of Native American Educators: Integrating History, Culture and Language to Improve Learning Outcomes for Native American Indian Students* seeks to fill this enormous gap in the literature by providing a variety of appreciative research on best practices for Native American students, and a voice for Native educators and scholars seeking a better world for their children and future leaders.

American Indian Education: A History of Resilience and Self-Determination

By Vincent Whipple, Ed.D.

The American Indian Education Unit within the California Department of Education (1982) offered the following observation regarding problems American Indian students were faced with in public schools:

> Because of their different culture and value systems, Indian students often have problems identifying with the middle-class values imposed on them in the classroom. For American Indian youth, being Indian is, in itself, no problem; but being an Indian in a non-Indian world frequently can be a problem. (*American Indian Education Handbook*, p. 33)

This cited resource points out that not only is poor academic performance by American Indian students a concern, but also their performance in society. The statement signified the prime tenet of American Indian Education: American Indian students. In Indian Education, a major qualifying component within the field is an overarching concern and culturally-based advocacy for the well-being of Native American students in communal, familial, and educational contexts. Native American history has demonstrated a definitive clash of cultures, philosophies, pedagogies, and worldviews between American Indian communities and the larger non-Indian society. This chapter will examine the salient features of American Indian Education as well as offer a Native perspective into challenges faced by contemporary tribal communities across the United States.

The field of American Indian Education denotes a body of knowledge comprised of a myriad blend of public policy issues, legal considerations, cultural aspects, investigative research, and educational praxis. Further, American Indian Education spans a range of educational levels from Pre-Kindergarten all the way through graduate level university programs. The field also represents both a historical reality and factual experience in the collective and individual lives of American Indians. In this chapter, I will focus on K-12 areas and the multiple meanings manifesting in grass-roots community contexts and professional educational settings to offer an operational and pragmatic view of American Indian Education in general terms. I will further investigate some of the most urgent contemporary issues confronting Indian Country educators and school professionals.

Throughout this chapter, various sets of terms appear in the research literature and will be used interchangeably to denote the same meanings. One of these is the set of reference words comprised of *American Indian, Alaska Native, Native American, Indian*, and *Indigenous*. Although there are numerous writings regarding the meanings, origins, and proper usage of each of these terms, a full discussion around these issues goes beyond the scope of this chapter. In the context of education, this author's preference is for *American Indian*; nonetheless, each term will be utilized according to its cited reference and quoted context. Another set of reference words is composed of *American Indian Education, Indian Education, Native American Education*, and *Indigenous Education*. This author's preference is for *Indian Education* in alignment with the federal government's current and historical usage as applied to its educational practices amongst the tribes of the United States. Again, each of these terms will be used according to its contextual usage as cited.

Also of significance, this chapter will underscore and concentrate on efforts and frameworks of analysis as applied to the Native peoples of the United States. Of particular relevance here, two emergent approaches in regards to the study of Native people require clarification. Huffman (2010) described the first approach as "a 'globalized' perspective and attempt to weave Indigenous peoples around the world together with an emphasis on shared experiences and challenges" (p. xii). This is the *Indigenous* movement. The second approach places emphasis on "the uniqueness of American Indian experiences and challenges" (p. xii). Various definitions of the term 'American Indian' exist; however, most would agree that the phrase refers exclusively to the Native American tribes recognized by the United States federal government.

In regards to who is or is not American Indian, the *No Child Left Behind Act* of 2001 (NCLB) offered this definition relative to educational contexts:

> The term Indian' means an individual who is — (A) a member of an Indian tribe or band, as membership is defined by the tribe or band, including — (i) any tribe or band terminated since 1940; and (ii) any tribe or band recognized by the State in which the tribe or band resides; (B) a descendant, in the first or second degree, of an individual described in subparagraph (A); (C) considered by the Secretary of the Interior to be an Indian for any purpose; (D) an Eskimo, Aleut, or other Alaska Native; or (E) a member of an organized Indian group that received a grant under the Indian Education Act of 1988 as in effect the day preceding the date of enactment of the Improving America's Schools Act of 1994 (NCLB).

Similarly, the Los Angeles Unified School District in California offered the following conceptualization of the term as applied to education:

For the purpose of this program, legislation defines "Indian" as "any individual who is (1) a member (as defined by the Indian tribe, or band) of an Indian tribe, or band, including those Indian tribes, bands, or groups terminated since 1940, and those recognized by the State in which they reside; or (2) considered by the Secretary of the Interior to be an Indian for any purpose; or (3) an Eskimo or Aleut or other Alaskan native; or (4) a member of an organized Indian group that received a grant under the Indian Education Act of 1988 as it was in effect in October 19, 1994." (Los Angeles Unified School District, 2003, para. 2)

The term *American Indian* itself connotes a political identity, and also a distinct racial group entity, shaped by the historic relationships established by the United States federal government with Native groups in formal government-to-government interactions. The term *Indian* appears in various forms in the U.S. Constitution, federal and state legislation, court decisions, executive orders, and congressional laws. A comprehensive study of these documents in relation to definitions of what constitutes an American Indian goes well beyond the scope of this chapter. Nonetheless, a specific terminology defining what is and is not an American Indian is essential to establishing individual eligibility for education benefits at federal, state, and local levels in the United States. The two descriptions described previous for the NCLB Act of 2001 and the Los Angeles Unified School District in California, provide an exemplary foundation for the purposes of this chapter.

Of note here, tribal groups have specific names for themselves in their own languages. For instance, the Navajo Tribe of Arizona refers to itself as *Dineh*, the Navajo tribal word meaning "the People." There are currently 565 federally recognized tribal governments in the United States (Bureau of Indian Affairs, 2011, para. 1). It would be a daunting task to detail the individual challenges each of these tribes faced; instead, this chapter will take a more holistic view of American Indian affairs as a systemic whole. It should also be mentioned that in the 2010 Census, 2.9 million persons indicated their racial identity as American Indian and Alaska Native alone; this equated to a total of 0.9% of the total U.S. population (U.S. Census Bureau, 2011).

What is Indian Education?

The reality of American Indian Education predated European discoveries of new lands in the New World. In his research on American Indian Education, Reyhner (2002) stated:

Before Columbus and the invasion of Europeans, North American Indian education was geared to teaching children how to survive. Social education taught children their responsibilities to their extended family and the group, the clan, band, or tribe. Vocational education taught children about child rearing, home management, farming, hunting, gathering, fishing, and so forth. Each tribe had its own religion that told the children their place in the cosmos through stories and ceremonies. Members of the extended family taught their children by example, and children copied adult activities as they played (p. 2).

The preceding passage described various aspects of traditional Native educational paradigms in cultural and environmental contexts. Such early Native pedagogies were concerned with the intergenerational transmission, societal practice, and retention of indigenous forms of knowledge.

The Mission system (1768-1853) and Boarding school complex (1823-Present) were forced institutional attempts at educational, religious, and ideological forms of dominion over Native peoples (California Missions Timeline, 2010, para. 1; *American Indian Education Handbook*, 1982, p. 21). Trafzer et al (2006) stated:

> Among North American Indians, the boarding school system was a successful failure. The practice of removing Native American children from their homes, families, and communities and forcing them into an educational system designed to assimilate them into American societies both succeeded and failed. Still the American Indian boarding school experience also resulted in many students living dynamic lives that forever changed American history and Native American cultures (p. 1-2).

Trafzer et al equated the boarding school experience with traditional American Indian stories and legends that told of mythic wars between good and evil. These stories recounted tales of heroes and of the epic battles they fought against monsters and malevolent forces. As instructive devices, these traditional stories were instrumental in teaching young people how to, and not to, live and exist in the world. They spoke of essential morality, communal ethics, individual virtues, proper group interactions, and correct intergroup relationships. Although the boarding school experience was at times harsh, American Indian students had been prepared by their culture for the prospective realities of unexpected hardships in life and for the specter of a cruel and unusual world. By referencing these tribal stories, young Native people held a psychological advantage as they knew how to face adversity in its darkest and most malicious forms. The extant survivors of the boarding school system were permanently scarred by the experience, yet their resiliency and will to live, sustained subsequent generations of Native peoples.

Beginning in the 1920s, a changed public mindset emerged relative to American Indians and education. Adams et al (2006) commented:

> The inability to effectively assimilate Indian children forced educators to rethink Indian policy. In 1928, publication of the *Merriam Report*, an investigation of Indian affairs, detailed the poor living conditions of Indian people, attacked the boarding schools and advocated that American Indian children be

taught within their own communities. Consequently, the Bureau of Indian Affairs (BIA) soon replaced boarding schools with day schools built on the reservations, so that Indian children could remain close to home. While the situation for Indian children had improved, they were still forbidden from speaking their languages, and educators continued to emphasize assimilation and "life adjustment" classes as opposed to more rigorous academic and cultural coursework (p. 7).

This period also saw a more systemic shift in National Indian Affairs. In 1934, both the Indian Reorganization Act (IRA) and the Johnson O'Malley (JOM) Act were passed by Congress (Hale, 2002, p. 45; *American Indian Education Handbook*, 1982, p. 75). The IRA allowed for the formation of tribal governments and the beginnings of contemporary political sovereignty, self-rule, and autonomous decision-making for Native communities. The JOM Act facilitated contracting by the Department of Interior with state governments in the provision of social and educational services for American Indians residing within their boundaries.

Beginning in the 1970s and continuing to the present time, the federal government embraced a public policy of self-determination for American Indian peoples in the United States. The National Advisory Council on Indian Education (1992) found:

> The self-determination era was ushered in with the 1970 Message of the President of the United States Transmitting Recommendations for Indian Policy Congress responded with the Indian Education Act in 1972 before it responded with the broader Indian Self-Determination and Education Assistance Act of 1975. The promotion and passage of this legislation fueled arguments that were taking place regarding the role of federal, state, and native governments with respect to education issues (p. 138).

The federal government had begun to reverse itself in terms of the historical patrimony and colonial dominance it had exerted for years over American Indians. In addition to the full establishment of the Bureau of Indian Education, other federal agencies were strengthened by this new legislation, including the Bureau of Indian Affairs and the Indian Health Service. Through the new legislative mandates, Indian Education support programs were created that operated nationwide in Native communities as well as in school districts servicing large populations of American Indian students. Recently, the *No Child Left Behind Act* of 2001 amended these acts under its jurisdiction as Title VII, Indian, Native Hawaiian, and Alaska Native Education. Under Title VII, Part A, Subpart 1, Section 7112, formula grants may be awarded to tribal groups and local educational agencies for the purpose of providing programs to Indian students at elementary and secondary grade levels.

The website Education.com (2011) provided a pragmatic definition of Indian Education as the "formal and non formal process of educating American

Indians to their own and to the broader society" (Glossary of Education, 2011, para. 1). Essentially, Indian Education represents both American societies institutional practice of schooling as well as Native communal traditions of indoctrinating American Indian students into knowledge. Smiley & Sather (2009) defined Indian Education "broadly to include any teaching practice, procedure, curriculum, or teaching guide having to do with educating the children of Native Americans" (p. 2). They further described Indian Education as "schooling in federal, mission, and public schools as well as culturally based education in American Indian and Alaska Native communities" (p. 2); additionally, they specified that "Indian education also refers to culturally based education of Native American children by their parents, relatives, and communities— traditionally and sometimes today in a native language" (p. 2). In their view, Indian Education was comprised of formal teaching pedagogies based in public, government, and historical frameworks and of communal educational practices centered in culturally relevant tribal paradigms.

In their research on educational inclusion, Reinhardt & Maday (2005) stated "these two aspects, the people and the content, tend to be what most people think of when the topic of Indian Education is discussed" (p. 3). In their view, *people* consist of "Native or non-Native, the teacher or the student" (p. 3) and *content* consists of "curriculum . . . topics or themes typically left out of a public school . . . as well as existing content which historically has been biased or inaccurate" (p. 3). Reinhardt & Maday offered an expanded description of Indian Education to additionally include:

> Pedagogies employed by Native American people, both historically and contemporarily, philosophies, values, and worldviews of Native American communities which inform both the intent and the content of education, and the historical and legal aspects of Indian education which give this type of education unique considerations (p. 3).

Indian Education is more than just Indian students, educators, and too often failed curricula; indeed, it is a unique phenomenon with an underlying cultural foundation. Approaches to teaching and learning developed by Native communities create distinct forms of culturally relevant educational practices that pervade current societal praxis and serve to potentially enhance the dominant system of education.

The University of Arizona College of Education (n.d.) stated:

> Formal education for American Indians and Alaska Natives is unique in that it has historically been a federal responsibility. Until very recently, that responsibility was carried out through the forced removal of Indigenous children from their families and communities to federal boarding schools, where punitive discipline and eradication of the native language and culture were explicit curricular and pedagogical emphases. The legacy of that experience has been hugely

disproportionate negative educational outcomes for American Indian and Alaska Native students. This singular socio-historical experience and its impacts define the field of American Indian/Indigenous education. (LRC Position Papers, n.d., para. 6 and 7).

In this view, contemporary Indian Education was rooted in the past, based in a historic calamity against Native peoples and also stemmed from a serious breach of federal trust. Further, dysfunctional governmental public policies, hegemonic teaching practices, and institutional social genocide served to undermine American Indian identity and culture. Collectively, these past experiences have led to the current dire reality manifesting in the poor academic achievement of Indian students.

What are some of the significant issues in Indian Education?

The Indian Nations at Risk Task Force (1991) made a study of the state of American Indian education and offered a report and recommendations for enhancing and improving Native student performance. Four causes of risk to Native nations were identified as:

1) Schools have failed to educate large numbers of Indian students and adults; 2) The language and cultural base of the American Native are rapidly eroding; 3) The diminished lands and natural resources of the American Native are constantly under siege; and 4) Indian self-determination and governance rights are challenged by the changing policies of the administration, Congress, and the justice system. (*Indian Nations at Risk Final Report,* p. iv)

The study gathered information from a number of direct sources, including: Indian educators, leaders of tribes, and parents of Indian students. The Task Force held consultation meetings and collected additional facts from individual first-person testimonials in states with high Native American populations, at school sites with educational leaders, at special sessions of the National Indian Education Association's national conference, and through position papers submitted by Indian Education experts. Among its conclusions, the study surmised that "the most important responsibility of any society is to ensure the health, protection, and education of its young children" (p. 33) and "the responsibility for improvement is shared by all those involved in the education of Native students— public, tribal, and federal school personnel and government officials; parents and students; and community members" (p. 32).

Report number GAO-08-679 was a 2008 document prepared by the United States Government Accountability Office (GAO) examining the accountability efforts of tribal groups in meeting the proficiency standards mandated by the NCLB Act of 2001. The report found:

The *No Child Left Behind Act* (NCLBA) requires states and the Department of
the Interior's Bureau of Indian Education (BIE) to define and determine
whether schools are making adequate yearly progress (AYP) toward meeting
the goal of 100 percent academic proficiency. To address tribes' needs for cultural preservation, NCLBA allows tribal groups to waive all or part of BIE's
definition of AYP and propose an alternative, with technical assistance from
BIE and the Department of Education (p. 2).

While tribes have generally adopted the academic content standards of the state
where the tribe is located, agreements had not been made between 12 out of 23
states and the Bureau of Indian Education. The importance of a tribal community's control over determination of its school system's Academic Yearly Progress amount is significant, as it allows a tribe the potential to more fully incorporate Native cultural dimensions into the creation of its educational content
standards. Although the *No Child Left Behind Act* of 2001 has been widely criticized in American Indian communities, this provision within the body of its legislative text provides the possibility for Native American tribes to have more
input into and control over the education of their children. Nonetheless, as of the
report's creation, only three tribal groups had even initiated the process of formulating their own community-based content standards as allowed under the
NCLB Act.

The National Indian Education Study of 2009 (NIES) examined the nationwide achievement results of representative samples of American Indian/Alaska
Native school children in the fourth and eighth grades. Part I looked at the results of these students on the 2009 National Assessment of Educational Progress
(NAEP) in the areas of reading and mathematics. Some findings for Part I of the
study included:

1) Average reading scores increase since 2007 at grade 8 but show no significant change at grade 4, 2) Performance of AI/AN students in reading sometimes differs from other race/ethnicity groups and by demographic characteristics, 3) Reading scores decrease since 2007 for AI/AN students in one state and
increase in another, 4) Average mathematics scores show no significant change
for AI/AN fourth- and eighth-graders, 5) Performance of AI/AN students in
mathematics sometimes differs from other race/ethnicity groups and by demographic characteristics, 6) AI/AN students in Oklahoma and South Dakota
make gains in mathematics (pp. 1-3).

Part II of the NIES presented information regarding AI/AN student experiences,
including data on family, community, and school environments. Additional findings for Part II revealed:

1) AI/AN students report varying levels of knowledge and exposure to AI/AN
culture, 2) AI/AN students find support at home as well as at school, 3) More

than one-half of AI/AN students attending BIE schools and public schools plan to go to college, 4) Students in BIE schools are more likely to be exposed to cultural themes and activities as part of the curricula, 5) Most AI/AN students receive instruction entirely in English, 6) Teachers of AI/AN students rely on state content standards in planning lessons, 7) Teachers of AI/AN students use a variety of techniques to assess students' progress, 8) Highest proportion of AI/AN teachers is in BIE schools, 9) Students are exposed to AI/AN culture in various ways, 10) Schools communicate with AI/AN families in a variety of ways, 11) Involvement of the AI/AN community in the school is more common in schools with high proportions of AI/AN students. (pp. 1-3)

Although the 2009 NIES also made comparisons of AI/AN student performance from the 2005 and 2007 NIES reports, it made no explanation for the resulting observed differences in reported performance levels by sampled American Indian students. The 2009 NIES indicated a caution in that the assessment tool examined was "not designed to identify the causes of changes or differences in student achievement or characteristics" (p. 7) and that "the many factors that may influence average student achievement scores also change across time and vary according to geographic location" (p. 7). The results, however, do indicate a lower academic achievement for American Indian students in specific academic areas and that the cultural experience of American Indian students in different social and academic environments is a variable experience.

In Huffman's (2010) work on academic success, he decried research of American Indian Education as too focused on the overall under-achievement and poor performance of American Indian students. He argued that research and study should be based in theory and offer some useful explication of presented facts, such as "A *theoretical perspective* can be defined as an intellectual framework containing a basic image of social life and associated assumptions that serve to integrate research findings in order to render meaning and guide explanations" (p. 3).

To Huffman, theory provided an explanatory framework for the observed phenomenon of low American Indian student achievement. He proposed that four existing theories effectively explained the range American Indian student experiences—these were: 1) "cultural discontinuity theory," 2) "structural inequality theory," 3) "interactionalist theory," and 4) "transcultural theory" (p. 12). In his view, theory enabled access to the underlying 'why' and offered sound reasoning for root causes of Indian student performance as opposed to simply relaying dismal numbers and statistics.

Brayboy (2005), likewise, was concerned with explaining the problems of American Indians in educational settings utilizing the application of a theoretical approach. He specifically wanted to privilege a Native American perspective that would "address the complicated relationship between American Indians and the United States federal government and begin to make sense of American Indians' liminality as both racial and legal/political groups and individuals" (p.

427). American Indians thus existed in a nebulous social position, ill-defined both in political and racial terms. Brayboy formulated Tribal Critical Race Theory (TribalCrit) and he summarized its various aspects as follows:

> 1) Colonization is endemic to society; 2) U.S. policies toward Indigenous peoples are rooted in imperialism, White supremacy, and a desire for material gain; 3) Indigenous peoples occupy a liminal space that accounts for both the political and racialized natures of our identities; 4) Indigenous peoples have a desire to obtain and forge tribal sovereignty, tribal autonomy, self-determination, and self-identification; 5) The concepts of culture, knowledge, and power take on new meaning when examined through an Indigenous lens; 6) Governmental policies and educational policies toward Indigenous peoples are intimately linked around the problematic goal of assimilation; 7) Tribal philosophies, beliefs, customs, traditions, and visions for the future are central to understanding the lived realities of Indigenous peoples, but they also illustrate the differences and adaptability among individuals and groups; 8) Stories are not separate from theory; they make up theory and are, therefore, real and legitimate sources of data and ways of being; 9) Theory and practice are connected in deep and explicit ways such that scholars must work towards social change (pp. 429-430).

As an offshoot of Critical Race Theory, Brayboy's TribalCrit approach offered less an explanation of societal problems based on the prevalence of racism, but rather on the unique historical experience of American Indian peoples with the United States based on the detrimental effects of colonialism.

Brayboy (2005) emphasized that American Indian frames of reference were culturally specific theoretical models and he viewed the genre of storytelling as particularly powerful:

> For many Indigenous people, stories serve as the basis for how our communities work. For some Indigenous scholars (and others), theory is not simply an abstract thought or idea that explains overarching structures of societies and communities; theories, through stories and other media, are roadmaps for our communities and reminders of our individual responsibilities to the survival of our communities. These notions of theory, however, conflict with what many in the "academy" consider "good theory" (p. 427).

Brayboy argued that an American Indian perspective was fundamental to truly understanding how Native communities operated. To view storytelling as a theoretical approach required a re-positioning and transformation of scholarship into an ontological structure of existence and being as told through the reality of Native culture and experience.

What is being done?

As mentioned previously, the Bureau of Indian Education (BIE) was established to carry out the federal trust responsibility to American Indians by administering educational programs in tribal communities in the United States. The BIE's (2010) stated mission is:

> To provide quality education opportunities from early childhood through life in accordance with a tribe's needs for cultural and economic well-being, in keeping with the wide diversity of Indian tribes and Alaska Native villages as distinct cultural and governmental entities. Further, the BIE is to manifest consideration of the whole person by taking into account the spiritual, mental, physical, and cultural aspects of the individual within his or her family and tribal or village context (BIE Mission, 2010, para. 1).

This approach supports the education of individuals and communities on a wide range of social levels, authenticates tribal identities, validates individual life experiences, affirms autonomous sovereign nations, and reinforces community social contexts. The BIE holds oversight for 183 schools at the elementary and secondary levels; of these, the BIE is directly accountable for the operations of 59 schools, while 124 of these fall under control of individual tribes (BIE Schools, 2010, para. 1). Additionally, the BIE is responsible for two college level schools.

Public advocacy groups have also emerged, such as the National Indian Education Association (NIEA), the National Congress of American Indians (NCAI), and the California Indian Education Association (CIEA). Each organization arose in response to American Indian community activism and the need for Native policy development in relation to the enhanced governmental support of Indian self-determination and tribal sovereignty. The NIEA organization described itself as:

> The National Indian Education Association is [a] membership based organization committed to increasing educational opportunities and resources for American Indian, Alaska Native, and Native Hawaiian students while protecting our cultural and linguistic traditions. Incorporated in 1970, NIEA is the largest and oldest Indian education organization in the nation and strives to keep Indian Country moving toward educational equity. Governed by a Board of Directors made up of twelve representatives, the NIEA has several committees that work to ensure native educators and students are represented in various educational institutions and forums throughout Indian Country and Washington, D.C. (NIEA, 2009, para. 1 & 2)

NIEA's goal of enhancing equitable opportunities for Native peoples is based in tribal forms of leadership with a community-centered focus. Political lobbying functions at federal, state, and local levels are also performed by American Indian advocacy groups. In a joint policy recommendation to the U.S. Department of Education, both NIEA and NCAI organizations stated:

> Children are our future. The health, well-being and success of Native children are central to tribal sovereignty. Tribal communities, supported by strong tribal governments, are responsible for raising, teaching and caring for children, and Native children in turn form the backbone of future tribal success. Indian nations have the largest stake in improving the education of their citizens. We must prepare them for active and equal participation in the global market. We must prepare them to be citizens in the 21st century. We must prepare them to be positive, involved members of our communities. And, most importantly, we must prepare them to be the future leaders of our governments. There is no more vital resource to the continued existence and integrity of Indian tribes than their children (National Tribal Priorities for Indian Education, 2010, p. 1).

This chapter has returned to the first prime tenet of American Indian Education as stated in this chapter's introduction—Native children. Proliferation of youth and the younger generations are essential to the survival of any family, community, and culture. In this light, the words of Chiago (1981) captured the essence of an inclusive approach to supporting American Indian students:

> Every Indian child is a unique person with most of the same educational needs as other children. Likewise as with other children, Indian children have many of the same educational non-needs. Both the needs and the non-needs should be viewed from a relative perspective. An approach that would be degrading to a non-Indian student should not be considered appropriate for an Indian student. Teachers and administrators need to increase their awareness of issues regarding Indian students if they are to begin to move toward serving the best educational interests of their students (p. 24).

Over time, the education of American Indians has undergone a marked evolution. From forced colonial practices of boarding schools to the current public policy of Indian self-determination, Native peoples have endured and shown marked resiliency against oppression. They have embodied the characters in their mythic tales of epic battles pitting heroes against terrible monsters in contemporary tales of struggle against the monstrous onslaught of such destructive federal policies as assimilation, termination, relocation, and even genocide. American Indian peoples have the current capabilities to effect the necessary changes required for the betterment of their home communities. Should they so choose, the ancient wisdom of their ancestors as well as the traditional knowledge of their tribal elders can be carried on through future generations.

References

Adams, N., Etter, T., & Hernandez, S. (2006). *Relationships, respect and revitalization: grantmaking strategies, a guide for Native American education and philanthropy.* Denver, CO: American Indian College Fund.

American Indian education handbook. (1982). Sacramento, CA: California State Department of Education.

Brayboy, B. (2005). Toward a tribal critical race theory in education. *The Urban Review, 37*(5), 425-446.

Bureau of Indian Affairs. (2011). *Tribal Directory.* Retrieved from the Bureau of Indian Affairs website: www.bia.gov.

Bureau of Indian Education. (2010). *Mission.* Retrieved from the Bureau of Indian Education website: www.bie.edu.

Bureau of Indian Education. (2010). *Schools.* Retrieved from the Bureau of Indian Education website: www.bie.edu.

Bureau of Indian education schools: improving Interior's assistance would help some tribal groups implement academic accountability systems (GAO-08-679). (2002). Washington, DC: United States Government Accountability Office.

California Missions Resource Center. (2010). *California Missions Timeline.* Retrieved from the California Missions Resource Center website: www.missionscalifornia.com/missions_timeline.html.

Chiago, R. (1981). Making education work for the American Indian. *Theory into Practice, 20*(1), 20-25.

Glossary of Education. (2011). *American Indian education.* Retrieved from the website: www.education.com/definition/american-indian-education.

Grigg, W., Moran, R., and Kuang, M. (2010). *National Indian education study 2009 – part I: performance of American Indian and Alaska Native students at grades 4 and 8 on NAEP 2009 reading and mathematics assessments* (NCES 2010–462). Washington DC: National Center for Education Statistics, Institute of Education Sciences, U.S. Department of Education.

Hale, L. (2002). *Native American education: a reference handbook.* Santa Barbara, CA: ABC-CLIO, Inc.

Huffman, T. (2010). *Theoretical perspectives on American Indian education: Taking a new look at academic success and the achievement gap.* Lanham, MD: AltaMira Press.

Indian education: a federal entitlement, 19th annual report. (1992). Washington, DC: National Advisory Council on Indian Education.

Indian nations at risk: an educational strategy for action. (1991). Washington, DC: U.S. Department of Education.

Los Angeles Unified School District. (2003). *Indian Education Program.* Retrieved from the Los Angeles Unified School District website: note-

book.lausd.net/portal/page?_pageid=33,1122775&_dad=ptl&_schema=PTL
_EP

LRC Position Papers. (n.d.). *Position Paper on American Indian/Indigenous Education.* Retrieved from The University of Arizona College of Education website: coe.arizona.edu/tls/lrc_position_papers.

Mead, N., Grigg, W., Moran, R., and Kuang, M. (2010). *National Indian education study 2009 - part II: the educational experiences of American Indian and Alaska Native students in grades 4 and 8* (NCES 2010–463). Washington, DC: National Center for Education Statistics, Institute of Education Sciences, U.S. Department of Education.

National Indian Education Association. (2009). *NIEA Profile.* Retrieved from the NIEA website: www.niea.org/profile.

National tribal priorities for Indian education. (2010). Washington, DC: National Congress of American Indians and National Indian Education Association.

No Child Left Behind Act of 2001. Pub. L. No. 101-110, Title VII, Supbart 5, Section 7151.

Reinhardt, M., & Maday, T. (2005). *Interdisciplinary manual for American Indian inclusion.* Tempe, AZ: Educational Options.

Reyhner, J. (2002). *American Indian/Alaska Native education: an overview.* Flagstaff, AZ: Northern Arizona University.

Smiley, R., & Sather, S. (2009). *Indian education policies in five Northwest Region states* (Issues & Answers Report, REL 2009-No. 081). Washington, DC: U.S. Department of Education, Institute of Education Sciences, National Center for Education Evaluation and Regional Assistance, Regional Educational Laboratory Northwest. Retrieved from www.ies.ed.gov /ncee/ edlabs.

Trafzer, C., Keller, J., & Sisquoc, L. (2006). *Boarding school blues: revisiting American Indian educational experiences.* Lincoln, NE: University of Nebraska Press.

U.S. Census Bureau. (2011). 2010 Census shows America's diversity [Press release]. Retrieved from www.census.gov/newsroom/releases/archives/ 2010_ census/cb11-cn.125.

The Dynamics of Native American Women and their Experiences: Identifying Ideologies and Theories that Help Explain Oppression

By Sandy L. (Kewanhaptewa) Dixon, Ed.D.

Being a Native American woman, I have always had an interest in the experiences of other Native American women. How similar are our experiences in daily life, work, and in opportunity? Over the years, I have met with many Native American sisters all across the United States. We have shared bits and pieces of our stories when attending Native workshops, tribal meetings, in educational settings, working together, or having dinner at a local cultural diner. We have laughed together. We have cried together. We have bonded through our experiences in many ways. Listening to other Native American women retell their life experiences influenced me to further investigate the life experiences of prominent Native American women, as related to success and oppression.

Native Americans have experienced oppression and structural inequality over the past 500 years. As the invaders came to the North American shores in pursuit of freedom of religion, wealth, and land, it was apparent that hierarchical systems accompanied the new world travelers. Two hierarchical systems, which made one of the largest impacts on the Indigenous groups, were patriarchy and colonialism. This review of the literature will focus on ideologies and theories that assist in explaining the experiences of oppression of Native American women by two systems. Upon defining these two systems, I introduce theories that assist in the maintenance of oppression and how they impact daily life, work, and experiences of Native women.

Hierarchical systems are considered a central feature of the social context of Western society (Moane, 1999). Through examination of these systems, domination and subordination theories will assist in describing how gender, class, and minority status are the key elements that lead to oppression of a group.

A hierarchy involves graded ranks marked by differences in power and resources. Inequalities are a feature of hierarchies, in that those near or at the top have more power and resources, while those at the bottom have relatively little. Gender, class, and minority group status are of key importance in influencing positions in the hierarchy and the possibilities of mobilization in societies (Bilton et al., 1996; Moane, 1999).

Miller (1986) argued that a dynamic of inferiority-superiority exists in hierarchical systems. For example, between a teacher and a student, or between an employer and employee, one is over the other. Miller suggested that once a group is defined as inferior, the superior or dominant group judges them to be incapable of performing roles that are valued highly by the dominant group. The dominant group assigns a lesser value role, usually one that provides service. The superior group sees the inferior groups' capacities as innate or natural, thus leading to stereotypes of the subordinates. These stereotypes include, "submissiveness, passivity, docility, dependency, lack of initiative, inability to act, to decide, to think" (Miller, 1986, p. 7). In turn, these stereotypes lead to oppression and structural inequality based on race, class, and gender.

Miller (1986) identified a second dynamic, which is the control by the dominant group of the *cultural outlook*. Here, the dominant group has the most influence on the cultural outlook, and it legitimizes and leads to myths such as biological inferiority of the subordinate group or in the case of women, suggests the "natural" place for women. The dominant eventually define what is normal, and convince themselves and others that "the way things are right and good, are not only for them but especially for the subordinates" (p. 9). They use this control to suppress conflict, since any questioning of the status quo was seen as threatening (Moane, 1999).

A third dynamic rests within the dominant groups' denial of their vulnerabilities and weaknesses in order to preserve the myth of superiority (Miller, 1986). For example, men are discouraged from showing weakness or helplessness, whereas women are encouraged to demonstrate this state in Western society. According to Anderson (1996), European American men, in order to preserve their dominance and continue the legitimacy of their dominance, would use racial difference to discipline women of their class and race.

This discussion so far illustrates the fundamentals of hierarchical systems. Next, a discussion looks at patriarchy and colonialism, which I consider as leading contributors to the oppression of Native American women.

Patriarchy refers to societies characterized by patrilineage (tracing ancestry through the father) and rule of women and younger men by older men through their positions as head of household (Moane, 1999). Walby (1990) referred to patriarchy as a "system of social structures and practices" wherein "every individual man is in a dominant position and every woman is in a subordinate one" (p. 20). Consequently, men are more likely to be favored by power differentials or dominating over women. These power differentials are related to social categories such as class, race, ethnicity, religion, sexual orientation, and other social statuses according to Moane.

In the Western context, or in reference to patriarchy in Western society in the United States, patriarchy can be viewed as a social system that is hierarchical and male dominated. Moane (1999) contends that those who have access to power are most likely to be White and heterosexual. This dominance can be seen in political systems in that the heads of state are usually male. In cabinet offices, for example, less than 10% are women (Seager, 1997). In economic systems, top financial institutions in business are held primarily by men. Religious systems are also male dominated. Within education and health systems, senior public servants and chief executives in education and medical institutions and organizations are predominantly male. Seager suggests even in the world of art, literature and mass media, executives, editors of papers and magazines, owners and directors of publishing houses, and television producers are almost all men.

Systematic differences also occur among children in the power and control that they experience throughout their school years. Percell (1977) identifies these differences as economic (the resources they receive), political (the influence their parents have on the educational process), ecological (where they go to school and with whom), interpersonal (the expectations teachers hold), or bureaucratic (the failure rate as well as a different authority or social relations children experience in the schools they attend).

Conclusively, for over two hundred years, the United Stated has been steered by male leadership who tend to lead from self-centered and self-preservation perspectives (Wilson, 2004). The expression "It's a man's world" points to male-dominated character of society which puts most of the political power in the hands of men or a male-identified system which then gives privilege to a certain group (White-middle-class-males). This group is then used as the standard of comparison that represents the best that society has to offer. Men are the cultural standard for humanity and women are just women (Johnson, 2001). As we see, male identity is woven into every aspect of social life, while women have less prominence. Johnson implies that most high-status occupations are organized around qualities that are culturally associated with masculinity such as aggression, competitiveness, emotional detachment, and control. Men of the dominant group belong to a system of privilege and benefit from this system. Privilege exists when one group has something of value that is denied to others simply because of the groups they belong to rather than because of anything they have done or railed to do. In many European societies the role of the woman was submissive to the Anglicized, European American men, who controlled all matters of importance. This hegemonic system, referred to as a "system of sexual hierarchical relations" by Eisenstein (1981, p. 19), was tied to reproductive functions of women in Western society (p. 14). According to Hurst (2004), once men dominated in areas outside of the family and gained the economic and political resources, women served the "material interests of men by serving as sexual partners, potential laborers, child-bearers, ornaments, and status enhancers" (p. 84).

Native American women did not fit into the classification systems of the European and Christian colonizers. Most Native communities often functioned harmoniously without the distinction of gendered social ranks that Christians expected. According to Ralstin-Lewis (2005), patriarchy left women dependent and vulnerable to male coercion. Many Native American cultures, by contrast, recognized women as autonomous beings: "This equality of gender struck European settlers as off, if not blasphemous" (p. 72).

Ford (1997) suggested that this patriarchal ideology from Europe was an ideological assault on Native Americans. Christian missionaries, schools, and ideology are all aspects of the thought-change process required in conquering a people culturally. Ford identified the major ideas of influence that affected Native Americans:

1. Patrilineal, father-dominated families with women dependent on husbands for maintenance,
2. Private property held in the name of the male head of household,
3. Female chastity and a double sexual standard,
4. An education system that reinforced limited gender roles, that is, women working in the home and men serving as the breadwinners (p. 57).

In a patriarchal society, women are often confined to an inferior status. Wall (1997) provided an example of how the Native American gender roles were modified to "civilize" the Native Americans at boarding schools. Wall noted that missionaries and reformers tried to teach Indian men to farm and women to sew as part of their total assimilation. They also encouraged both sexes to adopt Euro-American moral standards for the purpose of training Native Americans to accept the idea of individual ownership and restructuring the Indian society around patriarchal family units. This was part of the government's plan to launch the policy of 1887, called The General Allotment or Dawes Act. This policy converted tribal lands to individual ownership and was considered a means to bring Native Americans into *mainstream* American society by giving the U.S. President the right to divide reservation lands among individual Indians. However, most of the allotted land was taken by the U. S. government and sold to railroads and settlers. The proceeds were not given to the Native Americans, but held by the government to *educate* and *civilize* the tribes (Wall, 1997, p. 206). The Dawes Act also gave citizenship to Native Americans when they received their allotments. However, the citizenship did not afford equal rights to men and women. Gender roles were based on a European view organized around a patriarchal family unit and independent life. These ideologies were very different from many Native American matrilineal families. The Commissioner of Indian Affairs, Morgan saw the allotment program as a way to transfer Indians from "primitive" matrilineal to "civilized" patrilineal law (Wall, 1997, p. 207).

To further substantiate the impact of patriarchal thought, Johnson (2001) suggested that women are culturally *misidentified* with power, thus it was difficult for women to exercise power in any situation. Women, to have power in relation to men, are vulnerable for the mere fact that power in their hands lacks the cultural legitimacy of men's power. Hurtado (1996) suggested that, "in patriarchal societies all women are oppressed" (p. 24). Wilson (2004) contends that women are not seen as tough enough to be equal due to the male-oriented definition of "leader" and the entrenched and cultural ideals of female- sensitive and warm, self-sacrificing, and nurturing, good wife and mother. Male assertiveness and control continues to be in high demand. Johnson cited that female professors in today's society tell stories of having their authority, expertise, and professional commitment routinely challenged not only by colleagues but by students, men in particular. These Native faculty are few in number. According to the U.S. Department of Education, National Center for Education Statistics, in 2005, American Indians/Alaska Natives accounted for 0.5 percent of faculty in degree-granting institutions (DeVoe & Darling-Churchill 2008) Yet, women are 51% of the United States population and 47% of the labor force (mostly in the low rungs). Sixty percent of women have jobs, but are still responsible for domestic chores and childcare in 4 out of 5 marriages (Wilson, pp. 4-9). In 2006, thirty eight percent of American Indian/Alaska Native families were headed by females and in the same year the percentage of American Indian/Alaska Native female-headed households living in poverty was forty eight percent, higher than the poverty in the total U.S. population (DeVoe & Darling-Churchill, p. 20, 24) This evidence suggest that a patriarchal social system provides limited access to power for Native women. The next hierarchical system that contributes to the oppression of a group is colonialism.

Colonialism, the systematic domination of one territory by another is operated in a patriarchal context. According to Moane (1999), colonialism is gendered processed. She argued that violence, political exclusion, economic exploitation, sexual exploitation, control of culture, and divide and conquer is patterned differently for men and women in the colonial context. Defining colonialism as a Eurocentric paradigm, it is thus defined by Webster (1990) as, "control by one power over a dependent area or people" (p. 261). In this instance, human rights and self-determination are pushed to the side and colonialism is an obstacle to the desired liberty of the oppressed. Churchill (2003) contended that the term *colonialism* has historically been employed to describe a sort of relationship between nations, that is, structural domination and exploitation of any nation or people by another. Thus, indigenous people were often seen as being backward and too small in numbers to warrant the least solidarity in their quest to survive, much less assert independence. The role of colonialism, according to Churchill, is to "permeate trust authority over indigenous nations; the assumption by any nation of such authority over another's affairs and property" (p. 20).

Mohawk (2000) wrote that during the dominant phase of colonialism, European colonizers exercised the direct control of the colonized and destroyed the Native legal and cultural systems. European nations claim that they *owed* the benefits of their superior civilization to those less fortunate. This "obligation" to engage in armed aggression was termed, the "white man's burden" (p. 169).

Mohawk contends that these words gave legal rights to Europeans as the ruling class over everyone else in the world. The White man had rights to all the wealth, because he carried the burden of superior civilization. With this came the notion to solve all the problems of humankind. Whatever was necessary to exercise this right—murder, rape, kidnapping, torture, genocide—could be rationalized under this self-imposed mandate. Native environmental and political activist Winona LaDuke (1999) addressed the colonization of Native American women:

> We, collectively, find that we are often in the role of the prey, to a predator society, whether for sexual discrimination, exploitation, sterilization, absence of control over our bodies, or being the subjects of repressive laws and legislation in which we have no voice. This occurs on an individual level but equally, and more significantly on a societal level. It is also critical to point out at this time, that most matrilineal societies, societies in which governance and decision making are largely controlled by women, have been obliterated from the face of the earth by colonialism, and subsequent industrialism (p. 42).

Colonialism played a significant role in changing the Native society political and economic structures. Unlike other minorities in this country, who politically started with nothing and attempted to become a part of the existing economic and political structure, Native people started with a strong political and thriving economic base. Ralstin-Lewis (2005) suggested that the colonizers sought to transform Native Americans into mirror images of Europeans. During the early 19th century, federal policy demanded that Native women abandon their customary roles as familiar anchors and accept a life of male-dominated households. Prior to colonization Native American women in most tribes held important positions, leading through peaceful and arduous times adding to the industrious, economic communal balance that existed among gendered, tribal responsibilities. Ralstin-Lewis concluded that the effects of colonization disrupted Native American cultures, and "subsequently increased the power of Native men at the expense of women, who not only lost influence in their own domestic sphere but formal voting authority in some tribes as well. Moreover, the influence of Christianity and its redefinition of gender hierarchies, decreased women's autonomy by changing notions of sexual propriety" (pp. 72-73).

Many Native American researchers (Deloria, 1991; Joe & Lonewolf, 1994; Nichols, 2003; Mihesuah, 2003; Wall, 1997) have identified the education of Native Americans as one of the most devastating colonization practices of European-Westernized thought. By 1870, the Office of Indian Affairs devised a universal school system that was designed to change the Indian. Native Americans were expected to leave their cultural values behind in exchange for a *civilized* way of living. The people, usually by force were converted to Christianity, learned to speak English, change dress, and take on the gender roles of Westernized schools. The first reservation boarding school, Carlisle Boarding School in

Pennsylvania, functioned under the philosophy of full and immediate assimilation embodied in the same philosophy as the Dawes Act (Wall, 1997, p. 209). Joe and Lonewolf (1994) stated,

> The erosion of the role and position of Indian women began with missionization and education. Indian girls were forced to go to school to learn to be homemakers or handmaidens for non-Indian families. Others who dared to return to the reservations found themselves alienated until they either had to relearn traditional skills for survival and/or return to the non-Indian world to find work. This loss of values among Indian peoples was accelerated as more and more tribes were forced into paternalistic or wardship position with the federal government. The fabric of many tribal cultures, however, survived because in many instances women of the tribe used whatever means were available to protect their children and their men. Unfortunately, they were no match against the powerful arm of the federal government, an institution that was bent on "civilizing" the Indians. Tribes may have been able to save some elements of their language or their cultural traditions, but these efforts did not stem the tide of other changes, which have resulted in poverty and the loss of psychological well-being (p. 185).

Snipp (2004) suggested that the compulsory boarding schools for Native Americans sought to indoctrinate Indian children with the belief that tribal culture was an "inferior relic of the past and that Euro-American culture was vastly superior and preferable" (p. 356). Indian children were forbidden to wear their traditional attire, eat Native foods, speak their Native language, or practice their religion. Instead, they were issued uniforms, expected to speak English and become Christians.

Gradually, Native Americans who had everything they needed, lost much of what they had to an "advancing alien civilization" (U.S. Commission on Human Rights, 1981, p. 34). Today, colonization still continues in Indian country. Colonization efforts to separate Native people from their culture occurred in the 1940s by the government's efforts to move Native Americans from reservations to large urban settings. This relocation program separated families and saw additional children attend off-reservation boarding schools. Since the 1940s Native Americans have sought self-determination to manage their own affairs through involvement in politics, grassroots movements, and the development of tribal economic platforms to fight the stereotypical belief of being inferior that was established in earlier colonial United States.

Today, Native Americans struggle to keep separate government institutions in order to maintain the control and beliefs of the group. While other minorities seek integration into the larger society, much of Indian society attempts to retain its political and cultural separateness. To understand the impact of colonialism and patriarchy on Native women, a description follows on their roles within Native cultures before these two hierarchical systems influenced gender roles in traditional cultures.

The Role of Native American Women Within Native Cultures

Within many matriarchal tribal communities, Native people understood the power of women *and* the power of corn to be compatible. Corn symbolically represents life and is connected to all living things, including the land. The field (or earth) was and is the domain of all Native women. According to Mihesuah (2003b), Native women did not serve as tribal "leaders" per se. They did, however, control tribal activities by dictating the recipients of crops, declaring leaders, and serving as mothers, advisors, medicine women, midwives, and manufacturers of skins, hides, clothing, and implements. Native women did have religious, political, and economic power, not more then men but equal to them. Tribes were egalitarian, thus neither man nor woman was less important than the other. Women received recognition and compensation often in the form of controlling economic output. Work was never inferior to another's labor because all work was necessary. Women always had support from extended families and clans, which guaranteed a network of female relatives who lent support and companionship. Here, the matrilineal clans within the societies determined one's political alignment. Through clan membership, one received her or his social and political rights. Her or his mother determined a person's clan. For instance, I am a member of the Hopi tribe. My clan is my mother's clan, the Sun Clan. Our maiden name is not our fathers, but our mother's. This acknowledges Hopi lineage and place, which is important in Native matrilineal communities.

Many tribal "religions include a female divine spirit and positioning of women in prominent and respected positions" (Mihesuah, 2003b, p. 42). The Sioux have White Buffalo Calf Woman who gave the Sioux the gift of the pipe. A pipe is sacred and is the gift of truth (Allen, 1986). The earth is also considered female and in many tribes, such as the Okanagan, the earth was once a woman (Klein & Ackerman, 1995; Mihesuah, 2003). The earth is referred to as Mother Earth, because she provides for her people. Mentioned earlier was the power of corn. For Native American tribes such as the Cherokee and Tewa, corn is a prominent female being of the plant order and is the mother of all humanity. The Native American woman is a prominent member of Native life, engaging in cultural roles and practices. Following is a brief description of the responsibilities Eastern Woodland women had in the 1700s, which is reflective of other tribal groups. The Eastern Woodland tribes: Delaware, Iroquois, Creek, Shawnee, Seneca, and Wyandot nations, show a distinction between men's and women's respective places that reflect their conception of both the structure of the universe and the proper interaction given through sacred powers and its part. The women

1. Were the Keepers of the Village and the cultivators;
2. Directed, controlled, and performed the bulk of agriculture labor;
3. Had control of the food supply (Iroquois-Creek Tribes);
4. Had the roles of production: prepared arms and food for military campaigns as well as participated in active duty;
5. When the British negotiated with the tribes, they had to go through the women first; and
6. The Delegations of the Six Nations, Shawnee, Delaware, and Wyandots' women actively lent their support against the Americans during war campaigns (Klein & Ackerman, 1995).

These roles were very different from the cultures that had first contact with the Natives. European American men, through their limited field of vision, viewed Native men as being dependent upon the labor of women (Dowd, 1987; Mihesuah, 2003b). From a European American perspective, Indian men were viewed as lazy because women were seen tending the household and harvesting the fields. European Americans were unaware of the cultural roles and practices in matrilineal societies, and the egalitarian responsibilities Native American women held in the 1700s. Nor did they know that all tribal members had responsibilities tied to spiritual forces that created and sustained their social order and all else. Here, one can see how the superiority and dominating nature of European Western civilization utilized powerful and controlling forces to oppress another group. Amazingly, it was legal and had the blessing of the dominant church of Europe.

Colonialism and patriarchy played a significant role in changing the traditional gender roles of Native American women. Today, women still feel the effects of these ideologies within their tribes by the loss of equal power and control, respect from other Native men, and increasing violence and abuse within tribal communities. Removing women from their lands, homes, and families was an essential factor in depriving them of their personal liberty (Deer, 2010). However, Native American women are major contributors to their tribal communities today. The successful impact Native American women have achieved in tribal communities and other communities-at-large is reviewed in the next section.

Success and Native American Women

Historically, Native American women have been contributors to the survival of their tribal nations. Native American women have held leadership roles such as clan leaders, women society leaders, chiefs, medicine people, and spiritual guides. As a result of colonization and patriarchy, the roles of Native American women were lost due to the destruction of the practices, values, and beliefs of the tribal groups. Mohawk (2005) stated that,

Members of the British military noted that women were often present at peace negotiations. These were considered men's affairs and Indian men did do most of the talking, but there was a definite female presence. Europeans realized that women had a far greater role in Indian society than in white society. In European society of the early-contact years, a woman had no right to property, divorce, or even personal safety from her husband. Indian women of the northeast Woodlands enjoyed all of these. When young English women were captured or otherwise came to join Indian societies, they were treated with respect. Although the English found Indian customs of women's rights peculiar, the Indians might have pointed out that European practices excluding women were in fact impractical and rendered half of the society as marginally productive and deprived society of the wisdom of half its people (p. 18).

The destruction of tribes, which initially began in the 1400s, continues to present day, whereas tribes continue to deal with issues of tradition, change, and challenge. These issues include legal land claims, legislation and court actions, resources and economic issues, education, tribal acknowledgement, gaming and casinos, repatriation, religious sites and rights, sovereignty, assimilation, and identity issues, to name a few (Nichols, 2003; Barreiro & Johnson, 2005). Native American women are at the forefront of fighting such issues. Native American women are gaining and returning to their traditional roles that were once taken away by the colonizers, the U. S. Government, Christianity, and boarding schools (Deloria, 2001; Mihesuah, 2003; Nagel, 1996). An example of Native American women collaborating for their tribe occurred in1925 and 1943: The Menominee Chapter of League of Women Voters helped force the government to abandon the idea of allotting Menominee lands. In 1943, the depletion of the male workforce (because of World War II), threatened the Menominee lumber mill. Again, fifty Menominee women stepped forward and went to work in the mill, and many helped eradicate blister rust in the forest, thus saving the mills precious trees. (LaCourt, 2003, p. 297; www.menominee.nsn.us)

In 1974, Constance Redbird Pinkerton-Uri, a Choctaw/Cherokee physician, launched her own investigation into the forced and coerced sterilization of Native American women upon hearing complaints from women who were sterilized against their will. Uri's investigation led to a study of Indian Health Service records, which gave a mere glimpse into the severity of the problem. In 1978 female members of the American Indian Movement (AIM) established Women of all Red Nations (WARN), after seeing a need for more independent investigations into the sterilization of Native women and other Native women issues in general (Ralstin-Lewis, 2005).

Native American women have taken the role of leadership in elected positions. Lela Kaskalla served as Lieutenant Governor of the Nambe Pueblo in 1995, before serving as Governor from 1996-1997. She is credited with helping to stop anti-tribal legislation in New Mexico (Tedlock, 2004). The Institute of Women's Research Policy reported that as of October 2004, there were 10 Native American women serving in state legislatures in 5 states across the country. Success stories include people like Peggy Flanagan, a member of the White Earth Band of Ojibwe, who was elected to the Minneapolis school board; Lisa J. Billy, a Chickasaw woman elected to the Oklahoma House of Representatives; and Cecilia Fire Thunder, who was the first woman elected president of the Oglala Sioux Tribe ("Report Shows Status," 2004).

Native American women have shown marked growth in business. According to the National Women's Business Council, as of 2002, Native American and Alaska Native women in the U.S. owned 77, 483 privately held firms. On a national basis, 9.3% of Native Americans and Alaska Native women are entrepreneurs, compared to just one in eighteen of all adult women in the United States, giving Native American women and Alaska Native women the highest rate of ownership among the major ethnic groups (Center for Women's Business Research, 2002).

Native activist, Andrea Smith and Luana Ross address the Western notion of tribal sovereignty and Native Women's gender rights. They are committed to supporting tribal nations struggle against the colonizing influence of the United States in order to address violence against women (Ramirez, 2007).

This research suggested that Native American women are recognizing their roles and responsibilities and that these women are impacting many tribal communities. This may suggest that Native American men are being reintroduced to the female role and are recognizing the importance of women in leadership in politics, tribal governments, clans, education, and the overall survival of the tribe. I consider the resurgence of the woman's role a continuous battle for recognition, acceptance, and productivity due to the hierarchical systems of patriarchy and the *new colonizers* who continue to marginalize women of color. There are specific theories that I consider to assist in the maintenance of oppression of Native American women, which influence daily life, work, experiences, and opportunities. The next discussion will identify and define theories presented in the literature.

Theories of Oppression That Relate to Native American Women:

Connected Race, Class, and Gender Theory

The combination of these identities: race, class, and gender, shape the individual and locate him or her in society. Race, class, gender, *and* sex have been socially constructed in the United States as a *difference* in the form of hierarchy. Rothenberg (2001) explained that the meaning and values associated with those differences create a hierarchy of power and privilege. This process appears to be natural. Hence, it is used to rationalize inequality.

Specifically, the terminologies of race, class, and gender have individual and defining characteristics within the connected theory. First, race divides people according to biological or genetic similarities or differences. Socially constructed, the term "race" once had a popular connotation that people were born into different races with innate, biologically based differences in intellect, temperament, and character. This belief has not fully diminished from American society. According to Takaki (1993) race has been a social construction that has historically set apart racial minorities from European immigrants. Omi and Winant (1994) also see race as a more political category than a biological or scientific category and constructed for use in racial distinctions to correlate with economic and political changes in United States society. People of color are described as *different* from White people, but that difference, too, is understood as deviance from acceptable norms.

Rothenberg (2001) considered that white-skinned people of European origins have viewed themselves as innately superior in intelligence and ability to people with darker skin or different physical characteristics. However, Berreman (1972) implied that no society ranks people purely on a biological race, that is, on any basis that a competent geneticist would call *race*, which means based on distinctive shared genetic makeup derived from a common pool. Berreman implies that race is a foundation for special rank, and it is a socially defined phenomenon, which "very perfectly" corresponds to genetically transmitted traits. Race is a socially defined category and not physical differences that distinguishes groups of people and bars some from particular economic and interpersonal transactions. This description is often defined as *racial stratification* wherein groups of people are arranged into a hierarchal social structure based on race.

Shapiro (2001) noted that today most social scientists view race in a more subjective social category than a fixed definition of the past, wherein people are labeled by themselves or by others. Omi and Winant (1994) offered the theory, *racial-formation,* which views the social historical process by which racial categories were created, inhabited, transformed, and destroyed. Omi and Winant thus defined race "as a concept that signifies and symbolizes socio political conflicts and interests in reference to different types of human bodies" (p. 14). They concluded that race has both a biological and social component, and more specifically a dimension of human representation and social structure, linking racial formation to the *evolution of hegemony* or the way in which society is organized and ruled. In connected race, class, and gender theory race is interrelated to class, although it too has specific and different levels of structure. Again, class is a group of people, identified as *different.*

Shapiro (2001) defined a class system as a system of social stratification in which social status is determined by ownership, control of resources, and by the kinds of work people do. Marx's theoretical perspective emphasized the distinct relationship to the means of production (Marx & Engels, 1959). The people who own the means of production (capitalist) or sell their labor to earn a living (workers) place people in a system of production where one dominates the other. The class that dominates production also dominates institutions in society such as schools, businesses, media, and those institutions that make and enforce the rules. Marx concluded that they have opposing interest. This ownership and non-ownership is what divides the world into social classes. German sociologist, Weber (1958), also viewed the divisions between capitalists and workers and their assigned classes as the defining characteristics of social organization. He also included *social status* and even political party as part of the power closely tied to the economics.

The social construction of class can be considered analogous but not identical to race. According to Rothman (2002), class reflects a combination of economic, social and political factors, and occupation. He identified five social classes in contemporary American society: The elite who have unusual wealth, power, and social status. Membership is based on inherited wealth or institutional position. The elite travel in the same circles. Next, the upper middle class is predominantly composed of college-educated managers in the fields of science, computer specialties, law, and medicine. In addition managers and professionals who hold midlevel positions in large public and private organizations such as stockbrokers, systems analysts, and university faculty are included in the upper middle class. The third group is the lower middle class who collect, code, transcribe, file, record, and transmit data. Specific jobs would include bank tellers, data entry, and receptionists, secretaries, and retail/sales workers. Members of this class usually work for the upper middle class. The fourth class is the working class or blue-collar workers in factories, fields, garages, and mills. They work as manual laborers for products of distribution, production, and repair. Within this class, the wages vary from well paid to harsh working conditions with an unpredictable future. The last class is the poor, which includes members of society who work for low wages, have intermittent employment, and the chronically unemployed due to various situations such as lack of experience, skills, or lack of motivation. Some are disabled physically or mentally, while others have family responsibilities that limit employment. The majority of the classes do work, but for low wages that maintain a poverty level.

Fitzgerald (1997) contended that the very poor are considered by society to be "morally inferior" because of their situation (p. 132). There is also a tendency to equate being poor with race. For example, Fitzgerald described how the media over-exaggerates the number of Blacks among the working poor exaggerating more than twice the number of actual representation. As for Native Americans, initially, they were not even considered human. They were referred to as "savages," "animals," and "heathens." These terms were used by the initial invaders to this continent as a means of obtaining the land. Man could not take land from another man; however, man could take land from an animal.

The review of how class systems are stratified shows that income is only one factor associated with class positions, while working conditions, autonomy, and type of work are all related to status. Status often associated with class intakes economic position, which can accrue to a "higher" social status. However, Weber (1958) argued that status can only come from respect and honor that others are willing to give. Thus, status has a high personal quality. It is through the social construction of class and the *difference* between rich and poor that society justifies the unequal distribution of wealth and power that results from economic decisions made to perpetuate privilege.

Class status has been correlated with supposed *differences* in innate ability and moral worth. From this review of the literature, this author agrees that United States society is organized in such a way as to make hierarchy or class itself, appear neutral or inevitable. People are presumed to fit into a class and we come to believe that there should be a class of *difference*. We fall into the socially constructed belief rather than the given in nature. This leads to the next discussion of the third equivalent of connected race, class, and gender theory. Thus far, it is apparent that the social construction of race and class theories assists in the maintenance of oppression and social inequality. Does the gender theory have the same impact?

We know that the meanings and values associated with race and class create a hierarchy of power and privilege. For many United States citizens it appears to be *natural*. Again, this is how we rationalize inequality. Gender, too is seen as a *difference*. Two current definitions are provided by Rothenberg (2001, p.7) and Shapiro (2001, p. 5) respectively as follows: "Gender, which refers to the particular set of socially constructed meanings that are associated with each sex" and "the set of social and cultural characteristics, associated with biological sex--being female or male, in a particular society." Both of these definitions highlight the social construction, whereas gender *is* socially imposed (and biological sex is not). Lorber (1992) agreed that the *notion of gender* reflects a political and social decision rather than a distinction given in nature. These social scientists suggested that societies see males and females as distinct and opposed social beings. These beliefs transfer to the way people treat males and females *differently* and often in unequal fashion when it comes to political, social, and economic positions based on their sex or gender.

Bem (1994) proposed that the problem for women is being different from men in a social world that disguises what are really just male standards or norms as gender-neutral principles. She referred to this as an androcentric or male-centered world. A world in which almost all politics and practices are so completely organized around male experiences that they may fit men better than they do women automatically transforms any and all male/female differences into female disadvantages. For instance, during World War II, White women were laid off to make jobs for demobilized servicemen (White servicemen), losing the gains in employability they had made during wartime. The GI Bill was also aimed at assisting male, Euro-origin GIs. White males were able to take advantage of their educational benefits for college and technology training so they were particularly well positioned to take on the opportunity of the new demands for professional, managerial and tech labor. Willenz (1983) suggested that opportunities were not intended for women of any race. Native women were considered to be of the lower class, and "trained" to stay in a subservient role. Boarding schools for Native Americans trained young girls in vocational trades such as ironing, brass polishing, laundry, and other housecleaning duties. They spent their summer working for White families without pay and returned the following school year to take classes in advanced trades such as etiquette, cooking, and sewing.

Blood quantum has also been referred to as identifying class. Here, the amount of blood quantum gives Natives prestige or acceptance over another. A full-blood is seen by some Native people as more "Indian," than say a racially mixed-blood or lower degrees of Indian blood. This was not always the case and yet it remains an identity for Native people. In the 1850s, girls who attended the Cherokee Female Seminary clashed with each other over blood quantum. The social atmosphere at the seminary contributed to conflicts among Cherokee girls from progressive, mixed-blood families and those from more traditional, uneducated backgrounds. Those girls with mixed-blood believed themselves to be more "enlightened" because of their White blood and education. The darker-skinned Cherokee believed themselves to be more Cherokee and therefore a higher cultural class. The lighter-skinned also believed they were the higher cultural class and God favored them (Mihesuah, 2003b). It is important to note that the United States Government's Office of Indian Affairs helped establish, formally, the socially construed identity of class among Native Americans by initially assigning tribes through their self-governance to stipulate what qualifies one to be a member of a tribe. Each tribe has its own criteria. This criterion varies from 100% blood to 32/100. Some tribes have placed limits on their tribal roles to include non admission. Within Native communities, Tribal Councils, and schools for Native youth, blood quantum issues are always present. For instance, the Bureau of Indian Affairs (BIA) requires at least ¼ blood quantum for acceptance in all of their schools, even if the child lives on tribal lands. It is apparent that blood quantum continues to be about identifying class and not necessarily about community.

As United States society rationalizes and justifies race and class inequality, we see the same dichotomy with gender stratification. The dominant society is patriarchal, which gives men the ability to control institutional arrangements that bestow power and privilege on men. Very few women occupy corporate boardrooms or executive, CEO positions of significant political power. According to Higginbotham (2001), a fully employed woman still earns around 70 cents for every dollar a fully employed man makes. In 1996, a fully employed woman had a median income of $415 a week or 75.2% of the $552 median for men (United States Department of Labor, 1996). Morrison, White, Van Velsor and the Center for Creative Leadership (1992) considered that a barrier exists in corporate America. This barrier, called a *glass ceiling* is not there because of individual inability to handle a higher-level job. Rather, the glass ceiling applies to women as a group who are kept from advancing higher because they are women. When women do break through the glass ceiling, they are faced with another barrier -- a wall of tradition and stereotype that separates them from the top executive level, or those who hold the greatest power.

The Bureau of Indian Affairs (BIA) in the mid-1950s employed many Native American women. During their employment, many women were unable to advance into higher-level positions because of the patriarchal thought of a woman's place. Native women were often employed as dorm matrons or maintenance workers. Eventually many were hired as secretaries and teachers; however, few Native women held management positions. Even today, many Native women employed by the BIA work in the dorms in off-reservation boarding schools. Interestingly, many of these women are former boarding school students.

Identity Theory: Indian Life Stages Theory

Identity theory suggests that many Native people have been educated with an inaccurate picture of their own tribal relatives and other tribal groups. American education was designed and implemented from a dominant society perspective, which led to ongoing racism and negative stereotypes of Native Americans. Here, it is suggested that *Native Identity* can be considered as a constructivist view, as it reflects the social construction or reconstruction of Native identity. Mihesuah (2003b) presents a model of Indian life stages, an identity development model that takes into account issues of socialization, physical appearance, blood and cultural heritage, social and political conditions, prejudice, and discriminations. Mihesuah identifies four stages:

Stage 1: Pre-encounter

1. Natives are well aware of themselves as Natives, yet they know little about their tribal history and culture, much less anything about Natives or about the political, economic, and social state of tribes in general.
2. Do not necessarily identify with Whites, although some do.
3. Others see themselves as racially or culturally Native.
4. Some believe they are inferior to Whites and at fault for their economic, social, and/or political conditions. Others have no feelings of inferiority, are fulfilled, in addition, satisfied with their place in the world and never seek an identity.

Stage 2: Encounter

A Native person encounters a positive context about indigenous history and culture and is so moved to learn the correct history and truth about herself, with three basic goals in mind, focusing on any or all aspects of identity such as appearance, cultural traditions, or kinship:

Goal 1: Becoming an Indian. Natives who had little or no direct ties with the Indian family or community. They are culturally unsatisfied, marginally Native, and their distinctive Native appearance disallows them from being White or fully accepted by the dominant culture as equal. Many Whites after attending a "ceremonial" event such as a sweat lodge ceremony are so moved and then want to become a member of an indigenous group. They claim "Indian-ness" to try to fit in, to get a job, gain prestige, or write a book with an "authoritive voice." Most often, they desire some monetary value, while others seek attention that they did not get as a non-Native. Others engage in "symbolic identification." For example, some become Indian when Natives are in the news, a topic of conversation, or whenever it is popular.

Goal 2: Becoming More Indian or Rediscovering Indian-ness. This goal applies to Natives who have lost touch with their heritage and, through numerous events such as having a well-informed teacher who is able to share a rich and positive history or attending a traditional wedding, are moved to learn more about their religion and culture. Many Native women who are aware of their heritage and want to know more about it, or are unaware of issues of the tribe and other tribes, will take the role of an activist and may join an activist group like the American Indian Movement (AIM) or Green Peace.

Goal 3: Becoming Less Indian. Here, some Natives do not seek a Native identity, but after searching, seek an identity that is more White-oriented. They may do this by marrying a White person or a Native with light coloring. Not all women who marry outside their group want to become non- Natives. For example, a Navaho woman interviewed in a special series in the *Arizona Daily Sun*, "The Edge of the Rez" (1995) which focused on Native-White relations said, "I am a traditional Navaho. My first language is Navaho. I went to a mission school and all that, and was baptized a Catholic-- but that was when I was in school. But being Navaho is really my tradition. I tell my children, I tell students, you live by the values of your tradition."

Stage 3: Immersion-Emersion

1. This stage often causes anxiety, depression, and frustration over attempts to become the "right kind of Indian." The person attempts to change by getting rid of the old version and attempts to become the newer Indian.
2. Some Natives deny their non-Native racial and cultural aspects of themselves and become hostile toward non-Natives (Whites especially) and other Indians who do not conform to their ideas of "Indianness."
3. Some Natives adopt the "Redder Than Thou" attitude, while others may choose the opposite, "Whiter Than Thou" attitude.

Stage 4: Internalization

1. The Native person develops inner security about her identity. She is able to discuss racial issues in a rational manner with members of other racial or ethnic groups. This is also referred to as being culturally successful. She has come to a satisfactory con-

clusion as to who and what she is.
2. Others may not agree with her choice, but she is secure about her identity. Although she more than likely will have "internalized oppression" often due to rejecting a part of her heritage, that is also a part of her (pp. 83-110).

It is apparent that Mihesuah's (2003b) Indian life stages demonstrate an identity development model that is focused directly on Native people and their dealings with oppression from a Native person's perspective. As with other groups, there exist inequalities and discrimination among tribes, inter-tribally and intra-tribally. The following theories are evident in Native communities.

Culturalism Theory

Culturalism is a form of oppression that dovetails with racism (Mihesuah, 2003b). Factionalism (a group working against other such groups for its own ideas and goals) among tribes is viewed as being intertribal between those who cling to tradition and those who see change as a route to survival. The following are components of culturalism in Native societies in general:

1. Power Positions: Natives in power positions– political, economical, or social, often use expressions of culturalism against those who do not subscribe to their views.
2. New Value Systems: After some Natives adopted new value systems, members of a single tribe often viewed each other as being from different economic and social "classes."
3. Acculturation: Natives with a high level of acculturation might view themselves as "more enlightened" than others who they deem less enlightened, "uncivilized" or "heathen."
4. Tribal Leadership: Some who hold tribal leadership positions (usually a mixed-blood, educated and wealthy) see themselves as morally superior to the uneducated, non-Christian and less wealthy traditionalist. Their White-blood also contributed to their feelings of importance. They are the superior "class" (Mihesuah, 2003b, p. xvi introduction).

The culturalism theory also includes inequality by class. It is important to note here, that as we begin to consider class theory, *class* among Native Americans is quite different from inequality class theories among other groups. Among Natives, class does not always refer to money issues. It can also refer to levels of cultural knowledge and blood quantum. Today, Natives who know more about tribal traditions, speak the language, and are participants in ceremonies, and day-to-day community life may be considered a higher class in a more traditional sense. Native women and men who are educated, live in the urban setting, have a better earning status, and commute to their homeland as work allows to participate in ceremonies and family events are considered in a *different* class, rather than a better class by Natives living on reservations, from this author's observation. For instance, many who are not living on tribal lands for various reasons often experience inner conflicts and issues of acceptance as they seek to find the "right" way to give back and become a more acceptable presence at home on the reservation. They are often referred to as "apples," that is, red on the outside and white on the inside. They have left their home base, usually for an education, which is encouraged now more than ever. However, as they return home, they face more scrutiny and trust issues because they have come back with White man ideologies and ideas of change. For some, it is a thin line between two worlds. Going home so others see you more frequently helps to develop trust and acceptance on a regular basis, but this is not always possible. For example, this author has found it difficult to go home as often and as frequently as needed. The fast pace of the dominant culture encapsulates urban Indians as they seek employment and degrees. These attributes of gainful employment and doctorate degrees are important in the Western competitive culture. Going home frequently, bringing with me the sacks of flour, several cans of coffee for my family, and helping to prepare the food for the dances, has far more value to my Hopi mother and aunties than a degree hanging on my office wall. Even today, my mother is unaware I have completed a doctorate program and now, applying for tenure

This author considers the issues of contemporary Native American women as complex. A review of the literature thus far, and my own observations, reveals that Native American women are continuing to seek acceptance, and when they do receive the acceptance from their own people, it is valued beyond the acceptance from the dominant society's rewards and accomplishments. For instance, this author was asked to be the keynote speaker for the Hopi Education Symposium for the Hopi schools. The rewards came from the hugs of acceptance and all the "new" relatives who claimed me and welcomed me home again, on that particular day. I was able to share my expertise in education and leadership with schools, parents, and teachers, thus it was beneficial for the tribe.

Internalized Oppression

Like colonized groups throughout the world, Poupart (2003) contended that Native Americans learned and internalized the practices of the colonizers. These practices included social, political, economic domination, and sexual violence which enforced cultural codes of *otherness* upon Native Americans. Through formal education, conversion to Christianity, and assimilation into Euro-American culture and the capitalist economy, tribal people learned to speak the language and to interpret and reproduce the meanings of the oppressors. At the same time, the Native American cultures of North America were simultaneously devastated (Poupart, 2003, Smith, 2003). For survival, many succumbed to patriarchal power and aided in the loss of culture, language, lands, resources, and labor.

Continued oppression eventually turns the oppressed against each other. Friere (2003) explained this concept further: "The oppressed, instead of striving for liberation, tend themselves to become oppressors, or "Sub-oppressors." The very structure of their thought has been conditioned by the contradictions of the concrete, existential situation by which they were shaped. Their ideal is to be men; but for them, to be men is to be oppressors. This is their model of humanity. This phenomenon derives from the fact that the oppressed, at a certain moment of their existential experience, adopt an attitude of "adhesion" to the oppressor. "The oppressed, having internalized the image of the oppressor and adopted his guidelines are fearful of freedom" (p. 45).

When the oppressed turn against each other, a form of self-hate develops in the oppressed until eventually they internalize their oppression and as the sub-oppressors go against one another. History has many examples of this. For example, the most feared guards in the Nazi death camp were Jews and The U.S. Calvary used American Indians as scouts to help find fellow Native Americans who were eventually taken to prison, beaten, or killed. Today, Natives in conflict with one another often refer to the oppressor by calling each other names, such as, *white man's Indian, bureau Indian,* an *apple* (red on the outside and white on the inside), or that they have "sold out." I consider these forms of internalized oppression among Native people.

Cleary and Peacock (1998) suggested a more subtle internalized oppression is of one's self. The sub-oppressor attempts to destroy his or her own self through acts of self-destruction: alcoholism, drug abuse, suicide, and all of the other vestiges of internalized oppression. High rates of suicide and alcoholism in some Native American communities are examples of internalized oppression. Freire (2003) termed this as *self-depreciation.* This characteristic of oppression, "derives from their internalization of the opinion the oppressors hold of them. So often do they hear that they are good for nothing, know nothing and are incapable of learning anything—that they are sick, lazy, and unproductive—that in the end they become convinced of their own unfitness" (p. 63).

Some Native women experience internalized oppression by turning the violence against themselves or inward because of the severe repercussions of turning it against the colonial culture. Chinook (2004) relays the following in describing her internalized oppression from domestic violence and rape:

> Internalized Oppression: That my Native American heritage played a significant role in the rapes was an extremely agonizing recognition. In America's history of the colonization of Native peoples, rape has been used as a weapon of warfare, ethnic cleansing, humiliation, and oppression against us. In turn, Native peoples have internalized this oppression and passed it down through the generations. My Native grandmother's shame and oppression was passed down to my mother, who passed it on to me to the point that I blamed myself entirely for everything that happened to me. An example of how whites use rape as a colonial tool of domination against Native women is embedded in my

memory as a severe flashback. I thank my Creator for allowing me to remember the details only when I am in a safe place" (p.35).

The root of the anger is at the oppressor, but any attempts to direct it toward the oppressor is halted and consequently directed towards a family member (Duran & Duran, 1995). Domestic and sexual violence against women and children is not only linked to internalized oppression but also to race and class. Native women are considered inferior under patriarchal domination and are four times more likely to be abused than White women. One of the most devastating forms of oppression was the mass sterilization of Native women in the 1970s. Between 25 and 50 % of Native women between the ages of 15 and 44 were sterilized (Smith, 2005). In an attempt to rationalize this act by the Indian Health Service, the following account was taken from one doctor: "People pollute, and too many people crowded too close together cause many of our social and economic problems. These in turn are aggravated by involuntary and irresponsible parenthood...We also have obligations to the society of which we are part. The welfare mess, as it has been called, cries out for solutions, one of which is fertility control" ("Oklahoma" 1989, p. 11).

Other examples of harshness toward women occur when nature is also attacked. For example, on the Akwesasne Mohawk reserve, one of the most polluted areas in the country, the PCBs, DDT, Mirex, and HCBs that are dumped into their waters are eventually evident in women's breast milk. In the areas where there is uranium mining, such as in Four Corners and the Black Hills, Indian people face high rates of cancer, miscarriages and birth defects. Children growing up in Four Corners are developing ovarian and testicular cancers at 15 times the national average. In addition, the women on the Pine Ridge reserve experience a miscarriage rate six times higher than the national average (Harden, 1980; Tallman, 1992).

Summary

It is clear that Native American women and children are among the most economically, socially, and politically disenfranchised groups in the United States as seen in the literature reviewed. I reviewed two hierarchical theories: patriarchy and colonialism. The literature described how patriarchy and colonialism are leading contributors to the oppression of Native American women. Upon reviewing the specific theories: connected race, class, and gender, Indian life stages, culturalism, and internalized oppression, I considered these theories as being contributors to the maintenance of oppression of Native American women. Finally, the literature provided in-depth information on the roles of Native American women within their Native cultures, and how patriarchy and colonialism played a significant role in changing the traditional roles of Native American women and men. It is my hope that future studies may provide further insight into many educational and cultural aspects that influence the well-being and success of women Native American communities and societies.

References

Allen, P. G. (1986). *The sacred hoop: Recovering the feminine in American Indian traditions*. Boston: Beacon Press Books.

Anderson, K. (1996). *Changing woman*. New York: Oxford University Press.

Barreiro, J., & Johnson, T. (Eds.). (2005). *America is Indian country: Opinions and perspectives from Indian country today*. Golden, CO: Fulcrum .

Bem, S. L. (1994). In a male-centered world: Female differences are transformed into female disadvantages. *The Chronicle of Higher Education*. pp. B1-B2.

Berreman, S. (1972). Race, caste and other invidious distinctions in social stratification. *Race 13*, 385-414.

Bilton, T., Bonnet, D., Jones, P., Skinner, D., Stanworth, M., & Webster, A. (1996). *Introduction to sociology* (3rd Ed.). London: Macmillan.

Brawer, F. B. (1996). *Retention-attrition in the nineties*. (Report No. EDO-JC-96-06). Washington, DC: Office of Educational Research and Improvement (ED). (ERIC Document Reproduction Service No. ED 393 510).

Center for Women's Business Research. (2002). *Native American and Alaskan Native Women-owned businesses in the United States, 2002: A fact sheet*. Retrieved February 12, 2006 from *http://www.womensbusinessresearch.org/minority/ Native American.pdf*

Churchill, W. (2003). *Acts of rebellion*. New York: Routledge.

Cleary L. M., & Peacock, T. D. (1998). *Collected wisdom: American Indian education*. Boston: Allyn & Bacon.

Contaminated milk in Mohawk women. (1994, April). *Sojourner*, p. 11.

Chinook, R. (2004). My Spirit Lives. *Social Justice , v. 31* (no. 4), 31-39. Retrieved from, http:// 0-vnweb.hwwilsonweb.com.opac.library.csupomona.edu.

Deer, S. (2010). Relocation Revisited: Sex Trafficking of Native Women in the United States. *William Mitchell Law Review , 36* (no2), 621-83. Retreived from, http://0-vnweb.hwwilsonweb.com.opac.library.csupomona.edu.Deloria, V., Jr. (1991). *Indian education in America*. Boulder, CO: American Indian Science and Engineering Society.

DeVoe, J. &.Darling-Churchill, K. E.. (2008). *Status and Trends in the Education of American Indians and Alaska Natives: 2008* (NCES 2008-084). National Center for Education Statistics, Institute of Education Sciences, U.S. Department of Education. Washington, DC.

Dowd, G. E. (1987, Fall). North American Indian slaveholding and the colonization of gender. The Southeast before the removal. *Critical Matrix, 3*, 1-9.

Duran, E., & Duran, B. (1995). *Native American postcolonial psychology*. Albany: SUNY Press.

Edge of the rez. (1995, June 2). *Arizona Daily Sun*, p. 8.

Eisenstein, Z. (1981). *The radical future of liberal feminism*. New York: Longman.

Fitzgerald, M. (1997). Media perpetuates a myth. *Editor and Publisher, 13*, 130-134.

Ford, R. (1997). Native American women: Changing statuses, changing interpretations. In E. Jamison & S. Armitage (Eds.), *Writing the range: Race, class, and culture in the women's west* (pp. 42-68). Norman: University of Oklahoma Press.

Freire, P. (2003). *Pedagogy of the oppressed* (30th ed.). New York: Continuum.

Harden, L. (1980). *Black Hills PAHA sapa report*. Rapid City, SD.

Higginbotham, E. (2001). Women and work: Exploring race, ethnicity, and class. In T. M Shapiro, *Great divides: Readings in social inequality in the United States* (2nd ed.). Mountain View, CA: Mayfield.

Hurst, C. E. (2004). *Social inequality: Forms, causes, and consequences* (5th ed.). NewYork: Pearson Education.

Hurtado, A. (1996). *The color of privilege*. Ann Arbor: University of Michigan Press.

Johnson, A. G. (2001). *Privilege, power and difference*. New York: McGraw-Hill.

Joe, J. R., & Lonewolf, D. L. (1994) Cultural survival and contemporary American Indian women in the city. In M. B. Zinn & B. T. Dill (Eds.), *Women of color in the U. S. society*. Philadelphia: Temple University Press.

Klein, L. F., & Ackerman, L. A. (1995). *Women and power in Native North America.*Norman: University of Oklahoma Press.

Lacourt, J. A. (2003). Descriptions of a tree outside the forest: An Indigenous woman's experience in the academy. *The American Indian Quarterly, 27,* 296-307. Retrieved from, http://muse.jhu.edu.cardinal.fielding.edu

LaDuke, W. (1999). *Last standing woman*. Stillwater, MN: Voyageur Press.

Lorber, J. (1992). *The Cheryl Miller lecture*. Woodland Hills, CA: Sage Publications.

Marx, K., & Engels, F. (1959). *Marx and Engels: Basic writings on politics and philosophy.* Garden City, NY: Doubleday.

Mihesuah, D. A. (2003a). Activism and apathy: The price we pay for both. *The American Indian Quarterly, 27,* 325-332. Retrieved January 21, 2006, from http://muse.jhu.edu.exproxy.fielding.edu/journals/american_indian_quarterly/v27/27

Mihesuah, D. A. (2003b). *Indigenous American women: Decolonization, empowerment, activism.* Lincoln: University of Nebraska Press.

Miller, J. B. (1986). *Toward a new psychology of women* (2nd Ed.). London: Penguin.

Moane, G. (1999). *Gender and colonialism: A psychological analysis of oppression andliberation.* New York: St. Martin's Press.

Mohawk, J. C. (2000). *Utopian legacies: A history of conquest and oppression in the Westernworld.* Santa Fe, NM: Clear Light.

Mohawk, J. C. (2005). Three Indian contributions to western civilization. In J. Barreiro & T. Johnson (Eds.), *America is Indian country: Opinions and Perspectives from Indiancountry today* (pp. 16-18). Golden, CO: Fulcrum.

Morrison, A.M., White, R. P., Van Velsor, E., & The Center for Creative Leadership. (1992). The ceiling and the wall. In T. M. Shapiro, *Great divides: Readings in social inequality in the United States* (2nd ed.), (pp. 303-311). Mountain View, CA: Mayfield.

Nagel, J. (1996). *American Indian ethnic renewal: Red power and the resurgence of identity and culture.* New York: Oxford University Press.

Nichols, R. L. (2003). *American Indians in U. S. history.* Norman: University of Oklahoma Press.

Oklahoma: Sterilization of women charged to I. H. S. (1989, Mid-Winter). *Akwesasne Notes,* pp.11-12.

Omi, M., & Winant, H. (1994). Racial formations in the United States: From the 1960s to The 1990s (2nd Ed.). New York: Taylor & Francis, Routledge.

Percell, C. H. (1977). *Education and inequality: The roots and results of stratification in America's schools.* New York: The Free Press.

Poupart, L. M. (2003). The familiar face of genocide: Internalized oppression among American Indians. *Hypatia, 18,* 86-96. Retrieved July 28, 2005 ProQuest database.

Ralstin-Lewis, D. M. (2005). The continuing struggle against genocide: Indigenous women's reproductive rights. *Wicazo Sa Review, 20,* 71-95. Retrieved January 23, 2006, from *http://muse.jhu.edu.cardinal.fielding.edu*

Report shows status of Native women. (2004, December 17). *The Native Voice,* p. D1. Retrieved January 27, 2006, from ProQuest Database.

Rothenberg, P. S. (2001). *Race, class and gender in the United States* (5th ed.). New York: Worth.

Rothman, R. A. (2002). *Inequality and stratification: Race, class and gender* (4th ed.).Upper Saddle River, NJ: Prentice Hall.

Seager, J. (1997). *The state of women in the world atlas.* London: Penguin.

Shapiro, T. M. (2001). *Great Divides: Readings in social inequality in the United States* (2nd ed.). Mountain View, CA: Mayfield.

Smith, A. (2003). Not an Indian Tradition: Sexual Colonization of Native Peoples. *Hypatia , 18* (no. 2), 70-85. Retrieved from, *http://0-vnweb.hwwilsonweb.com.* opac.library.csupomona.edu.

Smith, A. (2005). *Conquest: Sexual violence and American Indian genocide.* Cambridge, MA: South End Press.

Snipp, C. M. (2004). The first Americans: American Indians. In M. L. Anderson & P. H. Collins (Eds.). *Race, class, and gender: An anthology* (5th ed., pp. 354-361). Belmont, CA: Wadsworth/Thomson Learning.

Takaki, R. (1993). *A different mirror: Multicultural American history.* Boston: Little, Brown.

Tallman, V. (1992). Toxic waste of Indian lives. *Covert Action,* 17, 16-22.U.S. Department of Justice (1999). *American Indians and crime.* Retrieved January 20, 2005, From *http://www.ojp.usdoj.gov/bjs.*

Tedlock, J. (2004). Female Pueblo governors honored. *Native American Times, X,* 6. Retrieved January 27, 2006, from ProQuest Database.

U.S. Commission on Human Rights. (1981). Washington, DC.: U.S. Government Printing Office.

U. S. Department of Labor. (1996, October 24). *Usual weekly earning of wage and salary workers, third quarter of 1996.* [Bureau of Labor Statistics release]. Washington, D.C.: U.S. Government Printing Office.

Walby, S. (1990). *Theorizing patriarchy.* Oxford: Blackwell.

Wall, W. (1997). Gender and the "citizen Indian." In E. Jameson & S. Armitage (Eds.), *Writing the range: Race, class, and culture in the women's west* (pp. 202-229). Norman: University of Oklahoma Press.

Weber, M. (1946/1958). *Essays in sociology.* (H. H. Gerth & C. Wright Mills, Trans. & Eds.). New York: Oxford University Press.

Webster's Ninth New Collegiate Dictionary. (1990). Springfield, MA: Merriam-Webster.

Willenz, J. A. (1983). *Women veterans: America's forgotten heroines.* NY: Continuum.

Wilson, M. C. (2004). *Closing the leadership gap: Why women can and must help run the world.* New York: Viking Penguin Group.

Navajo College Students' Perceptions of the Impact of Western Education on Retention

by Freda B. Garnanez, Ed.D.

The purpose of this research was to examine the problem of the seeming lack of anticipation about higher education protocol that exists among Navajo college-bound students and their perceptions of its impact on their retention in higher education. This study was based on the theory that the lack of understanding terminology unique to higher education affects their compliance with higher education protocol that in turn, affects their retention in higher education.

What is presented in this paper represents a small portion of a larger study that was conducted in 2001. This paper seeks to examine, explain, and clarify understanding about the experiences and changes in life that the Navajo people endured as a result of their introduction to Western education. The effects of these experiences and changes linger in the lives of the Navajo people today. This is evidenced in the way Navajo college students continue to need support and assistance to meet, endure, and conquer the challenges of higher education. Oftentimes, this is the alleviation or resolution of the seeming lack of anticipation about higher education protocol that exists among Navajo college-bound students and its potential effects on their retention in higher education.

The Effects of the Introduction of Western Education on the Navajo People

The tremendous effort expended by the Anglo people to deliver Western education to the Navajo people is important in understanding the assumed lack of anticipation about higher education protocol that exists among Navajo college-bound students and its potential effects on their retention in higher education. The delivery of Western education to the Navajo people took years of experimental modus operandi which is still going on today. Disguised by Article 6 of the Navajo Treaty of 1868 between the Navajo people and the United States Government, education was assured to the Navajo people, not for the sake of equality in knowing about the Anglo people's way of life, but rather, for the sake of changing the Navajo people's way of life to that of the Anglo people (Navajo Treaty of 1868). This tremendous effort expended by the Anglo people was never fully accomplished. Instead, the Navajos resisted Western education, and this resistance, according to Gilliland (1995), "endured from generation to generation" (p. 213).

The Navajo people's resistance to Western education is conspicuously evident throughout their history, but the masks of a good education often suppress the Navajo people's defiance. Their open and bold resistance was an intuitive reaction to the Anglo people's idea of civilization, that is, the acculturation and assimilation of the Navajo people to the Anglo way of life. A historical review of civilization according to the Anglo people showed that the Navajo people were intimidated and humiliated in the change of their lifestyle.

Acrey (1979) related that boarding schools were the most noted method for immersing Navajo children into the Anglo way of life. Navajo children were forcibly taken from their traditional and cultural environments and placed in frightening foreign environments—that of military-style boarding schools. In these boarding schools, they were harshly disciplined and used as slaves to defray the cost of the federal government boarding school operation. They were placed with Anglo families during school vacations to keep them away from their traditional and cultural home environment.

Sixty-two years after the Treaty of 1868 was signed, the Anglo people were still pressuring the Navajo people to assimilate and acculturate to the Anglo way of life. The application of this pressure forced the Anglos to incorporate innovative approaches in delivering Western education to the Navajo people. Acrey (1979) related that in 1930 the federal government designed and implemented a new approach to curricula in schools. The motive of this educational change was that if Navajo students saw themselves in a learning situation, they would have a much easier time learning "about other cultures" (p. 213), namely that of the Anglo society. Therefore, a bilingual, bicultural curriculum was designed and implemented in the schools.

Various approaches to delivering Western education to the Navajos continued 80 to 110 years after the signing of the Treaty of 1868. Roessel (1979) discussed the various educational delivery approaches including boarding schools, day schools, trailer schools, border-town boarding programs, public schools, mission schools, model demonstration schools, contract schools, community schools, and a 2-year college. Each school had a purpose on which its mode of operation was based. Six schools were boarding arrangements and four of them were commuter arrangements, from home to school and return. Although the commuter arrangements made it appear that the federal government was easing up in their attempt to assimilate and acculturate the Navajo people, the federal governmental authority to continue changing the lives of the Navajo people still pervaded. Roessel wrote, "Education on the Navajo reservation was a weapon used by non-Navajos to teach Navajo young people to become Anglos—to reject their heritage and culture and accept the identity and culture of the dominant society" (p. 17).

Finally, between 81 to 91 years after the signing of the Treaty of 1868, a significant increase in Navajo student enrollment in federal boarding schools occurred. Roessel (1979) wrote that between 1949 and 1959 there were 50,249 Navajo students who at one time or another were enrolled in the Navajo Special Program offered at 11 off-reservation Indian boarding schools. These schools were located in several states from Oregon to Oklahoma. The Navajo Special Program delivered education to Navajo children who were behind in academic grade level but needed some schooling and a vocational skill. This program failed in that purpose because many Navajo children who should have been enrolled in regular schools were enrolled in the Navajo Special Program at one of the off-reservation schools.

After 97 years of trying to deliver Western education to the Navajo people, the federal government finally relented on their absolute power and authority and consented to build schools that would "demonstrate . . . ideas about Indian education" (p. 205). Roessel (1979) wrote that the first school of this kind was established and put into operation at Lukachukai, Arizona during 1965 and 1966. The purpose of this school was to incorporate Navajo control over education in areas such as school boards, curriculum, community interaction, and student support services. However, "Navajo control" was not literally Navajo control. The concept of this school was still based on Anglo thought. After one year of operation, the lack of collaboration between the Navajo Nation and the federal government, namely the Bureau of Indian Affairs (BIA), on management functions and administrative issues led to the school's demise. However, the Navajos remained firm in their desire for Navajo control over Navajo education. In 1966, the Indian education concept was implemented at the Rough Rock Demonstration School in Rough Rock, Arizona. Roessel (1979) wrote that the Rough Rock Demonstration School was founded on a tripod configuration: "local control . . . educational excellence and innovation, and . . . Navajo emphasis" (p. 209).

The Navajos rapidly established a second school demonstrating their ideas about Indian education. In 1968, the first higher education institution, specifically for the Navajo people, was established at Tsaile, Arizona. This higher education institution, then known as Navajo Community College, is now known as Diné (The Navajo People) College. Although the college was based on the ideals of Western education, the emphasis of its academia was to integrate these ideals with Navajo history, culture, and language.

Since 1868, the federal government has expended tremendous effort to change the way of life for the Navajo people through Western education. Acrey (1979) and Roessel (1979) wrote a well-documented historical account of the many different ways the federal government devised and delivered Western education to the Navajos and how the Navajo children were forced to participate in it. These acts of force committed upon the Navajo people denoted to them that power and authority rested with the federal government, who were the Anglo people. It is no wonder that today the Navajos continue to resist Western education in many subtle ways including the assumed lack of anticipation about higher education protocol and its potential effects on their retention in higher education. This resistance to education still resonates today in the hearts and minds of the Navajo people. As Gilliland (1995) wrote, "many Indians had, and still have a negative attitude toward 'white' education and attend school in 'body' but not in 'spirit'" (p. 213).

The Transition to College

Making the change of life from a traditional and cultural home environment to a college cultural environment can be a dramatic experience for Navajo college-bound students. These students have much to be anxious about when entering college. They face a new way of life and need much support and assistance in dealing with the protocols of entering higher education. Rendón (1996) wrote, "college can be a time of great disequilibrium" (p. 19). It is a time when students need "structure and direction" (p. 17) to ease the confusion caused by engaging in an activity they have never experienced. Rendón referred to students who are transitioning to college as "border crossers" (p. 19) who will "learn more about their struggle to claim a place in the academic borderlands . . . reshaping identity and adapting and surviving in a new culture" (p. 19).

As pre-border crossers, Navajo students need assistance and guidance to comply with the requirements of entering college. The pre-border crossing stage, identified by Diltz (1980) as before "matriculation" (p. 241), is a stage that is crucial for Navajo college-bound students. It is a critical time for students to have educational and career goals set and to have all the technicalities completed for college entrance, including admission, financial aid, academic advisement, and college entrance testing requirements. Kalna (1986) emphasized that student success in college is associated with "goal identification" (p. 274). Therefore, Navajo students need assistance during their pre-border crossing stage or non-matriculation stage in planning their college careers and setting educational goals, insofar as how to complete their college education.

Diltz (1980) studied the assistance rendered to students in the non-matriculation stage and found that attention given to students during this time contributed to their success in college. This study was conducted on a "Pread-missions program" (p. 241) organized as a reciprocal admissions activity. The program both provided information to non-matriculated students about services and programs offered by the university where the study was conducted and had students provide information about themselves to the university, for its ability to service counselors and instructors. Diltz (1980) compared the matriculation of three groups of students consisting of a "preadmission control group, home visits [group], and phone visits [group]" (p. 241). All students in these groups had applied for admission to the university but had not yet registered for classes. The preadmission control group received no special attention. The home visits group received special visits at home from the admissions or counseling staff. The phone visits group received special telephone calls from the admissions or counseling staff. A comparison of the results indicated that the more personal attention that was given to students, the more likely it was that they would register for classes. (p. 241) The study also indicated that students who received special attention "became better persisters" (p. 241) in college.

The implications of the preadmission study conducted by Diltz (1980) are that colleges that give special attention to non-matriculated students are most likely to have them enroll, and that attention given to students during the non-matriculation stage also gives students encouragement to be better academic performers. So as Navajo college-bound students make the transition from their traditional and cultural home environment to the college environment, the support and assistance that they have received prior to college enrollment will help them respond more positively to their college experience.

"Validating and Invalidating Experiences" (Rendón, 1994)

Rendón (1994) coined the phrase "validating experiences" (p. 192) from which derives its opposing phrase, "invalidating experiences." L. I. Rendón (personal communication, February 23, 2001) defined validation as "an enabling, confirming and supportive process initiated by in- and out-of-class agents that fosters academic and personal development." Rendón explained "The Role of Validation" as the "wide range of experiences [that students go through] ranging from invalidation to validation which were the result of interacting with in- and out-of-class agents such as faculty, friends and relatives." Rendón's examples of validation that college students experience included "Faculty who worked closely with students and pushed them to excel," "Faculty who encouraged students to work together and help each other," "Spouses who provided support and encouragement," and "Faculty who treated students as equals and respected students." The examples of invalidation that Rendón gave as experiences of college students included "Faculty and staff who discounted [the students'] life experiences," "Faculty who appeared not to care," "Friends who teased students about not attending a 'real college,'" and "Out-of-class friends who did not care about academics and wanted the students to socialize with them" (L. I. Rendón, personal communication, February 23, 2001).

L. I. Rendón (personal communication, February 23, 2001) lectured that validation does the most good when it is afforded to students at the beginning of their college experience and is extended to students on a consistent basis throughout their college career. She explained that students who experience validation feel "they were cared for as a person, not just as a student," and that validating experiences "appeared to help students make the transition to college, get involved in institutional life, and become powerful learners." With the support of validating experiences, students "become motivated to succeed against all odds" (L. I. Rendón, personal communication, February 23, 2001).

The Navajo college-bound students certainly need validating experiences that provide moral support and engender enthusiasm for a positive college experience. Validation is particularly necessary for Navajo students who seem to demonstrate inadequate skills in anticipating higher education protocol. Rendón (1994) stressed that students cannot be expected to seek and become a part of the "academic infrastructures of an institution" (p. 45) when they do not have the skills to go about doing so. She wrote that students needed a validating experience that "affirms, supports, enables, and reinforces their capacity to fully develop themselves as students and as individuals" (p. 45).

To validate students is to remove the harnesses that constrain them in adapting and surviving in college. Rendón (1994) referred to this concept as "unleash[ing] the power of learning" (p. 47). Learning is knowledge, a powerful key to survival in difficult and uncertain situations. Knowledge is an esteem builder and brings with it confidence, competence, assurance, motivation, and security. Elkind and Weiner (1978) defined self-esteem as "the value people place on themselves and the extent to which they anticipate success in what they do" (p. 260). Navajo college-bound students who seemingly lack anticipation about higher education protocols need to be validated and given knowledge to provide them self-esteem to survive the higher education experience.

Language Issues Related to Understanding Navajo College-Bound Students
Young (1967) wrote, "as culture changes . . . those change reflect in language" (p. 11). Shonerd (1995) added that while languages are always in a "state of change" (p. 16), they change to accommodate the "changing needs of its speakers" (p. 16). When the federal government imposed Western education upon the Navajo people, a great change occurred, not only in their way of life, but also in their language. The federal government's imposition of Western education upon the Navajo people became a need for the Navajos to learn the English language. The most noted way the federal government forced a change in language for the Navajo people was through the boarding school concept. It was compulsory that Navajo students speak English while residing in boarding schools. Students who were heard conversing in the Navajo language were severely punished by boarding school staff members (Acrey, 1979).

The Navajos soon learned the English language and even adopted English words into the Navajo language. Shonerd (1995) called this practice "Navajo English" (p. 16). Navajo English is a form of Navajo dialect using a corrupt pronunciation of an English word. For example, the English word "Washington," referring to the federal government, became the Navajo word, "Wááshindoon" (Young and Morgan, 1987, p. 744). However, Shonerd (1995) emphasized that Navajo English is not a language deficit, but a language difference in which Navajo English is only a variety of the English language developed by the Navajo people.

As the Navajo college-bound students begin the process of transitioning from their native traditional culture to the college culture to fulfill their need for a college education, the language they have to understand and speak is the language of higher education. However, it is still unheard of to form Navajo English words out of higher education terminology in order to help students understand the terminology in their own dialect. Higher education terminology is difficult; its difficulty makes it a technical language. The technical terms make it difficult to learn, understand, and speak. For example, to form Navajo English words out of "unofficial transcript" as was done to the word, "Washington," would be difficult to do because the words have little significance to Navajos in terms of their definitive, illustrative, and expressive meaning. It would also have little significance in terms of translation or interpretation into the Navajo language.

Unlike higher education terminology, the Navajo language is a highly descriptive language. Young (1967) explained that there is much explanation that takes place when speaking the Navajo language. He further explained that interpreting what is said in English into Navajo is not a literal translation. The words "unofficial transcript" cannot be translated word for word in Navajo. Young wrote, "Full understanding [for a Navajo] happens only with full description in-depth and detail" (p. 12). Therefore, when Navajo college-bound students deal with higher education protocols, they require in-depth and detailed explanations of the terminology used by college personnel. For example, some Navajo college students do not understand the term, "Financial Need Analysis." To explain Financial Need Analysis in Navajo would entail lengthy explanations of life examples, such as the correlation of the word "financial" to the monetary worth of livestock, jewelry, homes, arts, crafts, and other possessions. The word "need" would be explained in terms of the things they do not have use for, not their wants and desires. The word "analysis" would be explained as slowly looking at the situation and carefully thinking about it. After an understanding has been established in Navajo, then the term would be explained to the students as a "paper" that is required by the Office of Navajo Nation Student Financial Assistance (ONNSFA) to demonstrate the state of their financial need in attending college. Then another lengthy explanation of the financial need calculation is required and even further explanation of whether or not students have a financial need. If there is no financial need, then the situation is clarified by re-explaining it from the beginning.

The definition of "Financial Need Analysis" in the English language is simply to take the resources, such as scholarships, grants, student loans, savings, and parental or student monetary contribution that students have acquired to offset their educational costs, and subtract the costs of education that includes tuition, books, housing, transportation, and personal expenses. If this calculation indicates that financial aid resources exceed the cost of education, then students have no financial need. If the calculation indicates that financial aid resources are less than the cost of education, then students have a financial need.

The unique Navajo language issues for Navajo students are not fully understood by college personnel, including faculty members. The cliché that it takes longer for Navajo students to understand classroom instruction because they are translating what the instructor is saying is not what is occurring. Young's (1967) concept that Navajo students are interpreting, not translating, what is being said is actually what is occurring.

So the issue of the Navajo language presents a dichotomy in that those representing the higher education institutions do not appear to fully understand the complexities associated with the Navajo language, and the Navajo students do not appear to fully understand the complex terminology of higher education. Although both could attempt to teach one another, it is a matter of who needs to understand the other more. The answer is obvious. Navajo students need to understand the language unique to higher education.

The language unique to higher education institutions is like a measure of control by the higher education institutions. Wheatley (1992) explained that this is the nature of a defensive organization. Organizations that operate defensively are like "impressive fortresses" (p. 16). Fortresses are built with a great degree of control to protect them from any possible intrusion. Higher education institutions operate like fortresses to protect themselves from invasion. This implies that they do not have a communicative understanding with anyone but themselves. They have developed a language that is specific to their needs and a language that only they can fully understand.

It is unfair for Navajo students entering college to be expected to understand higher education terminology, particularly when they did not anticipate doing so, and to converse intelligently with college personnel who know the terminology as a condition of their job. The students' lack of understanding the terminology of higher education and comprehending a conversation in which it is used can cause anxious feelings, discomfort, and uneasiness that can lead to dropping out of college. Rendón (1996) emphasized that this language problem can be intimidating or discouraging to new students.

If Navajo students are to be assisted in learning and understanding the terminology of higher education, the barriers that hinder their understanding must be removed. To be consistent with Rendón's (1994) validation of students, it is necessary to provide students with access to knowledge of higher educational terms. Therefore, having terminology written for reference by students and holding formal classes to help students learn the terminology would be extending effort toward removing barriers to understanding the terminology of higher education. Knowing and understanding higher education terminology will enhance their knowledge, abilities, and skills for surviving in the world of higher education.

Learning from Other Ethnic Groups

In 1981, Tatum (1987) studied the experiences of Black families coping in a dominant White society. In interviews conducted with Black families, she sought understanding and empathy as to how it is to live in the midst of an alien society, but in which it is necessary to achieve, thrive, and prosper. She questioned whether or not living amidst a predominately White society meant "opportunity, success, the American Dream realized, or is it rootlessness, isolation, and alienation?" (p. 1). In general, her interviews showed a combination of these elements. It depended much on the way Blacks managed and handled their lives. However, the reoccurring message that Tatum found was that success was contingent upon the value placed on family and extended kinship. Families and kinship provide a network of support, as well as an important link to the past and the future.

The Navajo people also lived by the principle that the family was the center of their life. Sadly, the federal government altered much of this important value of family, extended kinship, and cultural clanship when it imposed Western education upon the Navajos. The Anglo people used Western education to break the traditional and cultural ties of family, kinship, and clanship. They did this by forcing family separation upon the Navajos. They took the Navajo children away from their family, relatives, and homes and placed them in boarding schools great distances away (Acrey, 1979).

Rendón (1996) gave personal testimony that family roots among Hispanic people run so deep that going to college presents difficulties with family separation. Very often, this kind of situation brings people back to the basics of their lives reminding them that there is culture, a way of life. For Navajo students to deal with family separation, it might be best for them to take Rendón's advice that they "find animate and inanimate objects in the new college culture that might evoke a sense of comfort that originates in their early cultural upbringing" (p. 19).

Rendón's (1996) advice offers a source of comfort and relief for Navajo students who leave home for college and experience difficulty adjusting to family separation. Navajo students who enter college for the first time might find strength in Navajo cultural teachings. A Navajo cultural teaching, Diné T'áá Bí Át'éego (A Well-Directed Person) developed by Begishe (n.d.), is a philosophical concept about the upbringing of a person who strives for him or herself with the strength and power of sensible characteristics and behavior. These characteristics and behaviors were based on three factors: "not [being] lazy," a "strong foundation (in thinking)," and "not [being] externally constrained" and included variables pertaining to disciplining oneself in order to attain a good direction in life. These variables included "enthusiasm," "obedience," "endurance," "identity," "thinking," and being "bi-cultural and bi-lingual" (Begishe, n.d.).

Black people and Hispanic people, like the Navajo people, have a culture of values that encourage family and kinship and cultural teachings. Navajo cultural teachings must continue to emphasize the value of family, kinship, and clanship as the core of life. In their early history, the Navajos cared for one another and taught one another knowledge and skills to survive and prosper in life. (Gilliland, 1995, p. 253) This same concept can be put into action again by helping Navajo students gain knowledge and skills that will make them informed students of higher education.

Schema and Instantiations—The Storage Bin of Experiences

The experiences of the Navajo people are rich and deeply rooted in history. Howard (1987) related that life experiences such as the historical experiences of the Navajo people are stored in their schemata, the storage information system of the brain. He stated that a schema is "like a concept . . . a representation abstracted from experience, which is used to understand the world and deal with it" (p. 31). He also stated that experiences consist of "instantiations" (p. 32). Instantiations are examples or illustrations that build up to experiences in life. Eby (1998) explained that as experiences in life accumulate, the schema "expands to include many more facts, ideas, and examples" (p. 187). For example, in order for students to comprehend an instantiation so that it could be dealt with appropriately or accordingly, the brain scans their schemata and retrieves the knowledge of experience pertinent to what they are attempting to comprehend. If the schema that the students select does not contain the appropriate information or does not provide enough information to deal with the instantiation, it can cause them uncertainty or a lack of understanding of the situation. Eby (1998) explained that this happens when the "schemata are vague and sparse" (p. 187) caused by not having prolific experiences in life. The concepts related to the information that the students are seeking are neither clear nor "richly detailed and well-organized" (p. 187) in their schemata.

Navajo students who have never had the experience of dealing with the protocols of entering college or who have limited experience in dealing with these protocols are confused or bewildered when college personnel speak to them in the language of higher education. They experience uncertainty or a lack of understanding because this language does not exist in their schema. They do not have the language of higher education in their schema because they did not anticipate having to know a new vocabulary when they began the process of enrolling in college. On the other side of the issue, many college employees assume that Navajo students enter college familiar with the regulated language system of higher education and therefore, speak to Navajo students as if they know and understand the terminology of higher education. Consequently, they do not offer in-depth and detailed explanations of college-related situations to Navajo students.

Navajo College-Bound Students—Changing to Survive

Perhaps an intriguing thought, in terms of the eventful history of the Navajo people, is what might have happened if the Anglo people had not brought them Western education to change their lives. There is much to imagine about this, but even the possibility of ever returning to a truly independent, self-governing nation again as it once was before the arrival of the Anglo people is nil. The Navajo people had to make significant changes in their lives in order for them to survive the encroachment of the Anglo people upon their lives. Capelle (1979) stated that human systems "need to be able to change in order to survive" (p. 13). It is the nature of mankind as a system, and more specifically as a social system, to change.

In order to survive, the Navajo people need to examine the other side of this matter and realize the benefits of their changed society. Freire (1998) wrote about this kind of change experienced by people of a third world country in Latin America. He wrote about bringing hope to people who felt conquered due to the oppression imposed by their government. Their hope was realized through his efforts to educate them in the Western sense. Of significance was that Freire helped these citizens who believed they were forever situated in a "culture of silence" (p. 12) gain the confidence of a new self-awareness. Their new self-awareness empowered them to take a critical view of the world and to express their views of their situation in it without fear.

Freire (1998) presented two theories: the theory of anti-dialogical action and the theory of dialogical action. The theory of anti-dialogical action explained the concept of being a conquered people. According to Freire, it meant being oppressed, manipulated, imposed upon, and inhibited in creating by one "who dominates by virtue of conquest" (p. 148). The theory of dialogical action explained the concept of free, transformed people who are able to speak with open "critical analysis" (p. 149) of their situations.

If Navajo college students demonstrate the qualities of life as explained in the anti-dialogical action theory, they could succumb to being college "non-survivors." They could become a conquered people that are defeated by the realities and complexities of higher education. If the Navajo college students demonstrate the qualities of life as explained in the dialogical action theory, they could experience the freedom to be successful at their higher educational endeavors. Just as Freire worked to create "a new underclass" (p. 9) of educated people against the wishes of an oppressive government, the Navajo students can also become a new people and survive in higher education as a free, transformed people while maintaining their identity and culture.

The problem of the assumed lack of anticipation about higher education protocol that exists among Navajo college-bound students and its potential effects on their retention in higher education does not have to dominate and dictate the lives of the Navajo students. They can change or be assisted to change from this bondage and released to move on in their college careers with a newness of spirit and enthusiasm. Wheatley (1992) discussed different ways in which this change can happen. He said it could occur through "autopoiesis" (p. 20). The word, "autopoiesis" has a Greek derivation meaning "self-production or self-making" (p. 20). Autopoiesis is the process by which organizations self-organize, self-renew, and self-reference, but continue to remain unchanged in structure. Jantsch (1980) defined autopoiesis as "the characteristic of living systems to continuously renew themselves and to regulate this process in such a way that the integrity of their structure is maintained" (p. 7). Navajo college-bound students are autopoietic organisms. They can change by learning skills and acquiring knowledge to help them cope with the intricacies of higher education so that they can be better performers in academia but remain as Navajo students.

Wheatley (1992) further explained that change happens by leaps and bounds. This is called quantum theory. This theory is based on the principle that organizations seek and maintain order by changing or adjusting themselves in leaps and bounds. This occurs through sudden, unplanned changes or adjustments. It is possible for Navajo college-bound students to take quantum leaps by adjusting or changing their assumed lack of anticipation about higher education protocol to one of being anticipatory about higher education protocol and acquiring other positive aspects of being college students.

Finally, Wheatley (1992) related that change is actually "order" (p. 22) that occurs through chaos. This means that chaos is a "full partner" (p. 22) to order. Order in chaos comes through the observance of its patterns, motions, shapes, and stories. The assumption that Navajo college-bound students lack anticipation about protocols for entering higher education may seem to be chaotic, but according to Wheatley, there is order in this chaos. If the Navajo students' patterns of behaviors, motions of life, shapes of lives, and stories of experiences about higher education are heard and observed, changes can be made so that positive and encouraging things can happen to these Navajo college-bound students.

The appearance of Navajo college-bound students to lack anticipation about protocols of higher education is not a hopeless situation. Wheatley (1992) gave hope when she wrote, "growth is found in disequilibrium, not in balance" (p. 20). She explained that disequilibrium is caused by distractions and disturbances in the environment, such as the lack of anticipation about higher education protocols. Distractions and disturbances are mediums for change and growth that can reinvigorate or rejuvenate organizations, or in this situation, Navajo college-bound students. In the common vernacular, it can be said that students learn and grow from the experiences that shake up their status quo or equilibrium.

The Navajo people have survived the chaos brought about by the encroachment of the Anglo people upon their autonomous lives, have endured great changes to their way of life resulting from this encroachment, and yet have maintained stability in their identity as a Native American ethnic group. The

Navajo people's endurance is amazing, yet there is wonder about the current depth of this endurance and stability. The seeming lack of persistence of Navajo students to remain in college until they earn a college degree could be an indication that the characteristics necessary to survive chaos, endure changes, and maintain stability have weakened.

Brown and Kurpius (1997) studied Native American student persistence in higher education. Their study identified several "psychosocial factors" (p. 9) that helped Native American students persist in college. Of significance among these factors was "aspirations" (p. 9). Students who had aspirations had good grade point averages, "good study habits, and regular class attendance" (p. 9). Another factor that Brown and Kurpius concluded as important in the higher education of Native Americans was financial aid. This is a crucial factor in the success of Native American college students, many of whom face and contend with difficult financial challenges while in college.

Padilla, Trevino, Gonzales, and Trevino (1997) studied factors that contributed to the success of minority students at a university in southwestern United States, in spite of the many variables that could have made them unsuccessful in higher education. They found that the students' success was based mostly on "heuristic knowledge" (p. 126) or "practical" (p. 126) knowledge. Heuristic knowledge, in this situation, is information about college experiences that students pass on to another student who did not meet the scholarship application deadline, but submitted their application to ONNSFA anyway. As a result, these Navajo students know that they have a good chance of being awarded a Navajo scholarship, in spite of the lateness of their application.

As a result of their study, Padilla et al. (1997) developed the "local model" (p. 125). This consisted of four "categories of barriers" (p. 129) to the college education of students. The barriers included (a) "discontinuity barriers" (p. 129) hindering a problem-free transition to college, (b) "lack of nurturing barriers" (p. 129) indicating an inadequacy or shortage of services that help students adjust or adapt to college, (c) "lack of presence barriers" (p. 129) pertaining to the low number of minority population on campus and insufficient programs or curricula specific to minorities, and (d) "resource barriers" (p. 129) relating to the lack of funds for a college education.

As evidenced by these studies, although the problems of retention are complex and multitudinous, every effort must be attempted to curtail problems with Navajo student retention in higher education. It is not only the responsibility of higher education institutions to put forth this effort, it is also the responsibility of all concerned and all who have a vested interest in Navajo students. In addition, these studies support the significance of the fact that Navajos, as an enduring people, successfully survived change in many aspects of their lives. As survivors of change, Navajo students can certainly learn to anticipate and comply with the protocols of higher education. By anticipating these protocols and complying with them, Navajo college-bound students can be better prepared to meet, endure, and conquer the challenges of higher education. Currently, students continue to be vulnerable to many problems associated with the lack of retention. Therefore, it is necessary to continue studying ways to help these students meet, endure, and conquer the challenges of higher education and experience success in college.

Methodology

For this action-oriented, qualitative study, a college preparation training program and a student handbook were developed to intercept the seeming lack of anticipation about higher education protocol that exists among Navajo college-bound students and its potential effects on their retention in higher education. A training session was held utilizing the student handbook to familiarize Navajo freshmen with the terminology. The student handbook is a resource book to which students can refer for information on the procedures and processes of protocols and seek definitions, explanations, and illustrations of terminology unique to public higher education institutions, particularly in the state of New Mexico.

A total of 19 Navajo freshmen students participated in this qualitative study. They were placed in one of two groups. Group A consisted of 7 student participants who attended the training, and Group B consisted of 12 student participants who did not attend the training. Subsequently, a qualitative study using open-ended questionnaires was conducted with the two groups of Navajo freshmen students. All participants were given an open-ended questionnaire to complete, which sought to determine how they perceived their college preparation and its impact on their retention in college.

This research study as a step toward the retention of Navajo students in higher education contributes to the field of Navajo education in several ways. First, the study creates awareness about student retention and the lack thereof among the Navajo students of higher education. Second, the study promotes consciousness about helping Navajo students experience and attain success in college. Third, the study generates information about the needs of Navajo students entering higher education, such as the need to have anticipatory skills to comply with the protocols for college enrollment and for a successful college experience. Fourth, the study brings attention to the necessity of students meeting higher education expectations and requirements in order to be successful in higher education. Fifth, the study establishes emphasis on language and its importance in understanding and conceptualizing higher education terminology. Sixth, the study imparts mindfulness that responsibility and accountability are absolute for Navajo students of higher education. It fills a huge void in the literature on Native American education. In addition, the results which emerged will prove useful to those looking for strategies to help retain and graduate Native American students.

Findings

Responses to the open-ended questionnaires by student Group A and student Group B, provided the data for analysis from which the findings and the conclusions of this study were drawn. Student Group A had attended the college preparation training and each student received a student handbook of definitions, explanations, and illustrations of terminology unique to public higher education institutions in the state of New Mexico. Student Group B had not attended the college preparation training and, therefore, had not received student handbooks.

The two groups of students were surveyed to see if there were any similarities or differences in their view of the seeming lack of anticipation about higher education protocol that exists among Navajo college-bound students and its potential effects on their retention in higher education. However, the results of the data showed that there were more similarities than differences. These similarities were characterized as the needs of the students.

The analysis of the data provided composites from which the following findings are presented:

1. A representative number of students from both groups indicated a need to know and understand higher education terminology. The use of language, particularly the English language, is an important aspect in understanding and conceptualizing higher education terminology. Although both groups of students indicated a predominate comfortableness in speaking English and also indicated that they spoke English and Navajo equally in their homes or that they spoke English more than Navajo in their homes, they did not show full knowledge or understanding of higher education terminology. A considerable number of students indicated that they had not understood conversations with college employees upon their initial enrollment, did not give a response when asked to list higher education terminology they had heard during their enrollment process, and did not give a correct response when asked about their enrollment status in college. Although a good number of students knew their major, they could only describe their degree program. When asked to discuss the meaning of higher education student retention, numerous students responded with varied interpretations and literal translations. The student participants of this study also did not respond to many questions in the questionnaire or responded inappropriately to questions.

   A considerable number of students who had attended the college preparation training and received the student handbook stated that the handbook provided them information or defined the terms that they needed to know. Many of these students stated that they had already referred to the handbook for information they needed to know and understand. They also stated that they would have been more informed and prepared for college and would have better understood conversations with college personnel if they had received the handbook as a reference source prior to college entrance.

2. The students expressed a need for information and training on the terminology of higher education. Data indicated that a good number of students mentioned dictionaries, thesauri, and the Internet as sources to seek out the meaning of terminology they did not know or understand. A considerable number of students stated that if they did not know the meaning of a word used by a college employee, they would ask the person speaking, a friend, a college staff person, the Native office staff, or write it down to look up at a later time.

   Many of Group A students indicated that the student handbook was a valuable informational resource and recommended that the college preparation training be required for entry-level students. The data analysis also showed that numerous students indicated that training related to enrollment processes and academic skills would have helped them prepare to enter college.

3. The students expressed a need for assistance and guidance during their preparation for college. A number of students considered receiving financial aid for college as being assisted and guided to prepare for college. Although this is a tangible form of assistance and guidance, it is the intangible assistance and guidance in the form of understanding and direction given by counselors, academic advisors, educational funding advisors, or anyone with a genuine interest in the college education of students that was lacking. A high number of students indicated this lack of assistance and guidance by stating that if they had the opportunity to change the process of their enrollment in college, they would apply for scholarships early, review the catalog for "better idea[s]" of fields of study, be more aware of the differences among the kinds of degrees offered, seek an advisor for advice on "classes [and] degrees," seek information on colleges, and follow up on admission activities with the college in which they were enrolling.

   Although many of the students made plans for college and prepared for college in ways that they felt were appropriate, they demonstrated a need for assistance and guidance as they experienced college for the first time. The majority of students experienced anxiety upon entering college and expressed feelings of insecurity, doubt, and a feeling of not fitting into the college atmosphere.

   Data revealed that both groups of students gave indication that assistance and guidance inferred from cultural knowledge was diminishing. Students of both groups, were unable to identify their Native and tribal clans of various stages of decent. Knowledge of clan relationship is one of cultural identity. Cultural identity helps to strengthen personal identity. A strong, positive personal identity would give the students greater confidence to do well and succeed in college.

Many students indicated a need for assistance and guidance in understanding their role in college. Although the students knew their major field of study, a considerable number of them did not know their degree program. Instead, the students described their degree program referring to it, for example, as a "general requirements and the transfer program."

The students also indicated a need for assistance and guidance as they cited the causes associated with the lack of retention in higher education. A high number of students had insightful generalizations about the causes of students not returning to college and indicated that these were situations in which students needed assistance to remain in college. They offered suggestions as to ways that students could adjust to college and indicated their concepts of skills, attributes, and requirements needed to do well in college.

4. The students expressed a need for support of their aspirations that will help them gain meaningful opportunities in life. Data showed that both groups of students indicated a desire to graduate from college and then continue with their college career. Among several goals that the students listed, completing a college degree and continuing their college education were two of the three most desired goals. Other goals that both student groups listed within their top five were gainful employment for a better living, support of a family, a life of happiness, and independence from the parental home situation.

Group A students expressed a need for opportunities to become informed. They stated they would have been more informed and prepared as students if they had received the college preparation training and student handbook before they started college.

Roessel (1979), Acrey (1979), and Gilliland (1995) provided information and understanding about the experiences and changes in life that the Navajo people endured as a result of their introduction to Western education. The effects of these experiences and changes still linger in the lives of the Navajo people. This is evidenced in the way Navajo college students continue to indicate a need to know and understand higher education terminology, need for information and training on higher education protocols, need to be assisted and guided during their preparation for college, and need in the support for their aspirations that will help them gain meaningful opportunities in life.

Summary of the Findings

Based on the findings of this study, the conclusions for this study are presented as follows:

1. Acquiring knowledge and understanding of higher education terminology become challenges when Navajo students make the transition from a non-college culture to a college culture. When a cultural change is made, a change also happens in the language. This is a familiar situation to the Navajo people. Their history is an account of the many changes that they had to make in their way of life, including having to learn a new language—the English language. Shonerd (1995) wrote, "language changes to serve the changing needs of it speakers" (p. 16). So Navajo students who feel they need a college education make a change in their lives when they enroll in college. It is during the enrollment process that they hear terminology they do not know or understand.

The lack of knowing or understanding higher education terminology becomes evident during their dialogue with college employees about protocol issues. As one student wrote, "I didn't really understand what they (Admissions Office) were saying. Especially as a new student, they told me what to do, but I couldn't imagine it." Rendón (1996) found during interviews conducted with "first-year community college students" (p. 16) that students do have a concern about their lack of ability and skills to dialogue with college personnel. In an interview with a nontraditional student, the student told Rendón, "An academic life is much different than that of life at home or in the business world. So sometimes terms are not familiar to you" (p. 17). Rendón wrote that terms used by higher education personnel "can be very daunting to a new student" (p. 17) especially when the student has not had an opportunity to learn the words "at home or from peers or school" (p. 17).

Although opportunities to learn the higher education terminology in the non-college culture may be limited, students can learn the terminology through the experiences of others such as siblings, peers, friends, and classmates. Padilla's model, the "Expertise Model of successful college students" (as cited in Padilla, Treviño, Gonzales, & Treviño, 1997, p. 126) substantiated this. The model showed that students enter college with two kinds of knowledge: theoretical knowledge, that is knowledge acquired through "coursework and formal study" (p. 127); and heuristic knowledge, that is "practical knowledge" (p. 127) that is "acquired experientially" (p. 126) such as through the experiences of other students. Students communicate heuristic knowledge from one to another and thereby educate one another with practical knowledge about higher education.

Padilla et al. (1997) conducted an assessment of "heuristic knowledge of successful college students" (p. 127). This assessment revealed four "barriers" (p. 127) that successful students dealt and coped with throughout their college experience. These are the (a) "discontinuity barriers," (b) "lack of nurturing barriers," (c) "lack of presence barriers," and (d) "resource barriers" (p. 129).

The Navajo students' lack of understanding and knowing higher education terminology falls in every barrier category. As a discontinuity barrier, the lack of understanding higher education terminology prevents students from making a "smooth" transition to college. As a "lack of nurturing" barrier, the students' lack of understanding higher education terminology does not appear to be a problematic concern to higher education institutions. As a "lack of presence barrier," courses specific to learning higher education terminology are not offered for students. As a "resource barrier," an informational document such as the college preparation training student handbook that defines, explains, and illustrates higher education terminology in the vernacular of Native American students, specifically Navajo students, is currently unavailable.

2. Informing students about higher education terminology through training is a way to improve the quality of students entering college and to enhance the success of students in higher education. It is also a way to balance the dialogue between college employees and students.

Providing information and training for entry-level college students is consistent with Tinto's (1993) concept of "what works in retaining students" (p. 153). Tinto discussed student orientations as a method to provide that information and training. However, he stated that when higher education institutions hold student orientations they give "formal" (p. 159) information to students and often neglect to give students the "informal" (p. 159) information, such as the social network of the college.

The college preparation training and the student handbook contain formal information as well as informal information to students. The students are given formal definitions of higher education terminology and informal information regarding who to call upon for assistance, how to handle situations, and how to comply with processes and procedures, and why compliance with processes and procedures is necessary. The college preparation training and student handbook are means to help students acquire skills that can increase their confidence about higher education protocol. Tinto (1993) advocated for these types of qualities of students entering college. Tinto's model of institutional departure showed "skills and abilities . . . [as] pre-entry attribute[s]" (p. 114).

Tierney and Jun (2001) supported Tinto's concept of introducing students to higher education. They developed a college preparation program for the "low-income, urban, minority, youth" to introduce students to higher education through "cultural integrity" (p. 211). Cultural integrity is based on positive strengths, such as cultural "knowledge, skills, and abilities" (p. 210). This college preparation program demonstrated that the positive aspects of culture aided students in succeeding in higher education.

The purpose of providing information and training on higher educational matters is to enhance student retention. Brawer (1996) indicated in her study on retention and attrition that intervention retention strategies must be formulated and implemented even though students continue to leave college for reasons such as, but not limited to, inadequate financial aid, transportation problems, child care assistance problems, family problems, alcohol and drug abuse, and academic failure. These retention strategies included "orientation programs," "mentoring programs" (para. 5), and "multiple strategies" (para. 9) pertaining to creative and imaginative methods of retaining students in college.

3. Assisting students with matters pertaining to higher education protocol and guiding them through their apprehensions about entering college is vital to their success in college. Providing assistance and guidance to students in higher education protocol matters is consistent with Rendón's concept of validating students. She stated that when students are validated, they are given positive support during their preparation for college (Rendón, personal communication, February 23, 2001). Rendón's (1994) study emphasized that validating students helps them overcome feelings of "self-doubt" and expectations "to fail" (p. 36). This validation can also remove the mysteries of higher education that, as indicated in the questionnaire responses, included filling out admissions and financial aid forms, registering by way of a computerized system, and wondering about the college campus setting.

   Students who are provided with assistance and guidance are more likely to overcome the assumed behaviors of indifference, procrastination, lack of goal setting, and lack of assertiveness. Assistance provides students with help in properly performing and complying with the sequences and processes of the protocols of entering college and remaining in college. One student who had received no assistance and guidance with these processes stated, "I didn't know what to ask or what I should do. I was embarrassed to not know what was going on."

4. Aspiring to fulfill hopes and dreams and gaining opportunities afforded in life are students' goals. Kalna (1986) emphasized that student success in college is associated with "goal identification" (p. 274). Both groups of students expressed aspirations to graduate from the college and to persist in their educational goals toward higher college degrees. They also expressed seeking opportunities to improve their lives in ways such as obtaining employment with good pay and fringe benefits to enable them to support and care for their families and gain personal status to live a happy life.

   These aspirations and opportunities are consistent with the findings of Brown and Kurpius (1997) in their study regarding Native American persistence in higher education. Brown and Kurpius identified "aspirations" (p. 9) as one of the "psychosocial factors" that influences Native American students to remain in college (p. 9).

Recommendations from this study

There is a significant need to help Navajo students acquire the skill to anticipate higher education protocol. This need can be fulfilled by educating the students on terminology that is unique to higher education so that they can gain the confidence in dealing with the protocols of higher education and become competent in dialoguing with college employees with whom they interact during their enrollment process. This action-oriented project and research, consisting of a college preparation-training program and a student handbook of terminology unique to public higher education institutions in the state of New Mexico, were attempted as intervention strategies to help the Navajo students acquire the skills of awareness and knowledge so that they could be successful in higher education. The following recommendations are made as a result of this study:

1. A student handbook comprised of all higher education protocols, such as the example shown in Appendix A, be developed by public higher education institutions in New Mexico.

2. A freshmen seminar course using this student handbook as a text for the course be instituted by public higher education institutions in the state of New Mexico, and that this course be offered to all college entry-level students who demonstrate a need for it.

3. The New Mexico Commission of Higher Education (NMCHE), the Tribal Commission of Higher Education (TCHE), and the Office of Navajo Nation Scholarship and Financial Assistance (ONNSFA) sponsor the development of this student handbook and ensure its implementation as a freshmen seminar course in all public higher education institutions of the state of New Mexico.

Recommendations for Further Research

The retention of Native American students in higher education, addressed specifically in this study with regard to Navajo students, is a great concern to tribal leaders including Navajo Nation tribal leaders and educators. The study of retention and the lack thereof must continue in order to alleviate or resolve these concerns. Although Carney (1999) indicated that there have been just as many methods suggested for relieving or resolving retention problems, as there are problems with retention, efforts must continue to help Navajo students experience and attain success in higher education. Therefore, recommendations for further research on retention and the lack thereof existing among Navajo college students are presented in no particular order as follows:

1.   More research should be conducted on variables that foster retention problems and variables that enhance retention in higher education. In this study, the variables that seemed to have a negative effect on the anticipation skills of Navajo college-bound students in regard to higher education protocols, as well as their retention in higher education are identified as indifference, procrastination, lack of goal setting, and lack of assertiveness. Other variables that affect Navajo college student retention or lack thereof should be researched.

2. A study on the training of high school and pre-college Navajo students on terminology unique to higher education and higher education protocols should be conducted. These students should be followed after training to observe the effects of the training upon their college matriculation.

3. A longitudinal study should be conducted on the effects of training Navajo college students on terminology unique to higher education and higher education protocols. Students who receive the training should be followed for at least one or more years after training to observe any impact on their persistence or non-persistence in college.

4. A study on language issues pertaining to Navajo pre-college students should be conducted to examine their facility of the English language in terms of verbal and written competency and comprehension skills level.

The literature review presented many researchers who have studied methods to enhance retention among college students or to encourage retention among pre-college students. These studies, as well as this study, are steps in making small, but significant contributions toward the retention of students in higher education. Studies on the retention or lack thereof existing among students of higher education must continue, and of particular interest in this study, ways to help Navajo students meet, endure, and conquer the challenges of higher education and experience success in college must continue.

Conclusion

A great assumption often made about Navajo students is that they know how to be college students. It is assumed that they know how to deal with situations, how to handle the unexpected, and how to communicate in the world of higher education; however, when these students enter college, they demonstrate that they have had very little preparation to cope with these situations. This is the reason that Navajo leaders and educators must continue to examine the various aspects of the lack of retention existing among Navajo college students, create awareness of its existence among Navajo college students, deal with it from their own Native and Tribal perspectives, and work on alleviating or resolving it.

A new goal has been established. It is one that will familiarize Navajo college-bound students about the terminology of higher education through a college-preparation training program and a student handbook. Providing students with information and training on terminology unique to higher education will assist and guide them in understanding and becoming familiar with things pertaining to higher education. Eventually, students will realize that their aspirations for a college degree can help them access many opportunities. They can overcome the seeming lack of anticipation about higher education protocol and the effects it has on their retention in higher education. Kauffman (1980) wrote, "After a new goal is invented, a new program must also be developed to achieve it, not always on the basis of pre-existing program, but often on the basis of insights" (p. 32).

References

Acrey, B. P. (1979). *Navajo history: The land and the people.* Shiprock, NM: Central Consolidated School District.

Begishe, K. (n.d.) *Handout at a Navajo Culture training session.* (1988 Spring).

Brawer, F. B. (1996). *Retention-attrition in the nineties.* (Report No. EDO-JC-96-06). Washington, DC: Office of Educational Research and Improvement (ED). (ERIC Document Reproduction Service No. ED 393 510).

Brown, L. L., & Kurpius, S. E. (1997). Psychosocial factors influencing academic persistence of American Indian college students. *Journal of College Student Development, 38* (1), 3-12.

Capelle, R. G. (1979). *Changing human systems.* Toronto, Canada: International Human Systems Institute.

Carney, C. M. (1999). *Native American higher education in the United States.* New Brunswick, NJ: Transaction.

Diltz, N. (1980). A good case for preadmission counseling. Journal of College Student Personnel, 21 (3), 240-242.

Eby, J. W. (1998). *Reflective planning, teaching, and evaluation K-12* (2nd ed). Columbus, OH: Prentice-Hall.

Elkind, D., & Weiner, I. B. (1978). *Development of the child.* New York: John Wiley & Sons.

Freire, P. (1998). *Pedagogy of the oppressed.* New York: The Continuum.

Gilliland, H. (1995). *Teaching the Native American* (3rd ed). Dubuque, IA: Kendall/Hunt.

Howard, R. W. (1987). *Concepts and schemata: An introduction.* Great Britain: MacKays of Chatham.

Kalna, J. R. (1986). The entering study survey: A high risk identification tool. *Journal of College Student Personnel, 27* (3), 274-275.

Kauffman, D. L. (1980). *Systems 1: An introduction to systems thinking.* Minneapolis, MN: Future Systems.

Navajo Treaty of 1868. In Acrey, 1979, *Navajo history: The land and the people* (pp. 319-325). Shiprock, NM: Central Consolidated School District.

Padilla, R. V., Treviño, J., Gonzales, K., & Treviño, J. (1997). Developing local models of minority student success in college. *Journal of College Student Development*, 38, 125-135.

Rendón, L. I. (1994). Validating culturally diverse students: Toward a new model of learning and student development. *Innovative Higher Education*, 19 (1), 33-50

Rendón, L. I. (1996, November/December). Life on the border. *About Campus*, pp. 14-20.

Roessel, R. A. (1979). *Navajo education, 1948–1978, its progress and its problems.* (Navajo History, Vol. III, Part A). Rough Rock, Navajo Nation, AZ: Navajo Curriculum Center.

Shonerd, H. (1995). "Semilingualism:" Stereotyping the Navajo child. In the Excerpts from the *Journal of Navajo Education* (Vol. 2).

Tatum, B. D. (1987). *Assimilation blues: Black families in White communities: Who succeeds and why?* New York: Basic Books.

Tierney, W. G., & Jun, A. (2001). A university helps prepare low income youths for college. *The Journal of Higher Education*, 72 (2), 205-225.

Tinto, V. (1993). *Leaving college: Rethinking the causes and cures of student attrition* (2nd ed.). Chicago: The University of Chicago Press.

Wheatley, M. J. (1992). *Leadership and the new science: Learning about organizations from an orderly universe.* San Francisco: Berett-Koehler.

Young, R. W. (1967). *English as a second language for Navajos: An overview of certain cultural and linguistic factors.* Albuquerque, NM: The Navajo Area Office, Bureau of Indian Affairs.

Young, R. W., & Morgan, W. (1987). *The Navajo language* (2nd ed.) Albuquerque: The University of New Mexico Press.

Adolescent Drug Use and its Impact on Schools in Indian Country

Susan Harness, M.A., Kimberly Miller, Ph.D., and Fred Beauvais, Ph.D.

Research conducted in the past three decades has found drug and alcohol usage among American Indian youth to be far higher, than their non-Native counterparts (Oetting & Beauvais, 1989; Beauvais, 1992; Kandel, 1995; Plunkett and Mitchell, 2000; Beauvais et al, 2004). However, many people, including educators, were still surprised to learn that in 2005, nearly one fourth of American Indian high school students admitted to having used drugs on the way to school or at school. This statistic was the result from the 2005-2006 American Drug and Alcohol Survey, given by the Tri-Ethnic Center for Prevention Research, at Colorado State University, in Fort Collins, Colorado. The negative results of increased drug use became apparent in the physical and emotional impairment of the individual; the dysfunctional relationships of the family, as well as, the social and learning disruptions that could happen at the school level (Brown & Tapert, 2004; Tapert et al. 2005; Masten, 2009; Lubman et al. 2005; Oetting & Beauvais 1987). With regard to youth drug and alcohol use in the community, there were increased health risks, such as traffic accidents, or physical harm resulting from instigating or being a victim of violence (Spicer, 1997; ADAS Survey, 2005-2006).

Schools, as one aspect of the community, can actively affect a student's attitudes and ultimately behaviors toward substance and alcohol use and their role in introducing and establishing social networks that can create risk as well as protective factors, has been well documented. Parents also play a role in shaping their children's attitudes, behaviors, and values with regard to alcohol and substance use. This chapter looks at the intersection where schools and parents establish children's values, beliefs, and attitudes toward substance use, and how environments, created by schools and parents, encourages or discourages use.

Survey Background

The Tri-Ethnic Center (TEC), formerly known as Western Behavioral Studies, was established in the late 1960s at Colorado State University, and housed within the Psychology Department. Although the name indicates there were three major ethnicities of study, the Center actually researched a wide variety of social issues among many different ethnic populations, including American Indian. In 1974, the Center received the National Institute of Drug Abuse's (NIDA) Indian epidemiology grant, and it has been the longest running research within the TEC. The study *Drug Use among Young Indians: Epidemiology and Prediction* allows researchers to explore the epidemiology, correlates and consequences of American Indian youth drug and alcohol use.

Two other research projects, University of Michigan's *Monitoring the Future,* which was also funded by NIDA in 1974, and the CDC's *Youth Risk Behavior Survey*, conducted surveys nationally among American youth, including American Indians. However, the TEC's study is the only long-term study that specifically focuses on American Indian youth attending schools on or near reservations, examining their substance use patterns, attitudes and behaviors, as well as exploring the roles that schools, friends, and families play in shaping those values, attitudes and beliefs. The fact that American Indian youth continues to be the focus of this research, makes this three and a half decades-long study a unique contribution to scholarship.

Developed by Eugene Oetting, Fred Beauvais and Ruth Edwards, The American Drug and Alcohol Survey™ (ADAS) measures drug use, attitudes, and behaviors, as well as assesses school and family environments within the population of American Indian youth. Over the years, the survey has been updated to reflect the changes in society. Since the rise of pharmaceutical branding, for instance, many drugs are currently known by their brand name, rather than their scientific name. The TEC's most recent ADAS survey consists of 109 questions that explore usage, attitudes and behaviors of American Indian adolescents in relation to tobacco, alcohol and drug use, including several illicit classes of drugs. Peer, family, school influences, as well as what the students believe will happen (perceived risk) if they use illicit substances, are important factors in exploring drug use. Within the survey, students are asked to describe the frequency of use, locations of use, as well as their perceived and real experience of negative outcomes after use. The survey does not assume every student in the school uses alcohol or illicit drugs, but rather seeks to adequately assess under what circumstances use does or does not occur. This information provides important clues for prevention strategies, which can then be initiated by communities, schools and families. To date, the ADAS has been given to over 70,000 American Indian youth attending schools on or near 150 reservations. It currently provides the most extensive and accurate exploration of American Indian youth drug and alcohol use in the continental U.S.

The TEC has actively worked with tribal schools and communities to provide them with accurate data of their students, through an individualized report that is given to each participating school. In an attempt to clearly communicate the survey results, the final part of the report contains graphs, charts and other illustrations that allow schools to present information to others in the community that may be interested in establishing, maintaining or evaluating prevention efforts. This invitation to parents and community members to become educated about and participate in prevention programs has proven invaluable in addressing particularly worrisome drug and alcohol issues among American Indian youth.

American Indian Drug and Alcohol Use

According to the ADAS survey given in the 2005-2006 school year to American Indian youth attending schools on or near reservations, drug and alcohol use was still significantly higher among American Indian youths, than their non-Native counterparts. However, in comparing this ADAS survey with ADAS surveys conducted in previous years, it was clear that some strides had been made in prevention, specifically in the use of tobacco, marijuana, inhalants, psychedelics and PCP (use of all of these substances has decreased since their peak usage in 1990-2000).

This discussion examined four substances used most frequently by American Indian youth—tobacco, alcohol, marijuana, and inhalants—as well as cocaine, one of the so-called 'hard' drugs, still evident in reservation communities. The 2005-2006 survey, conducted with nearly 1,200 7th through 12th grade American Indian youth, asked about prevalence, using the term 'ever used,' or 'ever smoked,' in the question. Answers revealed that almost 54% of Indian youth smoked cigarettes, and nearly 33% used smokeless tobacco. These numbers had dropped significantly since 1986-88, when those percentages were 78% and 58%, respectively. Of those who smoked cigarettes, 28% smoked less than once a day, and 19% used smokeless tobacco less than once a day. Slightly over 70% of American Indian youth drank any alcohol, while half said they'd been intoxicated. Again, these usage rates declined from a previously high rate of 81% using any alcohol in 1986-88, and 62% being intoxicated in 1990-92. Over 60% of American Indian youth used marijuana, down from a high of 75% in 1998-2000, and almost 14% used inhalants, down from a high of 25% in 1990-92. Typically, 'hard' drugs, like cocaine, have always been associated with relatively low usage rates, mainly because illicit drugs like this, occur as part of larger, more dysfunctional type of drug use. In 2005-2006, less than 10% of American Indian youth reported using cocaine, and less than 2% reported using it once or twice, in the previous thirty days.

There is one pattern that has been consistent over the years, that is of particular importance and somewhat disheartening. From the survey results, it is possible to identify a group of youth who use multiple drugs, and who use them at fairly high levels. For American Indian youth, this group is about 20% of the population (Beauvais et al, 2004). As might be suspected, this group also experiences high levels of other deviant behaviors, such as violence, poor school adjustment and family problems. Dr. Beauvais, who is the principal investigator of the study, refers to these young people as a 'clinical' population. They have multiple needs, and many of them may not respond to the usual prevention programs. Instead, they may need intense intervention from a number of different sources.

Alcohol and Substance Use and the Brain

The impact of tobacco, alcohol and illicit drug use were visible in the individual and the family, as well as the community, in factors such as health, relationships and the economy. Among the American Indian adolescent population, alcohol was by far, the most consumed substance available to youth. Negative impacts of youth alcohol consumption have been documented through a myriad of research studies. Research found that among adolescents who drink alcohol regularly, there was an associated increase of misuse and dependence, as well as an associated decrease in neuro-cognitive functioning (Brown & Tapert, 2004; Tapert, 2005; Masten et al., 2009). What makes alcohol use in adolescence even more disturbing is the impact on brain functioning, which may not be reversible.

In his examination of age and alcohol initiation, Faden (2006) found that alcohol use, defined as drinking a whole drink, began around 12-14 years of age, and binge drinking increased sharply between 12 and 21 years of age. The ADAS found a similar age of initiation, however, the measurement of prevalence (ever-used) had little meaning—one sip can mean 'ever-used.' Therefore, measures of destructive use can be found in the question relating to intoxication. Survey results of 2005-2006 survey indicate that while 44% of 7th and 8th grade students had never been intoxicated, 13% had been intoxicated by age thirteen (ADAS, 1975-2006).

Considerable research in both humans and non humans have been conducted on how alcohol affects the adolescent brain, specifically with regard to cognitive functioning. Dissection of non-human brains allows researchers to more fully assess the neurological nature of the impact, thereby adding significantly to our understanding of how long-term alcohol use affects brain functioning in youth.

Non-human research has found that adolescent animals were less sensitive to the negative effects of acute alcohol intoxication, such as sedation, hangover and loss of coordination. However, they were more sensitive to the effects of alcohol on social interaction and spatial memory. Sircar and Sircar (2005) found that administering ethanol to adolescent rats placed in a water maze, substantially impaired the rats' ability to successfully escape the maze. The adolescent rats not only took a longer time to locate the exit platform, but swam greater distances in their search for the platform. Most revealing, however, was the fact that their performance did not catch up with control rats after the ethanol period was over, indicating more long-term impairment. More disturbing was their following study in 2006, where they found that ethanol exposure during adolescence, produced alterations in specific regions of the brain that lasted into adulthood (Sircar & Sircar).

Researchers have found similar effects on the human adolescent brain. Heavy drinking in adolescence produces poorer neurocognitive functioning in relation to gender. Brown and Tapert (2004:241) found young women experienced adverse effects to alcohol, specifically in the areas of working memory and visuo-spatial functioning. Young men, however, experienced negative effects between verbal learning and substance involvement. Tapert, et al (2005) found youths who were chronically heavy drinkers, experienced alcohol use disorders that were tied to smaller hippocampal brain volume; an important finding because the hippocampus is critical to learning and memory formation.

Aside from brain function, alcohol had also been found to affect social development and academic competency as well. In fact, Masten and colleagues (2009) argued that underage drinking impacted every facet of a young person's life: it disrupts concentration, damages relationships and affects school attendance, none of which bode well for the individual.

Other substances besides alcohol have been shown to negatively affect the brain, as well as the central nervous system. Young people who begin using marijuana before the age of seventeen, seem to be more vulnerable to cognitive impairments as shown by reduced brain grey matter (Pope, et al, 2003). According to Lubman, et al. (2006), inhalant use provides an initial state of euphoria, disinhibition and excitation, however, it soon progresses to disorientation, slurred speech and weakness, as the central nervous system becomes depressed. Their findings of chronic inhalant use reveal structural brain abnormalities and cognitive deterioration, which at times can be permanent and irreversible. Although this chapter deals with adolescent use, Bartzokis, et al (2002) found that brain scans of adult human cocaine users showed damage in both the frontal and temporal brain regions, resulting in an interruption of memory, as well as loss in executive and affective functioning. Based on this study, inferences can be made from an earlier statement that suggested, the earlier the age of initiation, the more misuse and dependence can occur.

Alcohol and Substance Use and Social Networks

Substance use not only affects cognitive functioning, it also affects a child's social environment as well, which includes family, peers and schools. In their formulation of Peer Cluster Theory, Oetting and Beauvais (1987) considered the structure and behaviors of peers in predicting drug use among adolescents. Peer clusters, they argued, shaped the use, attitudes, beliefs, and behaviors of all members of the peer group, thereby, norming the group for drug use or non-use. In clusters where drug use was a requirement, even at low levels, drugs played an important part of identity and group definition. In clusters where drug use was discouraged, group definition and identity as non-users was established as well.

Peer clusters were really just a group of friends who came together because of shared values and beliefs around various cores of behaviors, including drug use. This group was such a dominant force in a youth's life, an adolescent would typically not leave a peer cluster, unless they were making a social transition where values might conflict, such as entering marriage; marriage is an institution where drug use is less likely to occur (Bachman, O'Malley, and Johnston, 1984).

Popularity, a much sought-after characteristic among teenagers, is a double-edged sword, especially in peer clusters and specifically in relation to drug and alcohol use. According to the findings of Allen and colleagues (2005), positive outcomes associated with popularity, resulted in higher levels of adolescent ego development, attachments, friendship competence and positive interaction with mothers.

Families are another important social network that can shape attitudes and behaviors toward alcohol and drugs. In the ADAS, where youth assessed their families as being strong - for instance, their family cared about them, and the family was intact - drug use was low. In families where there was a high level of disruption, drug use was significantly higher. One single major protective factor against drug use is families that have strong sanctions against such use (Oetting and Beauvais, 1987).

The school environment is a third social network that impacts drug and alcohol use among youth. Youths who said they experienced a negative school environment, such as school failure, not liking school and teachers not liking them, were more likely to use drugs and alcohol, than youth for whom school had been a satisfying and positively, challenging experience (Oetting and Beauvais, 1987). This sense of failure has a direct impact on school climate. Disengaged students can be disruptive to the students around them. Some substances, like cocaine, may intensify feelings of hostility, resulting in fights and violence that break out as a result of drug use. In its most destructive form, especially in urban school environments, violence over drug territories can escalate, causing students to avoid classes out of fear. In response to these issues, school boards and administrations have established substance use prevention policies and efforts to address the negative social aspects of substance use.

School Policies and Substance Use

Typically, drug use reduction within the schools has been addressed through social control, such as the creation of bans and policies, or education, such as prevention efforts. The purpose of school policies was to construct norms within communities and schools that relay the values and expectations for student behavior. There also needs to be documentation procedures that address violations of substance-use related events. School policies that are delivered effectively, in other words, clearly stated and clearly identified, with harsh penalties for violation have been shown to most successfully reduce student drug and alcohol use rates (Evans-Whipp, 2007). The terms *clearly stated* and *clearly identified* are key in successful usage reduction. When a portion of the population feels unknowledgeable about either the institution of policy or the outcomes of policy, effectiveness is severely hindered.

Finn and Willert (2006) surveyed 103 teachers in various middle schools and high schools in upstate New York, and found inconsistencies between teachers' awareness of drug use at school, and their reactions in the classroom. Although teachers knew a drug economy existed at school, they paid little attention, or rarely addressed it, because students' impairment didn't affect the teachers' teaching or classroom management. These findings were not so much about non-intervention of the teachers, but rather about their uncertainty with regard to their roles in addressing drug and alcohol use. Teachers were not always clear about schools' policies and practices regarding students' drug use on school groups, and they were also not clear about the level of support they could expect from school administrators. When purpose, action and support were stated clearly throughout the school community, from administration to students, teachers became very successful leaders in anti-drug efforts in the schools.

Policies that addressed tolerance of usage were varied in design outcomes. Typically, usage policies include sanctions, such as bans on tobacco, alcohol, and illegal drugs. According to the 2006 School Health Policies and Programs Study (SHPPS), policies dealing with tobacco use, alcohol use and illegal drug possession, either in school, on campus or at school events, have been instituted in some form by 95%-100% of the 461 districts were surveyed, (Jones et al, 2007). However, drug use still exists within the school environment. As noted earlier, twenty-five percent of American Indian adolescents report using drugs on the way to, or at school. Just because policy bans are in place, doesn't mean they are effective. Poulin (2007) in her research on school smoking bans found that bans did not actually decrease cigarette use, nor did they protect students in junior and senior high schools from initiating smoking. So what does produce reduction of use and protection against initiation?

Findings from the 2006 SHPPS have shown that consistently, clearly-stated consequences have been shown to reduce drug and alcohol use in school communities. However, there was uncertainty about how to effectively establish consequences that addressed the varying levels of offenses. Of the 1,025 schools nationwide that were surveyed, almost a third provided detention or in-school suspension for tobacco use, while about 20% of the schools had a detention policy for alcohol use violations, and slightly less than 13% provided in-school suspension for alcohol use. With regard to illegal drug use or possession, only

15% of schools placed violators in detention, while less than 10% placed violators into in-school suspension (Jones, et. al, 2007). This uncertainty was also apparent in policies between age groups.

According to reviews done by Evans-Whipp et al (2004), elementary schools tend to have fewer formal policies than those of middle or high schools, presumably from the belief that younger students are not as likely to use illicit drugs. National data, however, suggests otherwise. Studies conducted by the TEC between 1993 and 2003/2004 show that drug and alcohol use exists among American Indian 4th through 6th graders attending schools on or near reservations. The most recent research carried out in in 2003/2004 indicates that 4% of American Indian elementary school children have ever been drunk, 12% have ever used marijuana and 12% have ever used inhalants (Miller, et al: 2008). These findings of prevalence support the idea that elementary schools should establish and enforce formal drug policies.

However, there are no hard and fast rules for establishing and enforcing policies. Anecdotal evidence indicates that wide variation in school policies and enforcement currently exists among middle and secondary schools serving significant populations of American Indian youth. This variation could be a result of individual community needs being addressed, or the need for a community's cultural attitudes and beliefs to be supported. The existence of this variation also underlines the continued need for local schools to be able to establish and enforce policies that affect their students, rather than accepting an overarching national policy which may or may not reflect the culture of substance use that exist within their schools. For example, regular urine testing carried out in large, inner-city schools may not appropriately address the issues of the scale of use and delinquency seen in smaller, rural schools. Polices are not one-size-fits-all approaches to dealing with substance use; local schools should be able to establish their own policies based on the needs and concerns seen in their communities

Policies and consequences establish norms for tobacco, alcohol and substance use, but they are only part of the usage reduction issue. Effective prevention programs support those norms.

Prevention Efforts

Prevention efforts do not establish policy, nor do they establish how violations of those policies will be dealt with. Rather, prevention efforts educate the community, including teachers, students and parents, about the issues and outcomes of drug and alcohol use. Goodstadt (1989) argued that "educational strategies reflect trust in the rationality, reasonableness, and goodness of humankind" (247). Like policies, prevention efforts take many forms: public service announcements (PSAs), media and poster campaigns, symbolic messages that were displayed on clothing, or participation in classroom curricula. Substance use reduction was heavily intertwined with how much risk youths associated with tobacco, alcohol and drug use. Bachman, Johnston and O'Malley (1998), in their *Monitoring the Future* study found that as the perception of risk increased, usage decreased, and vice versa. This was evident in the TEC's research related to inhalant use. Beauvais, et al (2002) suggested that inhalant usage fell so drastically between 1988 and 1997—dropping from 28% to 15%—because of prevention activities, such as posters, conference information, and inhalant use prevention materials that were implemented in many American Indian communities, educating parents, school personnel, community members, and student themselves of the negative ,and sometimes deadly consequences of 'sniffing.'

However, results had not been so successful in other prevention efforts relating to drug and alcohol use. Over time, our data has consistently shown that alcohol use on the reservation remains high, with little significant change, when compared to non-Indian students. These numbers are indicative that American Indian youth do not perceive a huge amount of negative risk in regular alcohol usage. In fact, data from the 2005-2006 ADAS show that over a third of American Indian youth felt that regular use of alcohol resulted in some harm, and only a little over a quarter felt it resulted in a lot of harm. This perception of harmlessness may be the result of some youths whose frontal lobes had not been fully developed in adolescence; the function of the frontal lobe is to plan and organize behaviors, weigh the consequences of future actions and inhibit impulsivity. The silver-lining, however, is in youths' perception of harm with regard to intoxication: nearly 70% of youths indicated that being regularly intoxicated resulted in a lot of harm (Crews & Boettiger, 2009).

Adolescents' ages also play a role in the types of substances they use. According to the 2005 ADAS survey, given to 7th–12th grade American Indian youth, 7th and 8th grade youth indicated that nearly 45% had used tobacco, 30% had used smokeless tobacco, 32% had been intoxicated, 54% have used marijuana, 20% had used inhalants and 4% had used cocaine. That same year, when 9th–12th graders were surveyed, the substance use-rates were disconcerting. Of this age group 60% smoked cigarettes, 30% used smokeless tobacco, 60% had been intoxicated, 66% had smoke marijuana, 14% had used inhalants, and 12% had tried cocaine (Crews & Boettiger, 2009).

As adolescents age, they not only seek autonomy from their parents, but they also develop more complex reasoning processes. Therefore, cultural messages aimed at this age group can have a huge impact on their perceptions of approval or risk of drug use, for all legal and illicit substances. The alcohol industry spends millions of dollars a year attracting and maintaining consumers. Brown and Tapert (2004) found that in those youths exhibiting alcohol use disorders, or AUD, media images containing pictures of alcoholic beverages produced an increased response in those areas of the brain commonly associated with emotion, visual processing and reward. "Given the strong neural response to alcohol beverage advertisements among teens with AUD, it is possible that these media images may influence continued drinking among teens with alcohol problems, and may interfere with effective coping strategies in youths attempting to stop using" (Brown and Tapert, 2004:240).

Successful programs contained specific characteristics. In 1999, Tobler and colleagues looked at the effectiveness of school-based drug prevention programs for marijuana use, and found that the most successful programs were interactive and contained content which included knowledge, drug-related refusal skills, generic skills and safety skills. Successful programs meeting these criteria were shown to be equally successful with marijuana, alcohol and tobacco. Morgan et al (2003) found that public service announcements against drug use that contained intense images, sound saturation, an unexpected format, a surprise or twist ending, and an acting out of the consequences of drug use, rather than someone narrating those consequences, created stronger affective responses among high risk students. This group gave these types of messages a higher sensation value, indicating the message was something this group tuned into.

Not all campaigns are successful, and research has begun to evaluate the effectiveness of various efforts. In 2001, the Robert Wood Johnson Foundation awarded a grant to test the effectiveness of the Take Charge of Your Life coursework, that is given through DARE and found it not only ineffective, but there was a 3–4 % increase in alcohol and tobacco use among 11th grade students who were not using either substance in 7th grade (http://www.rwjf. org/pr/product.jsp?id=42049). Analysis conducted by Hornik and colleagues (2008) showed no effects from the National Youth Anti-Drug Media Campaign that was funded by the US Congress, who appropriated nearly $1 billion for the campaign. Why these results failed to surface are unclear, but the fact that these costly efforts contributed to slightly higher teen alcohol and tobacco use was especially troublesome.

As has been shown (Goodstadt), drug education will only be effective for some of the people, some of the time; there was no one-size-fits all approach to education. Therefore, the power of parents and families becomes a very important tool in decreasing drug and alcohol use, especially among American Indian youth.

The Role of Parents in Prevention

Research has shown that both nuclear and extended families can have a huge impact on their children's decisions to use, or not use, alcohol and illicit drugs. When exploring how peer groups work in relation to alcohol and drug use, Swaim and colleagues (1993) found that peer networks among Anglo adolescents, play a much larger role in predicting use, while among American Indian youth, family played a larger role. Cousins in the American Indian population had replaced the peer group, possibly as a result of living in isolation on reservations, and the proximal living arrangements of extended families. Being part of larger extended families, cousins tended to clump in similar age groups exerting pressure, similar to peer clusters, on one another to drink or use substances. The pressure, in this case, was thought to come from drug and alcohol use being initiated in the homes of friends and family, making it difficult, if not impossible, for offers to be declined, because familial pressures to 'fit in' and 'belong'. The types of drug used were closely related to youths' social and kinship network. Cousins were associated with marijuana use, hard drugs were associated with friends, and alcohol and cigarette use were associated with parents (Kulis, et al., 2006).

Although these findings of the negative influences of family in relation to drug and alcohol use are disconcerting, research has found that a decrease in drug use was related to strong family connectedness. Ford (2009) examined the reasons why close families had such an impact of reducing drug use. According to his research, teens felt that not only would drug use interfere with the close relationships they had established with their family, but that close families monitored their teens' behaviors, making deviant behaviors more readily recognized and punished.

There is a perception that in American Indian culture, children observe the adults or elders, and elders' model appropriate roles to youth. However, since the boarding school era, this cultural parent style may no longer be in existence, except in very traditional families. Swaim and colleagues (1993) argued that parenting style could be particularly effective in influencing children's attitude toward drug and alcohol use; therefore, it was imperative that families not only become informed about children's drug and alcohol use, but that they should also be aware about the messages they were sending their children, specifically. Hurdle and colleagues (2003) agreed that an American Indian youth's family as a whole, could act in very positive and supportive ways, especially in the realm of sanctions against drug and alcohol use. These sanctions in American Indian families could be specifically impactful, because drug and alcohol use are perceived to be so widely condoned. Therefore, consistent negative messages from all members of the family may be seen as not only unique, but important because of their very uniqueness.

Schools and Families Together

When families team up with schools, drug use prevention was even more effective. Ford (2009) noted that a student's strong bond with school, created an investment in conformity, and thus, students became involved with conventional activities, such as academic development, artistic development or athletic development. Crosnoe,(2009) found that adolescents who had claimed close relationships with their parents, who came from well-organized homes, felt emotionally close to teachers, and performed well in school and valued school achievement, were protected from the negative influences of deviant friends.

The numbers related to the 2005-2006 ADAS findings, showed that there was work to do in the American Indian community to address drug and alcohol use among youth. According to 7th through 12th grade American Indian students who participated in the 2005-2006 ADAS, their schools were not places of engagement for them, nor did they create a productive challenge. Almost 50% liked school "some," 53% said they liked their teachers "some" and a little over 50% felt that teachers liked them. Only 16% indicated school was fun. Ironically, more than half felt their grades were good and they were good students. What was most important, however, was what the numbers do not say. Year after year, the graduating year of seniors was approximately half the population of incoming sophomores. This was indicative of a drop-out rate of nearly fifty percent.

The 2005-2006 ADAS survey also indicated that educational support from families was relatively low. Only a third of families attended a lot of school events, while a little over a third never attended school meetings. About half of the families had communicated information about intoxication, inhalants, marijuana and other drugs, while only about 40% talked about tobacco. This latter statistic was an indication of the high tolerance of tobacco use in the culture.

There was good news, however. In the 2005-2006 ADAS survey, results showed slightly over 80% of American Indian 7th through 12th graders felt their families cared about them "a lot," while 83% of this group said they cared for their families "a lot." These numbers had the feel of family closeness, which, according to the previous research, was invaluable in addressing substance use issues. This closeness, when added to a school's effective policies and prevention efforts, could have a significant impact on drug and alcohol use among American Indian youth.

Conclusion

Previous research has found that tobacco, drug and alcohol use are significantly high in American Indian youths in 7th through 12th grades attending schools located on or near reservations. For some substances, such as tobacco and alcohol, the tolerance level was relatively high in the communities and the families, making it difficult to address. For other substances, like inhalants and cocaine, tolerance was extremely low, and youths had exhibited a significant decrease in use over recent years.

The importance of addressing tobacco, drug, and alcohol use was apparent in terms of health, both physiologically and emotionally. Not only do drugs have a negative impact on the physical body, deteriorating such organs as the lungs, liver, heart and brain, but they also damage friendships, intimate relationships, as well as the ability to work and economically contribute to the community.

Schools' attempts to address the issue of drug use, have been centered on the establishment and institution of policies and consequences for violation. Although they form norms of tolerance and intolerance, they are limited in their scope to actually decrease use, or decrease the initiation of use by youth. The role of families and parents in reducing drug use was especially impactful as they can send strong, unified messages against use which teens, if they have a close relationship with their families, may pay closer attention to. When schools and parents come together, they can be a formidable force in addressing drug use. Strong protective factors against alcohol and drug use are seen in adolescents who feel they are close to parents, close to teachers and have a sense of academic achievement.

References

Allen, Joseph P., Porter, Mary Frances R., McFarland, F. Christy, Marsh, Penny, McElhaney, Kathleen Boykin. (2005). The Two Faces of Adolescents' Success with Peers: Adolescent Popularity, Social Adaptation, and Deviant Behavior. *Child Development*, 76(3):747-760.

Bachman, J.G., O'Malley, P.M., & Johnston, L.D. (1984). Drug use among young adults: The impacts of role status and social environment. *Journal of Personality and Social Psychology,* 47:621-645.

Bachman, J.G., O'Malley, P.M., & Johnson, LD. (1998). Explaining Recent Increases in Students' Marijuana Use: Impacts of Perceived Risks and Disapproval, 1976 through 1996. *American Journal of Public Health*, 88(6):887-892.

Bartzokis, G., Beckson, M., Lu, P.J., Edwards, N, Bridge, P., Mintz J. (2002). Brain maturation may be arrested in chronic cocaine addicts. *Biological Psychiatry.* 51(8): 605-611.

Beauvais, F. (1992). Indian adolescent drug and alcohol use: Recent patterns and consequences. *American Indian and Alaska Native Mental Health Research.* 5(1):1-67.

Beauvais, Fred, Wayman, Jeffrey C., Jumper-Thurman, Pamela, Plested, Barbara, and Helm, Heather. (2002.) Inhalant Abuse Among American Indian, Mexican American, and Non-Latino White Adolescents. *American Journal of Drug and Alcohol Abuse,* 28(1): 171-187.

Beauvais, F., Jumper-Thurman, P., Helm, H. Plested, B., & Burnside, M. (2004). Surveillance of drug use among American Indian adolescents: Patterns over 25 years. *Journal, of Adolescent Health*, 34(6):493-500.

Beauvais, F., Oetting, E.R., Edwards, R.W., Swaim, R., Jumper-Thurman, P. (2005). Inhalant Use in the United States. In E. Zvartaue, (Ed.), *Inhalants.* Saint Petersburg: Pavlov Medical University Publishing House, pp. 224-246.

Brown, Sandra A., and Tapert, Susan F. (2004). Adolescence and the Trajectory of Alcohol Use: Basic to Clinical Studies. *Adolescent Brain Development: Vulnerabilities and Opportunities.* Ronald E. Dahl and Linda Patia Spear, Eds., New York Academy of Sciences, 1021:234-244.

Crews, Fulton Timm, and Boettiger, Charlotte Ann. (2009). Impulsivity, Frontal Lobes and Risk for Addiction. *Pharmacology, Biochemistry and Behavior*, 93:237-247.

Evans-Whipp, Tracy J., Bond, Lyndal, Toumbourou, John W., Catalano, Richard F. (2004). A Review of School Drug Policies and Their Impact on Youth Substance Use. *Health Promotion International*, 19(2):227-234.

Evans-Whipp, Tracy J., Bond, Lyndal, Toumburour, John W., Catalano, Richard F. (2007).School, Parent, and Student Perspectives of School Drug Policies. *Journal of School Health*, 77(3):138-146.

Faden, Vivan B. (2006). Trends in Initiation of alcohol use in the United States, 1975-2003. *Alcoholism: Clinical and Experimental Research*, 30:1011-1022.

Finn, Kristin V., and Willert, H. Jeanette. (2006). Alcohol and Drugs in Schools: Teachers' Reactions to the Problem. *The Phi Delta Kappan*. 88(1):37-40.

Goodstadt, Michael S. (1987). Substance Abuse Curricula vs. School Drug Policies. *Journal of School Health*. 59(6): 245-250.

Hornik, Robert, Lela Jacobsohn, Orwin Robert, Piesse, Andrea and Kalton, Graham. (2008). Effects of the National Youth Anti-Drug Media Campaign on Youths. *American Journal of Public Health*, 98(12):2229-2236.

Hurdle, D.E., Okamoto, Scott K., Miles, Bart. (2003). Family Influences on Alcohol and Drug Use by American Indian Youth: Implications for Prevention. *Journal of Family Social Work.*, 7(1):53-68.

Jones, Sherry Everett, Fisher, Carolyn J., Greene, Brenda Z., Hertz, Marci F., Pritzl, Jane. (2007). Healthy and Safe School Environment, Part I: Results from the School Health Policies and Programs Study 2006. *Journal of School Health*, 77(8): 522-543.

Kandel, Denise B. (1995). Ethnic Differences in Drug Use: Patterns and Paradoxes. *Drug Abuse Prevention with Multi-Ethnic Youth*. G. Botvins, S. Schinke and M. Orlandi, eds., Sage Publications, Thousand Oaks, CA, Pp. 81-101.

Kulis, Stephen, Okamoto, Scott, Sen, Andrea Dixon Rayle Soma. (2006). Social Contexts of Drug Offers Among American Indian Youth and Their Relationship to Substance Us: An Exploratory Study. *Cultural Diversity and Ethnic Minority Psychology*. 12(1):30-44.

Lubman, D. I., Hides, L. Yucel, M. (2006). Inhalant misuse in youth: time for a coordinated response. *eMJA*. *http://www.mja.com.au/public/issues/185-_06_180906/lub11067 _fm. html.* Accessed 1/15/10.

Masten Ann S., Faden, Vivan B., Zucker, Robert A., Spear, Linda P. (2009). A Developmental Perspective on Underage Alcohol Use. *Alcohol Research & Health*, 32(1):3-15.

Miller, Kimberly A., Beauvais, Fred, Burnside, Martha, Jumper-Thurman, Pamela. (2008) A Comparison of American Indian and Non-Indian Youth to Sixth Graders Rates of Drug Use, *Journal Ethnicity in Substance Abuse*, 7(3):258-267.

Oetting, E.R. & Beauvais, F. (1987). Peer Cluster Theory, Socialization Characteristics, and Adolescent Drug Use: A Path Analysis. *Journal of Counseling Psychology*, 34(2):205-213.

Oetting, E.R. & Beauvais, F. (1989). Epidemiology and correlates of alcohol use among Indian adolescents living on reservations. In: D. Spiegler and D. Tate (Eds.) *Alcohol Use among U.S. Ethnic Minorities.* Research Monograph #18. Rockville, Maryland: National Institute on Alcoholism and Alcohol Abuse.

Plunkett, Mark, and Mitchell, Christina M. (2000). Substance Use Rates Among American Indian Adolescents: Regional Comparisons with Monitoring the Future High School Seniors. *Journal of Drug Issues*, 30(3):575-592.

Pope, H.G. Jr., Gruber, A..J., Hudson, J. I., Cohaine, G., Huestis, M.A., Yurgelun-Todd, D. (2003). Early-onset Cannabis use and Cognitive Deficits: What is the nature of the association? *Drug and Alcohol Dependency*, 69:303-310.

Poulin, Christiane. (2007). Smoking smoking bans: do they help/do they harm? *Drug and Alcohol Review*, (26:615-624).

Robert Wood Johnson Foundation. (2009). Evaluation of the D.A.R.E. School-Based Substance Abuse Prevention Curriculum, http://www.rwjf.org/pr/product.jsp?id= 42049. Accessed 3/3/2010.

Sircar, Ratna and Sircar, Debashish. (2005). Adolescent Rats Exposed to Repeated Ethanol Treatment Show Lingering Behavior Impairments. *Alcoholism: Clinical and Experimental Research*, 29(8):1402-1410.

Sircar, Ratna and Sircar, Debanishish. (2006). Repeated Ethanol Treatment in Adolescent Rats Alters Cortical NMDA Receptor. *Alcohol*, 39:51-58.

Spicer, Paul. (1997). Toward a (Dys)functional Anthropology of Drinking: Ambivalence and the American Indian Experience with Alcohol. *Medical Anthropology Quarterly.* 11(3):306-323.

Swaim, Randall, Oetting, Eugene R., Jumper-Thurman, Pamela, Beauvais, Fred, Edwards, Ruth W. (1993). American Indian Adolescent Drug Use and Socialization Characteristics. *Journal of Cross-Cultural Psychology*, 24(1): 53-70.

Tapert, Susan F., Caldwell, Lisa A., and Burke, Christina. (2005). Alcohol and the Adolescent Brain. *Alcohol Research and Health.* 28(4):205-212.

Zucker, Robert A., Donovan, John E., Masten, Ann S., Mattson, Margaret E., and Moss, Howard B. (2008). Early Developmental Processes and the Continuity of Risk for Underage Drinking and Problem Drinking. *Pediatrics.* 121(4):S252-S272.

Ah neen dush: Harnessing Collective Wisdom to Create Culturally Relevant Science Experiences in Pre-K Classrooms

Ann Mogush Mason, M.Ed., Mia Dubosarsky, Ph.D., Gillian Roehrig, Ph.D., Mary Farley, Stephan Carlson, Ph.D., and Barbara Murphy, M.A.

Introduction

Ah neen dush (roughly translated as 'why?' in Ojibwe) is a professional development partnership between the White Earth Reservation Head Start program in Northern Minnesota and the University of Minnesota's Department of Curriculum and Instruction. *Ah neen dush* aims to support and mentor teachers as they create engaging environments that weave discovery-based science activities with Ojibwe philosophy and tradition. Professional development workshops have unlocked stores of expertise previously contained within individual Head Start centers, allowing teachers access to one another's experiences and opportunities to reflect on their own work. This chapter serves as a partial chronicle of our projects first 14 months, a period during which the integration of science and culture became a new focal point in teachers' thinking about their work with students.

In the coming pages, we will first describe the theoretical framework that informs this project, situate our work in its local context with data and descriptions of White Earth Head Start centers, outline the conceptual framework of the research project, and then introduce you to three of the teachers. Through the voices of these teachers and a few others, we will share successes and struggles in the process of implementing a culturally relevant approach to teaching science on the White Earth reservation.

Theoretical framework: Culturally relevant pedagogy

Culturally relevant pedagogy is presented by a growing group of scholars as a way to address inequity in educational achievement (e.g. Aguilera et al, 2007; Cleary & Peacock, 1998; Demmert, 2001; Ladson-Billings, 1995; Yazzie, 2000). Many of these researchers adopt a cultural difference perspective, acknowledging that, for many students from non dominant backgrounds, the culture of schools and the culture of families are different. The work of culturally relevant pedagogues, then, is to design school experiences that offer a closer match between home and school culture.

According to Valenzuela's (1999) ethnography about U.S.-Mexican youth in a Texas community, schooling is subtractive any time that something the student carries into the classroom is either devalued or unrecognized. Valenzuela differentiates *education*, which is a holistic view of education as pervading all spheres, from a more detached notion of *schooling*, to which most students must learn how to adapt. When schooling is subtractive, young people can experience an atrophy of culturally based strengths, or assets.

In response to an educational environment characterized by subtractive practices, culturally relevant pedagogy takes aim at three goals: 1) to "produce students who can achieve academically; 2) to produce students who demonstrate cultural competence; and 3) to develop students who can both understand and critique the existing social order" (Ladson-Billings, 1995a, p.474). While individual teachers will forge unique paths to cultural relevance, Ladson-Billings (1995b) found that culturally relevant teachers share some general ideologies and beliefs that characterize all students as creators of knowledge who have the potential to succeed. Thus, culturally relevant pedagogy is less about a specific set of teaching methods, than it is about a way of looking at students and thinking about one's own teaching (Ladson-Billings, 1995a).

Many scholars of culturally relevant pedagogy (c.f. Gay, 2002; Delpit, 1998; Nieto, 2009; Valdes, 1996) advocate conceptions of teaching that consider the unique learning needs to diverse groups of students, and that favor a focus on teachers' attitudes and beliefs over discrete methodologies. Gay encourages educators to allow students "the right to grapple with learning challenges from the point of strength and relevance found in their own cultural frames of relevance" (2002, p. 114).

The 'funds of knowledge' approach advanced by Moll, et al (1991) challenges teachers of culturally and linguistically diverse students to view themselves as students of their students' backgrounds. By conducting home visits and interviews with family members, teachers can learn about what knowledge the students bring from home to the classroom, and teaching can be adjusted to facilitate a better match between home and school learning (Moll, et al, 1991). Li (2008) outlines a theory of culture pedagogy, which, like culturally relevant pedagogy, aims to empower students as cultural translators and build on funds of knowledge. Each of these theories operates on a belief that when students feel engaged and connected at school, they learn more.

For example, the Ka Lama Teacher Education Initiative in Hawaii trains Native Hawaiians to teach in their own communities (Au et al, 2008). By promoting an asset-based perspective that focuses on community-specific needs and interests, Ka Lama is able to prepare teachers who recognize the need for culturally relevant instruction for their primarily Native Hawaiian students (Au, 1980). Vogt, Jordan, & Tharp (1987) strengthened Au's argument by modifying her model in a Navajo cultural setting. In both cases, schooling has been designed to fit the students, instead of the other way around (Ladson-Billings, 1995b).

A potential pitfall in this approach to cultural relevance, however, is that it could lead to a 'checklist' mentality in which educators simply place an existing formula into their setting with minor local modifications. This may lead to an over-reliance on static, versus dynamic, definitions of culture. In addition, this approach can encourage a focus on the micro level of practice without explicitly addressing structural issues.

Moving beyond the checklist mentality, Gonzalez, et al refer to students' funds of knowledge as "strategic and cultural resources" (2005, p. 47), arguing that these resources constitute the information that educators and policymakers need, in order to create pedagogical, evaluation and assessment models that work for diverse students. Such an approach can transform perceptions of culture from static to dynamic, which makes it easier and more meaningful to incorporate culture as prior knowledge that can inform curriculum and classroom practices. The authors also cite the transformative potential of an asset-based perspective on students' families, particularly in terms of how teachers view the responsibility of figuring out how schools and families can relate and communicate (Gonzalez et al, 2005). In the same chapter, teacher-researcher Amanti (Gonzalez et al, 2005) takes critical aim at typical conceptions of multicultural education as an 'add-on' to normative approaches that work from Eurocentric viewpoints and view cultures as static.

While each member of the Ah neen dush University research team entered this project with her or his own interpretations of the research and theory around culturally relevant pedagogy, a key goal of the project was to work toward a local definition of cultural relevance as conceived of, and enacted in, the Head Start classrooms in White Earth. Thus, we hope to add depth and, of course, relevance, to theoretical conceptions of cultural relevance, by describing the process of negotiating its definition in one unique setting with one unique group of teachers and researchers.

Community context

Data presented by the Minnesota Department of Education show that Native American students lag behind state achievement averages. On the White Earth reservation, 34% of third graders either partially meet or do not meet state mathematics standards; statewide, only 18.6% of students fit into those categories. In reading, 29% of White Earth third graders either partially meet or do not meet the state standards, compared to 21% across the state. Of White Earth fifth graders, 86.3% do not or just partially meet the Minnesota science standards, compared to 60.9% statewide. A Native American student in Minnesota is three times more likely to drop out of school, than the average Minnesotan. Sadly, this is a representative picture of educational achievement among Native American students across the United States (Bowman, 2003; Lynch, 2000).

The educational disadvantages that Native American students face can be compounded by teaching methods that do not acknowledge Native epistemologies (Nelson-Barber and Estrin, 1995). Some researchers refer to Native American emphasis on storytelling as a way of passing information (Ballenger, 1997; Eder, 2007). Stories told within a familiar epistemological perspective are more comprehensible to children (Bock, 2006) and assist the maintenance of cultural integrity (Eder, 2007). When Westby and Roman (1995) describe an approach for teaching Native American elementary school students how to comprehend mainstream narrative texts, they discuss in terms of using Native American discursive styles as a bridge to mainstream styles. Above all, they argue, Native American children should learn to value Native forms of discourse, while also learning to navigate mainstream narratives' structure, content, and style. To further complicate conceptions of successful teaching that incorporates Native American culture, Hermes (2005) asserts that Native American language must be an essential component of teaching culture. Ismail and Cazden (2005) suggest finding common ground between native and Western epistemologies to facilitate learning opportunities.

The White Earth tribal council, on the reservation's main website, puts it this way: "...learning about the past can help us understand our present. In search of such understanding, let us pick up the story of the Chippewa in those distant times when, as they say, the earth was new and tribal people reigned supreme in North America" (www.whiteearth.com).

Head Start serves most of the preschool-aged children who live on or near the White Earth reservation. While no data are available for White Earth's Head Start students, NAEP reported that almost all children in grades K-12 received free or reduced price lunch in 1998 and 2000, a figure that likely remains consistent. The White Earth Head Start program includes 9 classrooms in 6 centers spread throughout the reservation, as well as two teachers who travel throughout the community to provide home-based services for Early Head Start (children from birth to age 3). The teaching staff of roughly 35 women is approximately one-half Ojibwe and one-half White or mixed heritage. With some variation, classrooms consist of a lead teacher, assistant teacher, and aide, and a Family Services Advocate.

In several ways, the relationships between University researchers and Head Start teachers in this project parallel those reflected in Gonzalez, Moll, and Amanti's (2005) work. In their case, teachers and anthropologists represent practice and theory, respectively, but they complicate that relationship by mutually informing one another. Rather than viewing research as informing practice in a linear, one-directional fashion, this approach to research acknowledges the back-and-forth relationship that actually exists between theory and practice.

Why early childhood?

While most research on culturally relevant pedagogy addresses K-12 and post-secondary settings, we argue that it is also necessary to acknowledge the incredible socializing power of early childhood settings. Thus, early childhood education has particular importance for marginalized students, whose schooling experiences can often be subtractive (Valenzuela, 1999). Research on early childhood intervention programs shows that children from disadvantaged families gain long-lasting benefits from high quality programs. Gains were found in school competence, development of cognitive skills, attitudes, and impact on families (Consortium for Longitudinal Studies, 1983). Head Start, specifically, has been found to lead to "sizable improvement in school success...persistent effect on achievement, grade retention, special education, high school graduation and socialization" (Barnett, 1995, p. 43. Referring specifically to Native American students, Demmert (2001) underlines the critical role of the early childhood environment and experiences:

> Ensuring a challenging and stimulating early environment for young children is associated with cognitive development and, later, achievement in the formal school setting. If improving academic performance for all Native children is a priority, we must take these findings seriously and pay attention to this period in a Native child's life (p. 07).

Ah neen dush conceptual framework

Ah neen dush is designed as a series of monthly workshops, a weeklong summer workshop and a group website that is used for mentoring and discussions. Each monthly workshop is hosted by a different Head Start center, and opens with a short presentation by the hosting staff. These presentations include photos and documentary evidence of the science activities the teachers have conducted during the month. The format of the monthly workshop allows all teachers to share interesting science activities they have done in their classrooms, and how culture was integrated into the lessons.

Building on best practices in early childhood education, our theoretical framework draws on and incorporates culturally relevant pedagogy, Demmert & Towner's (2003) six critical elements for culturally based education programs, Copley & Padron's (1998) professional development standards for early childhood teachers, and inquiry-based science pedagogy. Thus, *Ah neen dush* emphasizes:

1. A long-term commitment to working toward sustainable professional development;

2. Discovery-based science and mathematics curriculum rooted in Ojibwe culture and developed by the teachers with assistance from the program team;
3. Multifaceted learning experiences: teachers play the role of students during modeled lessons, teachers during curriculum development, and presenters during each monthly session;
4. Making connections to families and community members;
5. Mentoring: online mentoring as well as monthly classroom visits;
6. Learning communities: creating teams of teachers who work and learn together (Zech et al., 2000);
7. Reflective journaling (Schon, 1996) and;
8. Effective use of technology: enhancing the culture of learning communities and project dissemination via the project's website.

The holistic nature of this professional development sequence calls for a gradual introduction of diverse topics to the Head Start teachers. Research with primary-grade teachers has shown a need for improved knowledge in science content, science methods appropriate for young children, ways of representing and formulating science topics for young children, curricular activities, and administrative support (Kallery, 2004). Following this logic with early childhood teachers, Ah neen dush's first year focused on building foundations such as implementing inquiry-based science pedagogies. By beginning with concepts related to place-based learning and nature, we have helped orient teachers' work toward the American Indian standards for science education. Specifically, the 'science as inquiry' standard notes that students should develop awareness that "observations and understandings of nature and ecological relationships traditionally formed an essential base of knowledge among American Indian cultures" (Bureau of Indians Affairs & ORBIS Associates, 1998, p. 01).

This chapter reflects data collected and teacher's reflections on the first 14 months of *Ah neen dush* (January 2009-March 2010). During the 2009-2010 academic year, our goal has been to introduce the processes and concepts of scientific inquiry through a culturally relevant pedagogy that draws from and reflects Ojibwe culture. The Young Scientist series (developed by Education Development Center, Inc.) was chosen as a baseline science curriculum, because it integrates inquiry activities with observations and understandings of students' environments. This curriculum includes three modules focusing on nature, structures, and water. We chose to work on the nature theme first, noting the aforementioned link between nature and the American Indian science standards, as well as acknowledging the logical connections between nature and Ojibwe culture.

After establishing understandings of the inquiry process in early childhood science, the University research team and the Head Start teachers began exploring how to use these processes to learn about traditional and cultural Ojibwe practices. For example, during a unit on wild rice harvesting (outlined in greater detail below), White Earth Head Start teachers use elders' stories, pictures and field trips to demonstrate the 'ricing' process. Explorations of the wild rice plant and habitat connect the children not only with their natural environments, but also with a long-practiced tribal tradition that links families, communities, and economies.

At the heart of *Ah neen dush* is the goal of enhancing White Earth Head Start students' science experiences through improved teaching practices that are responsive to Ojibwe culture. Ultimately, we view teachers as agents of change who can affect children, their families, and the White Earth community.

Researcher positionality

Since the researcher is the primary instrument of qualitative research (Merriam, 2009), Peshkin (1988) argues that researchers should constantly consider how their multiple subjectivities shape the ways they interpret data. In this study, a diverse group of education researchers are comprised of 4 females, of whom two are graduate students and two are faculty members, and one White male faculty member in outdoor education. One graduate student is from Israel and the other is a White American. Both have experience in teaching and/or developing early childhood curriculum. One female faculty member is a White American with expertise in child development and early childhood education, and one is a White science educator from England.

Not surprisingly, the research team and the Head Start teachers share some cultural frames of reference but differ in many others. As educators, all stakeholders in this project share an orientation toward educational equity and a general care and concern for young people. Most significantly, as University researchers working in a Native American community, the research team runs the risk of reproducing the patterns of domination that contribute to the structural inequality this project hopes to combat.

In the next section, three focal teachers will be introduced. While by no means representative of the 35 White Earth Head Start teachers as a group, these three teachers are illuminative examples of the varying experiences had by Ojibwe, White, and mixed-heritage teachers in this setting. Observational and interview data came from the following sources: focus groups conducted in August 2009, individual and paired interviews conducted in February 2010, field notes taken when a group of teachers presented at a professional conference in March 2010, and observational field notes from classroom visits and professional development workshops between August 2009 and February 2010. While we rely as much as possible on the teachers' own words to describe themselves and their experiences, the University researchers acknowledge the mitigating effect of the interview and focus group processes, recognizing that any such account can only be partial.

Teacher A: Leah

> (This program has) taught us how to look with children. Don't just tell them, 'that's an ant,' get excited with them and ask questions. (Professional conference presentation, March 11, 2010)

Leah teaches in the farthest-flung Head Start center on the reservation. About one hour's drive from the primary Head Start building, the Rice Lake center has the least contact with Head Start coordinators and administrative staff. Several of the teachers at this center have worked there for the bulk of their careers. At this center, 3-5 year olds are together in one classroom with a very busy teaching staff! The Head Start room is connected to a community center that houses a gymnasium, exercise room, and senior center. Because of the physical link to elder community members, the Head Start children at this center enjoy relationships with multiple adults other than their families and teachers.

Long before the Ah neen dush project began, Leah, an Ojibwe woman, considered her classroom a place to share her passion for maintaining close ties to native traditions. This feeling is evident throughout the classroom: Ojibwe words label various classroom items, several bulletin boards feature Ojibwe stories, and Leah even has a birch bark canoe on display.

Teacher B: "Karen"

> (The language is) the hardest part for me, and I always worry about if I'm teaching it the right way, because I don't want to offend anybody either, so it's kind of like okay I really want to do this, but am I doing it right? (Interview, February 4, 2010)

This 4-5 year old Head Start classroom is the first you see upon entering the tribal Head Start headquarters. The energy of its young inhabitants reverberates even hours after the children have left for the day. Karen, the lead teacher, who is of mixed White and Ojibwe descent, has a stated commitment to developing culturally relevant practice. Karen's Head Start classroom consists of about 16 students, a White assistant teacher and two Native American aides. Karen has taught at White Earth Head Start for 13 years. Her classroom is spacious enough to include various marked-off areas for specific types of activity: kidney tables for meals and group work, a circular carpet for whole class meetings and games, a science area, a dramatic play area, a space for quiet reading, and ample storage.

Karen grew up on the edge of the reservation, not knowing until she was a young adult that her grandfather had been Ojibwe and had attended a boarding school. This realization was meaningful to Karen, especially as she began to discover the role that silence had played in her family's story: when her grandparent's generation was told not to speak the Ojibwe language or practice its traditions, the effect, two generations later, was that she became unaware of her own cultural heritage.

Teacher C: "Ruth"

"I came in this morning as one person, and I'm leaving as a changed woman."
(Spoken during professional development workshop, September 10, 2009).

Ruth is a White teacher who feels a deep connection to the Native Americans who first inhabited her community. Referring to the historical relationship between Native American communities and European colonizers, Ruth emphasizes that Native American individuals still carry a 'deep hurt' that traces back generations, a hurt that she hopes her work as an Early Head Start teacher might ease.

Ruth's position differs in many ways from the previous two teachers. Whereas their work is with children ages 3-5, Ruth visits children in their homes when they are between birth and age 3. Her role as an educator, then, involves work with families as well as children. She also invites families to 'socialization' events at her office, which is contained within one of the community schools on the reservation.

Strategies and struggles

Two strategies and one struggle came up consistently in the teachers' descriptions of and reflections on their work toward culturally relevant teaching of science concepts. Involving parents and the community and rethinking their approaches to teaching science were repeatedly described as key to the Head Start teachers' growing success in this work. Each in their own way, teachers have struggled with concerns related to authority and authenticity in addressing topics related to Ojibwe culture and traditions. In the coming pages, each strategy and struggle will be described through the teachers' words and stories.

Strategy 1: Parent and community involvement

During an interview (on February 4, 2010) about what sort of additional re-sources could enhance their work with Head Start children, the following con-versation occurred between Karen and another teacher:

1	Mary	Basically (involve) your elders, and I don't know a lot of
2		them, like I said in Calloway, they never talked about it or
3		did any of it, it was never an issue, so, yeah. I don't know.
4	Leslie	Like they always do a parent day, they should do a grand-
5		parent day. You know, I mean they should do if they were,
6		have your grandma or grandpa come in and tell what hap-
7		pened when they were young. That would be kinda neat.
8	Mary	Maybe we'll just have to do it on our own!
9	Leslie	I know, that 's what I was thinking too!

Excerpt 1.1

Excerpt 1 was particularly interesting because the initial question was actually about what resources from the University or the tribe could help the Head Start teachers, and Mary and Leslie responded with suggestions for ways *they* could harness the resources that already exist in their communities. In the following exerpt, Leah refers to the way her center has been able to gain access to elders' stories and perspectives, by inviting them to be part of the everyday life of the Head Start class:

1	Leah	I think it's important to keep the elders involved, because
2		like at Rice Lake we have elders coming in and out, pretty
3		much every day, and then we also bring in the wild rice,
4		take them on a field trip, let them see it, bring it in, cook it,
		eat it, we do, I mean they do a lot like that.

Excerpt 1.2

While Leah's setting with the community center down the hall provides a built-in resource for involving community members, in Excerpt 3, she and a colleague also discuss the amount of help they can receive from the reservation at large. Other teachers have shared stories about the Department of Natural Resources being available to help teachers arrange wilderness hikes and ice fishing trips, even cutting fishing holes and stocking a lake with small fish for the children to catch!

1	Patricia	…we have the advantage with, what, I'd say 97, 98% of our
2		class is Native American, so we have that access right there.
3		We don't do much besides Native American, we don't say,
4		like, this is how White people would do it.
5	Leah	We not only have our communities, but we have our reser-
6		vation, so there's lots of resources. And we have a biology
7		department now, and they're helpful, and we have all kinds
8		of different departments in place, so when we teach safety
9		we have tribal cops, and there's a lot of community re-
		sources out there.

Excerpt 1.3

In all, White Earth Head Start teachers seem to give much credit to their community connections for their success at integrating science and Ojibwe culture. This mindset is consistent with other educators' descriptions of culturally relevant pedagogy as relying on students' funds of knowledge (Gonzalez et al., 2005) to guide curriculum and teaching, as well as the principle of culturally relevant pedagogy as one that positions students as 'knowers,' or the experts of their own experiences (Ladson-Billings, 1995a).

Strategy 2: Rethinking science content

A series of focus groups conducted with Head Start teachers in August 2009, revealed that several non-Native teachers felt they lacked the knowledge of Ojibwe cultural practices required to respectfully implement a culturally relevant curriculum. With this in mind, the Ojibwe staff from the Rice Lake Head Start center organized an in-service day in September 2009, during which we were fully immersed in wild rice harvesting and processing. Native and non-Native teachers reported that this first-hand experience, enhanced by the fact that one of their colleagues had led it, helped them feel more prepared to teach and discuss wild 'ricing' in their classrooms. While this event came only 9 months into the Ah neen dush project, it served as a clear example of the ways the Head Start teachers have rethought their approaches to teaching science at the early childhood level. The following excerpt came from the same focus group meeting, and includes Leah describing how she realized that she had actually been teaching science topics, only had not realized or labeled it as such:

1	Leah	Teaching them that a lot of stuff they already know and al-
2		ready do is considered science and math. Like they go on
3		field trips, like going on a science field trip.

Excerpt 2.1

During her February 2010 interview, Mary expressed a similar sentiment about realizing that the Head Start content she was already teaching included scientific concepts, and that she only needed to shift her thinking a bit to present it that way to her students. Later in the same conversation, we discussed the role of culture in that process, of which a bit is included here:

1 2 3	Annie	So according to your experiences so far as a teacher and as part of this professional development, how would you give a definition for teaching science in way that's culturally rele-vant?
4 5 6 7 8	Mary	 I don't know, I think it's pretty easy, actually, just because the culture is a lot about nature. And you know I mean that's pretty much how they lived off the land and what they used to do and it's a lot of the science ties right into their culture so it's pretty, pretty easy I think, the science part of it.

Excerpt 2.2

Explicit teaching strategies have been impacted by teachers' changes in thinking about science content, as well. For example, Leah describes below how she has become more mindful of her planning about how she poses questions to the children in her class. Leah's attentiveness to her students as budding thinkers is evident in this excerpt, and it reflects her consistency with principles of cultur-ally relevant pedagogy, such as Ladson-Billings' (1995a) call for teachers to accept the knowledge and ways of knowing that children bring to school:

1 2 3 4	Leah	Another thing I've found interesting about this ((professional development)) is learning how to ask open-ended questions, have the children answer, because, I don't know, I did it, but I wasn't like prepared to do it, or something, so… I'm just more aware of it, just more aware of it.

Excerpt 2.3

For Ruth, shifting her thinking toward teaching science in a culturally relevant way has been as simple as putting 'a bug' in students' ears about the possible lives available to them. While, in her role as an early childhood educator, those futures are distant today, she considers it important that she works now with the future in mind:

1	Ruth	...Okay just go as far as you can, ((Ruth)), and hope the best
2		for these kids and you hope that maybe they'll go on to school
3		and do something more than just stay here, maybe they'll go
4		on and be a doctor and come back to this community, maybe
5		they'll go on and be a teacher and, you know, uh, carry that
6		culture to other places in the world, whatever. Um, but you
7		know and I try to tell them, you going to be a doctor when
8		you grow up? All right, let's talk about what you're gong to
		do. I try and put a bug in their ear for that one.

Excerpt 2.4

Finally, the following excerpt provides a snapshot of how one group of teachers describes the process of transitioning to a form of culturally relevant pedagogy that is integrated with science content, rather than one that treats each as a separate sphere within the Head Start curriculum:

1	Gillian	So it's a starting point, you're starting with the tradition
2		rather than the, like I'm going to teach, electricity.
3	Leah	and it's kind of not even a choice, because the Head Start
4		performance says ((performance standards say)) that we
5		have to teach cultural ((content)), so it, we start with num-
6		bers, and when we do the traditional stories, and from the
7		traditional stories there's never like a right or wrong way,
8		it's, it kind of leaves it open, but there's always a teaching
9		within that story, either how something's made or how
10		something came about, the ((creation)) stories are like that,
		it's like creation stories.
11	Patricia	Or like "how the bear lost his tail."
12	Gillian	So you'll start with the story or tradition and you'll put
13	Leah	science in...
14		
15		And then we have a lot of younger parents now than we did
16		before, so we'll put we always send home copies of stories
17		and stuff, I know it takes a lot of paper, but I always try to
		get the cultural things back home. So they get a lot of
18	Sally	books, and if you guys need any, XXXX, or whatever, you
19		guys come down and I'll give you a copy of them.
20		

| 21 | | And I also think it's really important that we keep this culture in the Head Start, because once our kids transition to the public school, they don't get it there. Its' gone. But they remember what they've been taught in Head Start. |

Excerpt 7

The above excerpts indicate growth toward a locally mediated, unique approach to culturally relevant teaching of science concepts. This in-process definition will be discussed in greater detail below, as now we turn to the primary struggle identified in the teachers' words and stories about their work related to the Ah neen dush project.

Struggles: Authority and authenticity

Like many professionals who work in settings where they consider themselves cultural outsiders, White teachers (and several teachers with Ojibwe heritage who report feeling disconnected from Ojibwe culture and traditions) struggle with concerns of speaking authentically and with authority about Ojibwe cultural content. Often, as described below, these struggles take shape in the form of questions about the Ojibwe language:

1 2 3	Annie	Can you think of a time when it's been a struggle ((to integrate culture and science content)), or when you've felt you were doing it and didn't really pull it off?
4 5	Krystal	Well when you talk in Ojibwe or say Ojibwe words, that's definitely, that's a struggle
6 7 8	Julie	That's the hardest part for me, and I always worry about if I'm teaching it the right way, because I don't want to offend anybody either, so it's kind of like okay I really want to do this, but am I doing it right?
9 10 11	Krystal	I'm like (laughter) and you can ask how to say it and stuff but still am I gonna remember this? You know because I don't have no Ojibwe, I mean my mom's Ojibwe (laughs)
12 13 14 15	Julie	Yeah. But it's a hard language to learn, there's no rhyme or reason to it, it's really a hard language to learn. It's like, it you know, I don't know. I'm just always scared of offending a family or making someone upset because I didn't teach it right. It's kind of a, do you do it or don't ya.
16	Krystal	Sometimes if you even say an animal wrong, kids'll say, no, it's this!
17	Julie	They know already. Yeah

18	Krystal	You get up here and tell us!

Excerpt 3.1

In addition, teachers referred regularly to the need for culturally relevant teachers to be astute observers and careful listeners. Learning to listen can be considered a strategy as well as a struggle, of course, but we include it at the end to remind readers that when we struggle to make culturally relevant teaching a reality, the struggle can probably be instructive. Indeed, much of what we need to know as teachers, Ruth, told me in a conversation in February of 2010, is contained within what we can hear and see from our students. Near the end of her formal interview, Ruth was asked, "given the opportunity to make a recommendation, what would you tell another White teacher who just started working with Native students?" She responded as follows:

1	Ruth	Listen…
2		
3		I think that's the key, and observe. And from there, with the
4		observations and that listening, you'll be able to develop a
5		lesson that'll work, because sometimes ((a child's)) objectives
6		and their family life are different than the objectives in another community…

Excerpt 3.2

Conclusions

As mentioned, one function of this project was to translate theoretical work on culturally relevant pedagogy into the realm of practice. This process was meant to result in a negotiated meaning of culturally relevant science curriculum and teaching. Preliminarily, the focus groups and interviews collected thus far indicate four (4) emerging collective definitions of culture relevance as:

1. Cultivating connections to nature and mother earth
2. Emphasizing language preservation through Ojibwe language development
3. Part of the everyday school experience that can be applied beyond school
4. Do-able, knowable, and losable

Clearly, this emerging definition reflects a composite, individual iterations of which will include some unique elements and exclude others. It represents a moment in time, but not the depth and complexity of work enacted by these and other teachers on a daily basis.

The White Earth Head Start teachers' work is unique and specific to its local setting. While it has transformative power for those of us involved, we cannot expect this work to be transformative beyond a local context. We can, however, expect it to contribute to the mounting response to calls for cultural relevance, responses that go beyond describing the need for culturally relevant pedagogies and begin to describe how teachers conceive of cultural relevance, enact it in their teaching, and make sense of their own roles in the process. At the same time, additional studies are needed to identify relationships between culturally relevant teaching and academic achievement. Likewise, any lasting social change that occurs because of these teachers' work, will likely not be visible until years from now; thus, this for now we can offer only a preliminary look at the effects of culturally relevant teaching. More projects like this one, along with longitudinal and comparative work, will help identify the potential, the complications, and the drawbacks of culturally relevant pedagogies.

References

Au, K.H. (1980). Participation structures in a reading lesson with Hawaiian children: Analysis of a culturally appropriate instructional event. *Anthropology & Education Quarterly, 11(*2), 91-115.

Ballenger, B. (1997). Methods of memory: On Native American storytelling. *College English, 59*(7), 789-800.

Barnett, W. S. (1995). Long-term effects of early childhood programs on cognitive and school outcomes. *Future of Children, 5*(3), 25-50.

Bock, T. (2006). A consideration of culture in moral theme comprehension: Comparing Native and European American students. *Journal of Moral Education, 35*(1), 71-87.

Bureau of Indian Affairs (Dept. of Interior), Washington, DC. Office of Indian Education Programs., & ORBIS Associates, Washington, DC. (1998). *American Indian standards for science education.*

Consortium for Longitudinal Studies. (1983). *As the twig is bent: Lasting effects of preschool programs.* Hillsdale, NJ: Erlbaum.

Copley, J. V., & Padron, Y. (1998). Preparing teachers of young learners: Professional development of early childhood teachers in mathematics and science. *Paper presented at the Forum on Early Childhood Science, Mathematics, and Technology Education (Washington, DC, February 6-8, 1998).* Retrieved May 10, 2008, from http://www.project2061.org/publications/earlychild/online/fostering/copleyp.htm.

Delpit, L. (1988). The silenced dialogue: Power and pedagogy in educating other people's children. *Harvard Educational Review, 58*(3), 280-298.

Demmert, W.G., Jr. (2001). Improving schools' academic performance among Native American students: A review of the research literature. Charleston, WV: *ERIC Clearinghouse on Rural Education and Small Schools.* Retrieved February 4, 2003, from http://www.ael.org/eric/demmert.pdf.

Demmert, W.G., Jr. & Towner, J.C. (2003). *A review of the research literature on the influences of culturally based education on the academic performance of Native American students.* Portland, OR: Northwest Regional Educational Laboratory

Eder, D. J. (2007). Bringing Navajo storytelling practices into schools: The importance of maintaining cultural integrity. *Anthropology and Education Quarterly, 38*(3), 278-296.

Gay, G. (2002). Preparing for culturally responsive teaching. *Journal of Teacher Education, 53*(2), 106-116.

Gilliard, J. L., & Moore, R. A. (2007). An investigation of how culture shapes curriculum in early care and education programs on a Native American Indian reservation: "The drum is considered the heartbeat of the community". *Early Childhood Education Journal, 34*(4), 251-258.

Gonzalez, Moll, & Amanti (2005). *Funds of knowledge: Theorizing practices in households, communities, and classrooms.* New York: Routledge.

Grande, S. (2004). *Red Pedagogy.* Lanham, Maryland: Rowman and Littlefield.

Hermes, M. (2005). "Ma'iingan is just a misspelling of the word wolf": A case for teaching culture through language. *Anthropology and Education Quarterly 36*(1): 43-56.

Ismail, S.M., and Cazden, C.B. (2005). Struggles for indigenous education and self-determination: Culture, context, and collaboration. *Anthropology and Education:* 36(1): 88-92.

Kallery, M. (2004). Early years teachers' late concerns and perceived needs in science: An exploratory study. *European Journal of Teacher Education, 27*(2), 147-165.

Ladson-Billings, G. (1995a). But that's just good teaching! The case for culturally relevant pedagogy. *Theory Into Practice, 34*(3), 159-165.

Ladson-Billings, G. (1995b). Toward a Theory of Culturally Relevant Pedagogy. *American Educational Research Journal, 32*(3): 465-491.

Li, G. (2008). *Culturally contested literacies: America's "rainbow underclass" and urban schools.* New York: Routledge.

Lynch, S. J. (2000). *Equity and Science Education Reform.* New Jersey: Lawrence Erlbaum Associates.

Merriam, S.B. (2009). *Qualitative research: A guide to design and implementation.* Jossey-Bass.

Moll, L. and Gonzalez, N. (2004). Engaging life: A funds of knowledge approach to multicultural education. In J. Banks and C. Banks (Eds.), *Handbook of research on multicultural education* (pp. 699-715). San Francisco, CA: Jossey-Bass.

Lomawaima, K.T. (1993). Domesticity in the federal Indian schools: The power of authority over mind and body. *American Ethnologist, 20*(2): 227-240.

Nelson-Barber, S., & Estrin, E. T. (1995). Bringing Native American perspectives to mathematics and science teaching. *Theory into Practice, 34*(3), 174-185.

Nieto, S. (2006). Solidarity, courage and heart: What teacher educators can learn from a new generation of teachers. *Intercultural Education, 17*(5), 457-473.

Peshkin, A. (1998). In search of subjectivity- One's own. *Educational Researcher,* 17(7), 17-21.

Schon, D.A. (1996). *Educating the reflective practitioner: Toward a new design for teaching and learning in the professions.* San Francisco: Jossey-Bass, Inc.

Tannen, D., S. Kendall & C. Gordon (Eds.) (2007). *Family talk: Discourse and identity in four American families.* Oxford: Oxford University Press.

Tuhiwai Smith, L. (2005). Building a research agenda for Indigenous epistemologies and education. *Anthropology and Education Quarterly. 36*(1): 93-95.

Valdes, G. (1996). *Con respeto: Bridging the distances between culturally diverse families and schools.* New York: Teachers College Press.

Valenzuela, A. (1999). *Subtractive schooling: US-Mexico youth and the politics of caring.* NY: State University of New York Press.

Vogt, L.A., Jordan, C. and Tharp, R.G. (1987). Explaining school failure, producing school success: Two cases. *Anthropology and Education Quarterly 18*(4), 276-286.

Westby, C. E., & Roman, R. (1995). Finding the balance: Learning to live in two worlds. *Topics in Language Disorders, 15*(4), 68-88.

Zech, L.K., Gause-Vega, C.L., Bray, M.H., Secules, T., & Goldman, S.R. (2000). Content based collaborative inquiry: A professional development model for sustaining educational reform. *Educational Psychologist, 35*(3), 20.

Acknowledgment: We would like to acknowledge the contributions of Bernadette Furey, Krystal Harstad, Leah Hvezda, & Julie Molacek to this manuscript.

Appendix 1:

Transcription conventions (adapted from Tannen et al., 2007)
((words))	transcriber's thoughts, comments
Carriage return	Each new line represents an intonation unit
-	Indicates a truncated word
!	Rising intonation (exclamatory)
.	Falling, final intonation
,	Continuing intonation
…	Silence
:	Elongated word
CAPS	Emphatic stress
(number)	Length (in tenths of seconds) of pause in talk
XXXX	Proper noun removed for purposes of anonymity

Collapsing the Fear of Mathematics: A Study of the Effects of Navajo Culture on Navajo Student Performance in Mathematics

Henry H. Fowler, Ed.D.

American schools are in a state of 'mediocrity' because of the low expectations in math (Nation at Risk Report, 1983, No Child Left Behind Act of 2001, Duncan, 2009). Trends in International Mathematics and Science Study (2007) reported that low achievement in mathematics was more prominent among minority groups, particularly among the Native American student population who were substantially behind the national norm in their mathematical achievement. The Arizona Instrument to Measure Standards (AIMS) shows that Navajo tenth grade students are not proficient in mathematics.

Overall, there has been much research on the academic achievement of American and Alaskan Indians (1999). However, there has been little research specifically on Navajo high school student achievement in mathematics from the Navajo perspective. The intent of this research was to explore the effect of implementing a math program based on the Navajo culture and teaching to increase achievement for Navajo high school students. This research examines the use of a Navajo cultural component in a high school math curriculum to improve the educational program for the Navajo high school students at Sand Stone High School (SSHS) on the Navajo Reservation. The purpose of this study was to explore an alternative method in teaching Navajo high school students to become competent in understanding mathematics based on the perspective of the Navajo culture. How does integrating Navajo cultural traditions in the math curriculum impact student achievement and students' learning? The goal of the Navajo Cultural Component Mathematics Curriculum (NCCMC) was to use the student's familiar environment as a bridge to mathematics achievement and understanding. Action research based on the teacher researcher perspective provides the framework for this research study which employs a quasi-experimental methodology using mixed methods of data collection.

Background of the Study

Empowering Ourselves as Native Teachers to Promote Cultural Content Lessons

Teaching mathematics is a challenging experience. At times, teaching displays itself as wonderful art pieced; colorful, refreshing, and appealing. But at other times, teaching exhibits an art piece that is unattractive.

My task is to teach mathematics to high school students. These students are my own people, the Navajos. When teaching them, I am approached with a wall of silence. I have observed the wave of unmotivated students with short attention spans to learn mathematics. This scenario created a difficult and challenge situation to promote the strength of understanding the mathematics literacy. The teaching practice that I have acquired from the university, I concluded that it has a small impact on teaching the Navajo high school with efficiency and success in mathematics. How to improve the Navajo high school achievement has been a concern throughout Navajo Reservation high school. As a result, the school district that I have worked with hired outside consultants to develop schools' curricula and streamlined outside knowledge and philosophy into how to teach the Navajo students. The educational program they bring forth does not fit into the cultural style of learning for Navajo students. The orientation that promises to close the achievement gap for Navajo students evaporates once the student drops out or fails because the teachers do not support the relevant needs of Navajo students.

The environment, habitat, regulations, policies and the quality relationship with modern social system has a protrusion influence on the quality experiences of the Navajo people and through these conditions the quality outcome of the lives of the Navajos exhibits. As a researcher, I ponder through these challenging times of the Navajo people; especially with a belief to improve the quality lives of the Navajos through mathematics literacy. I would think alone in my classroom and reflect on my teaching practices that mobilize my energy to generate cultural math activities, which I used as supplement materials to the math curriculum with a sense of anticipation for these materials to motivate my students to learn mathematics with understanding. Now is the time for the grass root stakeholders to take interest in decision making in formulating inquires to our own problems and seeking solutions to improve our quality of mathematics education. By implementing our own ideas as stakeholders we will enhance our cultural ways of life, as well as our educational programs. Since we understand our own unique way of life, we should be able to formulate appropriate solutions to our own inquires, questions, hypothesis, and issues. In this reform of education, we become the agent of transformation to deal with our own unique situations. The time is right for the Navajo educators to begin making our own unique educational materials for our educational system. In the area of mathematics at the secondary level, a new idea is especially needed that will help the

Navajo students to study mathematics with excitement and increase their math proficiency in algebra and geometry.

In 2001, Starko stated that new ideas are formed based on creativity. Creativity is developed based on the criteria of novelty and appropriateness. Novelty is enlightening an experience with new creative ideas. An example would be creating an innovative math lesson that is interesting and allows the students to explore mathematical ideas by doing. Starko defined appropriate in the context of creativity as meeting the goals or "criterion of a culture" (p. 6). He indicated that in order for creativity to formulate, it must be culturally appropriate in context. For example, math curricular for Navajo schools should offer appropriate opportunity to integrate Navajo culture in teaching important mathematical operations and standards. Davison (1994) discussed several cultural key components which are as follows: a) multisensory experiences and relevant to the situation; b) concepts taught are embedded with local situations, home, community or within contexts; c) it has energy that is exciting and interesting to the students that incorporates hands-on construction and drawing, group work and practical; and d) instruction is based on students seeing the whole picture, link to culture and rich relationships.

Formulating new ideas usually circulates from an open mind. Fowler (personal communication, May 12, 2003) stated that this open mindedness is referred to in Navajo as "t'aa w'ho' a'aji teego.'" T'aa w'ho a'aji teego' is initiated by inspiration, intuition, vision, or insight and results into a prototype. Fowler related that a creative individual uncovers the hidden meanings. She also added that creative persons look for metaphors, possibilities or alternative application in whatever is done, heard or learned. In the Navajo sense, those who search for creative ways are in harmony with them and can come up many different unique possibilities.

In approaching a problem with creative solutions from the perspective of an educator, people will lead in a manner that would best improve the quality of mathematics education for American Indian and Alaskan Natives students.

Navajo Learning Styles: Teaching from the Cultural Perspectives

Teachings of the Navajo culture originate from the Hogan (pronounced Hooghan). A Hogan is a Navajo home that is constructed by interlocking juniper tree logs to form a regular octagon. The door to the Hogan faces the eastern direction. Cultural teaching tenets are based on the Hogan; therefore, instructions for life begin in the Hogan. Fowler (personal communication, May 12, 2003) a traditional Navajo stated that life begins in the Hogan and from there, spirals in an ever-widening circle to broader, more complex realities, such as adulthood, *kinaalda* (a traditional ceremony), parenthood, clan, language, a Navajo name, rituals, and ceremonies. The teaching values associated with the hogan are universal. Fowler (2003) indicated that the essence of this reflects the importance of family and clan ties and the concept of *k'e*, which means the appropriate manner to respectfully fashion a relationship with others and nature. The teaching starts with the basic elements of life. Similarly to the Greeks, the Navajos believe there are four basic elements of life. It consists of fire, water, air, and Mother Earth.

According to Fowler (personal communication, May 12, 2003) that teaching in the Navajo community is integrally tied to life experience, the challenge for educators is to link the culture of the community to the culture of the school. In an interview to discern what elements of Navajo culture would be essential to the process of mathematics, Fowler (2003) reveals that Navajo weaving is a complex task that is integrally tied to Navajo culture, yet highly mathematical in nature. A Navajo weaving displays imagination that integrates mathematical ideas. Fowler indicated that to create a weaving she uses a picture developed in her mind and uses her body such her fingers, arms, and legs as a measurement to formulate a geometric rug design. She goes on to note that the Navajo notion of measuring comes into existence in reference to their task and its relationship to the environment. The body is used as a standard measuring device, which provides the first understanding of time and space. When Fowler weaves she numerates using her body to perceive the order of her design. For Navajos, numeration and locating is closely associated with the body. Navajos numbers system is related to their body. Fowler (2003) noted that she counts by putting her hands up in the air and starts from the left and crosses over to count to ten. She added, "then I count the same way with my toes to count to twenty." She indicated that this counting principle represents the body as a "whole." For Navajos, the importance of counting is an important part of living and living with nature. Numeration is the pivotal in the continuous living for the Navajos. The principle of counting is an art because its spirit will make things happen and it will generate things. For example, Fowler (2003) stated that she used numeration in every aspect of solving daily problems and relevant in her making Navajo rugs. For example, in her daily activities, she counts her animals and she uses numeration to make traditional pottery, make jewelries, build a looming frame for her weaving, and to prepare traditional meals.

According to Fowler (personal communication, May 12, 2003) that the internal experience of weaving is energized by an intimate relationship with the construction of the whole process of her weaving. Throughout the construction of weaving the weaver talks, numerates, sings, and prays to establish an oneness with her loom. Bonar (1996) and Fowler (2003) stated that a weaving comes alive through the weaver's thought, fork comb, batten, warps, wefts, spindles, songs, prayers, and the personal intimacy of mathematical concepts. Math concepts such as symmetry, congruent, geometric shapes, parallel lines, perpendicular lines, rotations, dilations, reflections, and slides evolve from making a Navajo rug. Fowler mentioned that the Navajo rug in Navajo is referred to as "dah'iistl'o". Bonar (1996) stated, "dah'iistl is a verb referring to the process of integrating the warp and weft in the art of weaving on a set-up loom" (p. 34). The patterns on the Navajo rug portray traditional symbols and legends that transmit sacred stories of Navajo Life.

Fowler (S. Fowler, personal communication, May 12, 2003) indicated that only through culture is their characteristic, behavior, emotion and learning is evolved. Without culture how do we become human and how do we act. Barkley and Cruz (2001) point out that many of the daily activities of human affairs are embedded with mathematics ideas. Lipka, Hogan, Webster, Yanez, Adams, Clark, & Lacy (2005) viewed that Native American and Alaskan Natives culture has rich context of mathematics. For example, the following activities have mathematics ideas: making fish racks, bead designs, rugs, potteries, home structures, and cultural artifacts. Lipka et al. (2005) argued that the symbolic of local knowledge and language of NA/AN is a necessary component in the mainstream Western mathematics education. Cultural component math program means to include the mainstream math content comprised of content knowledge and Navajo knowledge, pedagogy process from the Western perspective of teaching along with Navajo perspective, and contextual knowledge of school related information and with Navajo high school students experiences, prior knowledge, and community based knowledge. Cultural based math curriculum that comprised with home life experiences of NA/AN and Western knowledge provides NA/AN more relevant and meaningful education in learning mathematical ideas (Lipka & Wahiberg, 1998). Fowler contended that the Navajo way of life is an important connection in reforming math education. She indicated as a Navajo elderly that our cultural way is not acknowledged in mainstream academic curriculum. She contended that a new change is needed in how the Navajo children are taught in schools. She explained that how elders were taught by their forefathers to realize new information: a) observation is key component in learning. Observation is a key skill that is developed at a young age. This skill involves observing and watching then imitating the activity to learn the task at hand; b) working in cooperative effort involves learning by working together and talking things out and respecting each other's opinions; c) learning is actively engage in doing the activity; d) learning is acquired by comparing and contracting things; f) learning is acquired through the connection of senses that provides the ability to reason by involving hands-on project and experimental learning; g) storytelling provides the rich heritage stories which is communicated orally through Navajo language; h) songs and ceremonies guide the mind through a state oneness with the nature and self and learning is acquired through this force of energy; i) learning is gained by interacting with the environment and nature; g) visual aids contribute to learning; and h) Ke' is the cornerstone in gaining appropriate relationship with oneself, with others and nature, this notion offers blessings for intellectual growth (S. Fowler, personal communication, May 12, 2003).

These cultural notions are essential to be part of new direction of change in math education and how mathematics is learned for the Navajo high school students. Romberg (1992) explained that minority students' way of knowing should not be eliminated from school, however acknowledged in the school learning. Using this principle of ideas, a Navajo cultural math based program is a necessary component in teaching and learning mathematics for the Navajo students. For example, the cultural activity of weaving would provide based on incorporating ethnomathematics in constructing a math lesson that has relevance for Navajo students. By developing a math lesson that incorporates a cultural based math program, instructors would be able to create meaning in math that surpasses the boundaries of what traditional rote procedural skills can teach. The lesson on the weaving portrays of teaching mathematical concepts on rectangle, quadrilateral, symmetry, transformation, area, and perimeter. Romberg (1992) noted that when math concepts are taught to familiarity context of the students' schema, the students are likely to understand the procedure and concepts. Through cultural contextual pedagogy, the Navajo students will be able to construct their own mathematical meanings by formations of mathematical practice that is already developed in their culture. The cultural based math lessons will provide the students an opportunity to integrate new knowledge into a learning scheme that already exists through their knowledge of weaving and their situation.

This examination effectively demonstrates that by looking inward and investigating culture, relevant cultural paradigm that have prominence and pertinence to Native American students can be exploited for use in education. The challenge now is for educators to take the process to the next level and change the math education based on this perspective. Until this step is taken, Native Americans will continue to lag behind all other ethnic minorities in math educational attainment.

Personal Experiential Learning: Reminiscence of my Childhood

I was born into and raised in a family that believed and practiced the Navajo cultural and traditional ways. A subtle Navajo lady, my mother, Sally Fowler, instilled in me my values and beliefs. All her life she was nurtured by the Navajo way of life and, today, this is the only culture that has shaped who she is today. Today, her life is happy. Her happiness is seen in her attentive listening and heard in her soft voice. She learned from the Dine culture how to listen and how to speak softly and meaningfully. My mother often says, "When you listen to yourself, other people, and your environment, it contributes in shaping your life."

When I am attentive and listen keenly, I hear the gentle wind sweeping at the base of White Mesa and sheering out to the rolling plain toward the distance east where Black Mesa stands. Across the hills, the female gentle wind carries the thumping sound of my mother's weaving.

The sound of my mother's weaving is reminiscent of my childhood days herding the family sheep on the Western part of the Navajo Nation, near Page, Arizona. In this high, arid, desert region, I played with my mother's weaving loom while she systemically constructed her weaving. Every yarn she twined on her loom added a brilliant, symmetrical, geometric pattern.

As my mother wove her rug, I stayed by her side and created my own small world, my playground, by exploring nature in my surroundings. This childhood days of my life provided the foundation of my sense of space, language, physical skills, and emotional development. Playing around my mother's weaving revealed my experience in playing with twigs, sand and rocks. I collected colorful pebbles from nature and pretended they were my sheep. I formed circles with Navajo tea twigs that symbolized a sheep corral. Each day I counted my pebbles to make sure that I did not lose one. The damp earth added to my adventure of playing. I worked and kneaded the moist earth to replicate a hogan, our traditional Navajo home, and a sheep herding horse.

My mother weaved in the cool summer shade house that was covered with a blanket of juniper trees. Under this shade house, the spinning and stretching of the yarn breaks the silence. The stretching of the yarn and my interaction with my surrounding described how my family lived.

We processed new information and learned through active process. My mother Sally Fowler (personal communication, June 22, 2005) called this process of learning in Navajo taa' wa hwo aji t' eego. According to Fowler, it means that it is entirely up to an individual to actively construct their own understanding based on current and prior experiences that shape our cognitive structure. We depended on our cognitive structure to transform our ideas or concepts, draw inferences, inquire, build hypothesis and make decisions. Fowler stated that our cognitive structure provided meaning and organized our experiences in which a higher order of thinking is developed. Our experiences is defined and curved by nature and where we live. In this domain of living, my family lived a simple life.

My family did not have electricity and running water. We had to haul our drinking water from a nearby windmill. The windmill became the center stage for the Navajo people, young and old, to update each other on local news or events. As children, the windmill site was our play area. This is the place we had water fights and climbed the cylindrical water tank. Occasionally, we jumped into the water trough just to cool off from the hot desert sun.

When the snow fell in mid-December, we harvested our drinking water from melted snow. Water was precious to us. All year we harvested water like a precious grain. We stored, conserved, collected, and prayed for rain. Harvesting our water was a family oriented task. Each family member took part bringing in

the water for cooking and for drinking. We worked around the season to search
for water for our survival needs, as well as that of our livestock.

While my sisters and brothers were away at school, my clan cousins and I
herded the family sheep. During summer, we took the sheep out of the corral
before the sunrise. We followed an old trail that was once used to move horse-
drawn wagons over the glowing eastern horizon.

The sun rose when we would be near the canyon. At the rim of red rose
canyon, I heard echoes of cows calling for their new-born calves and smelled the
fresh morning air. At a distance, wild birds chirped from juniper trees that dotted
the canyon landscape. The canyon had endless features from which we could
create a full day of exciting activities. The activities were comprised of playing
grounds that stretched in every direction of the canyon and it became our laboratory to investigate our surroundings using our senses. Our surroundings and
prior experiences shape our perception and understanding about the world
around us. We jumped off the canyon ledge that peered out from the wash bed
and landed on the banks of the drifting sand. From this activity we learned from
our mental construction. We learned new information by putting it together with
what we already knew. We know from our mental construction of jumping off
canyon shear walls is to jump directly on the peak of the drifting sand that supported our weight so no injury was experienced. We napped on the ledge of the
sheering canyon walls and at the same time used it as our lookout tower. We slid
down the face of the ledge to reach the canyon floor. We played with the canyon
vegetations and other elements of nature. Playing in the canyon developed our
keen sense of space and time. The space and time of the canyon revealed the
pattern of the canyon and universe. In the summer months, we cooled off by
playing on the northern slopes of the canyon ledges. It became our natural air
conditioning. In the fall and winter, we played on the southern walls of the canyon to stay warm. The canyon floor also reflected many memories that my
mother valued. My mother is a large lady and well respected in the Navajo
community.

Then, just as it is today, my mother practiced the Navajo tradition. She
speaks only Navajo, but is full of energy and very intelligent. According to her,
everything around us contributes to our mental construction. Based on this principle, my mother woke us up each morning and required us to run toward the
eastern sky to greet our Deities, the Holy People. According to the Navajo way,
the Holy Person called Talking God is around in the early morning to bless us
with nice beautiful materials and a long strong healthy life. Also running in the
early morning light we practiced our ancient tradition.

The cool air brushed our face when we ran each morning. We let the Holy
People know that we were their children by yelling as we ran toward the eastern
horizon. While we were running we blessed ourselves with morning darkness.
My mother told us it represented our grandparents. By the time we returned
home, my mother would be standing by the Hogan entrance with the white

cornmeal ready. We prayed with the cornmeal offering to the eastern sky. In our prayer, we called out the four cardinal directions of our sacred mountains: Eastern Mountain is Mount Blanco; Southern mountain is Mount Taylor; Eastern Mountain is San Francisco Peaks; and the Northern Mountain is Mount Hesperus Peak. My mother indicated that these four cardinal directions represented the Dine Way of life and our Navajo knowledge. The East symbolizes thinking. In this component, reasons, imaginations, ideas, and comprehension arise. South, signature of the day time, is cognizant of the mind to improve one's life by planning and to act on those plans with full of energy. The West, marks the sunset and means to reflect back on one's journey on its earlier thought, plan, and action. North is the sign of darkness. In this component, it marks to rest and rejuvenate under the security of the Earth. In addition, we prayed to the air, rivers, earth and clouds for protection and guidance. These elements are here to teach and protect us. Living this way in connection with the nature we maintained in harmony with the cyclic of time and space. According to my mother, the cycle of Dine way of life is infused with totality, which is in rhythm with order of the nature and the cosmos. My mother indicated that to ignore these teachings is to ignore the purpose of life, understanding and the mean of existence.

Unlike my brothers and sisters who were raised by our grandmother, I was raised by my mother. She had her own descriptive way of speaking, like many traditional mothers. She told me I was born at the time the chill air of the winter had gone by, new grasses landscaped the rolling plain and the gentle female rain had ended. Also there were an abundance of new lambs, and shearing of sheep had started. When I started my formal education, I was told that I was born in May, but that month was essentially meaningless to me, not infused with activity, experience and life as my mother's way of speaking.

At the age of four, I was placed in a government boarding school at Kaibeto, Arizona. My older brothers and sisters attended this school too. I remember vividly my first day experience in being dropped off at the boarding school to receive a Western education. I cried and ran after my mother, but I was wrestled to the ground by a dorm mother. In the arms of the dorm mother, I heard negative words all around me and observed that the students were against the wall to maintain order.

The dorm mothers who took care of us were unfriendly and the students had to follow their commands. They drilled and moved us in a single line around the school campus like we were fighting soldiers who were getting ready for a combat mission. If we did not follow their orders we were verbally mistreated and punished by doing duck walks, push-ups, and scrubbing dorm walls. We walked in single file to lunch hall and classroom. In the classroom, the teachers were mostly White people. My first introduction to my formal education was difficult. It was frustrating to learn a new language and a new culture. The Western approach of teaching and learning was not parallel and feasible to how my mother had taught me. The instructor dominated the teaching environment in disseminating important educational information. The information was given in a lecture format in a classroom that was comprised of straight rows of metal desks. As students, our responsibility was to listen passively and assimilate the Western academic knowledge. Reading, writing, arithmetic, science, and spelling, penmanship, and manner classes embedded the Western academic knowledge areas. The discourses of these knowledge areas were taught from the Western textbooks. For example, the content of mathematics was taught by rote and drill. We learned our multiplication facts through multiplication cards and learned our numbers and alphabets through drill. This style of teaching did not register in our scheme, because it did not relate to our prior experience. In the course of the classroom lecture, the new knowledge that we were gaining evolved to be foreign, dull and senseless. The Western education had no relevant ties in how we processed information and ignored our cultural methods of teaching and learning. My mother and Dine way of teaching and learning empowered the learner. The learner explored, inferred, and reflected to internalize. In contrary, in the Western approach to education we work alone and mimic the teacher to learn. My experience of the Western education relied on a fixed curriculum and presented part to whole. I found this method of education a challenge to understand.

Through my years of Western education I had to work extra hard to learn their comprehensive curricula. Eventually, I had persevered in order to graduate from an off Navajo reservation high school. I graduated from Flagstaff High School in Flagstaff, Arizona. I continued my horizon of the Western education at Northern Arizona University. I had good understanding of the mathematical language in high school, which came with good grades, so I pursued my interest to study mathematics at Northern Arizona University. The curricula at Northern Arizona set a higher level of thinking and the pace went by too fast for me to understand the beauty of the mathematical relationships.

Navajo Education

By integrating the Navajo cultural aspects and the principles of connection and communication, constructivism, and ethnomathematics, the gap between achievement and underachievement in mathematics that Navajo students are now held in bondage of will either become closer or may even close. The realm of education for Navajos has been going with the flow with the mainstream content curricular. Research has indicated that minority students in particular the Hispanics and Black students in fourth-grade and eighth-grade math achievement have closed the gap between their White counterparts between the years 2005 and 2007. However, there is no significant change indication for the American Indians between the year 2005 and 2007 with their White counterparts in an improvement of math achievement for grades fourth and eighth-grade (National Assessment of Educational Progress, 2007). This gloomy result of American Indian students' scores in mathematics has an impelling impact in the future destiny of the career choices of students as well as the tribe's future technological and economic development. The history reveals that the Western education paradigm has been a challenge for the American Indian students. The early part of education for American Indians was melancholy to the point that the goal of the dominant Eurocentric education was to strip the identity of AI/AN and the federal government aim for a policy was to assimilate AI/AN into the dominant culture (Szasz, 1999). Reports such as Merriam Report 1932, Kennedy Report of 1969, and Indian Nation at Risk Task Force Report of 1990 all documented the failure of education for the AI/AN (Szasz, 1999, & Reyhner, 2009). A new direction of educational change is essential for the AI/AN for this twenty-first century, in particularly for Navajo high school students in the expanse of mathematics.

National Council Teacher of Mathematics (NCTM) (2000) called for "equity" education for all students that they have an opportunity and excess to study mathematics. Mathematics has been identified as the tool for success in the competing global economy (Spelling, 2006). Gauging how much mathematics an individual knows and understands contributes to their success and opportunities in a career. To elevate the promise and potentials of all the students, a reform is essential in teaching and learning mathematics. NCTM (2000) indicated that mathematics should be taught with understanding as well as from the ideology perspectives of progressive education, constructivism and ethnomathematics. The psychological and social process that course mathematics with boredom through drill and practice is no longer an option in this era of innovative technological world.

The educational system is sophisticated with innovative advancements in technology; it calls for best creative ideas of research practice to innovative (President Bush, 2006). A fresh innovative idea conveys a new way of doing business. At this critical time of our history, a new way doing business is desired in how mathematics is taught and learned by the Navajo students. This new frame of ideal practice will help close the achievement gap between their counterpart White students as well as improve performance achievement on the state standardized test.

Multicultural education is suggested in reaching to all capability levels of students to increase their social opportunities in learning. One form of reaching to all students is to create and implement instructional programs based on the cultural value and standards of the students (Gay, 1995). It is humanity in nature to diversify school programs and yield with justice and liberty for American Indian community to create its own educational school programs to advance their math programs and needs. Merriam (1928), Indian Education Act (1972), and Self-Determination and Education Assistance Act (1975) reminded the federal government that AI/AN has the entity to function and manage their own welfare. Although these Act and Report open opportunities for Tribes to run and control their school systems, the focus is mainly in maintaining and revitalizing the Tribal language. Eventually more measurable steps are necessary to improve the academic needs for AI/AN.

AI/AN social system is unique. They have a social structure that is based on oral tradition. Learning is creative integrated with the natural order of the universe. Learning is continuous with natural inclination drawn up by the force energy of the nature, environment, culture, and experiences. Learning is intertwined with the learners' prior experiences (Dewey, 1938). With this notion, for AI/AN, teaching and learning mathematics should be connected to their heritage, costume, norm, and values (Lipka, 1994). The concept of cultural based math curriculum connects with the Western math concepts to assist AI/AN with school learning.

The Setting of the Study

This study was conducted on the Navajo Indian Reservation in Arizona. Sand Stone High School was located in the Northeastern part of Arizona, near the Four Corners. The Navajo Reservation covers 24,000 square feet of the Southwest in the United States. The reservation includes all of Northeastern Arizona, portions of Northwestern New Mexico, and a portion of Southeastern Utah. The region of the reservation is defined by the Colorado River, San Juan River, and the Little Colorado River. This land mass is landscaped with mesas, rock formation towers, buttes, desert, pinnacles, canyons, and mountains. According to Census 2000, there were about 300,000 Navajos in the United States, which were the decedents of the Athapaskan Tribe. The members of the Navajo Tribe refer to themselves as Navajos or Dine which means "the people". They are the largest Native America Indian tribe with the largest Federal Trust Land Reservation in the United States.

The Navajo is a matrilineal society. The women are considered as the head of the household where they own all the personal possessions of properties and estate. The women are known for weaving rugs that depicts the Navajo landscapes. The men are known for making sterling silver jewelry, ranching, and horsemanship. The Navajo raised sheep, goats, horses, and cattle, which is an essence of their economy. There is about a 45 percent unemployment rate on the Navajo Reservation and over 150 schools that consist of public, Bureau of Indian Education, mission, Grant, parochial, and Charter schools (Szasz, 1999). The Navajo Nation Department of Dine Education oversees the operations of the Grant, Charter, Contract and Bureau of Indian Education schools. The Navajo Nation Department of Dine Education is comprised of 11 Boards of Education. Their function and duty is to regulate the educational program of the Navajo Nation. The Boards of Education were created in reference to Navajo Nation tribal code Title XII, which was enacted by the Navajo Nation Council Delegates in July 2005.

Sand Stone High School is a Contract School contracted through the Bureau of Indian Education. Contract schools are schools that the Bureau of Indian Affair (BIA) contracts with the local tribal community to operate their own educational institution (Szasz, 1999). The school is locally managed and lead by the community elected school board members. The six school board members have the responsibility to oversee the whole school operation, school educational programs, finances, and school's personnel in accordance to the Indian self-determination enactment of PL 93-638 which was evoked by President Richard Nixon in 1972. Sand Stone High School (SSHS) consists of K-12 grade with an average enrollment of around 450 students. The school emphasizes at all levels of grade, the development of writing, reading, and speaking the Navajo Language. The intention of SSHS is that by the time the student becomes a twelfth grader at SSHS, the student should be able to know how to converse in Navajo by writing, reading, and speaking the Navajo Language. It is believed that this environment of bilingual education will enhance student self-awareness and self-control, empower them with the identity of their culture, and better equip them to adapt and compete in the modern society.

SSHS has an average enrollment of 141 secondary high school students which is comprised of Junior High School with grades seventh and eighth grade and High School with grades ninth to twelfth grade. Each student needs 25 credits and was responsible to pass the Arizona Instrument to Measure Standards with a score that Meets or Exceeds in mathematics, writing, and reading to graduate from high school. The required educational courses are four credits in mathematics, English, science, and social studies. The additional courses are two credits of Navajo studies and seven elective classes. The high school offers eight classes for its instructional schedule with each class 50 minutes. School starts at 8:00 am and ends at 3:49 pm with a 30 minutes lunch break.

The Research Design

Description of the Data Sources

The control group consisted of nine participants (n=9) and the treatment group consisted of six participants (n=6). The participants were 16-19 years old. The control group was taught using the traditional pedagogical method of teaching and learning and the treatment group was taught using the NCCMC during their regular 50 minutes scheduled math class for a period of eight weeks from January 2010 to March 2010. The qualitative and quantitative data included a pre and post test, structured interviews, an 18 question Likert Scale Questionnaire, and a teacher journal to determine the participants' math achievement on the 11 Arizona math benchmark standards and to determine the participants learning experiences using the NCCMC.

In the Context of Navajo Language

The sociocultural perspective is an approach that frames the students to establish or formulate the cultural practice of mathematics by engaging in group activities or discussion, and explanation. Vygotsky (1978) maintained that learning is not accompanied by isolation, but in a form of context process and social interaction. He believed that cognitive development is supported by home life experiences which should be infused with school curriculum to help students with school learning. Vygotsky referred to this as cultural tools such as symbols and language that support cognitive development with understanding. Communication by language negotiates meanings of the higher order of thinking such as with problem solving. However, for the minority population their ancestral way of knowing is controversial in the mainstream school curriculum. The history of the American schools was to assimilate all immigrant children into the dominant Euro-society. In 1968, the federal government stepped in to help minorities acquire equal opportunity education by endorsing bilingual education with the passage of 1968 Bilingual Education Act. The role of Bilingual Education is using the first language of the minority students and along with English to increase their academic learning (Cummins, 1979). Cummins (1979) suggested that to increase the involvement of Native American students in school is to incorporate their language and culture into the content curriculum. Today, the Navajos have taken interest in preservation of their language.

Schools across the Navajo Reservation are emphasizing revitalizing and maintaining the Navajo language. To preserve the Navajo language, the Reservation schools are approaching with programs such as the full immersion program at lower grade levels from K-3 which means that more conversation are done in Navajo to continue the language or a Navajo language class is created as elective class that focuses on writing and speaking the Navajo language. However, at the high school the use of Navajo language is isolated from the academic content and only emphasized in Navajo language class.

For the Navajos, language is key part of learning and understanding their environment. The Navajo language holistically should be part of the fiber of the high school academic curriculum on the Navajo Reservation schools. Mathematics is communicated by a diversity of language in the world and generated to what math is at this time, creating a sophisticated technological society. Language is in every discourse of the human life. To the Navajos, language is scared and blessed with the highest quality of divine spirit. The Navajos used the Navajo language in every aspect of their lives. Thus, Navajo language should be used to teach high school math courses on the Navajo Reservation. This form of communication using the Navajo language, may give the Navajo students a sense of wholeness in learning mathematics with understanding.

This teacher action research was a quasi-experimental design using qualitative and quantitative data to explore the effects of the Navajo Cultural Component Math Curriculum (NCCMC) on Navajo high school student's math performance and learning experiences. The research was conducted on the Navajo Reservation using two groups.

Discussion of The Findings

The discussion will be presented in the following major themes of the research: Reflections, Culture in Mathematics, Mathematical Careers and the Future, Action Research, and Additional Findings of Activities. It will also discuss the implications for math education comprehensively based on the results of the findings. Recommendations will be made for future study and the chapter will conclude with a Navajo Education Model for Math.

Reflections

In conclusion, from the start of this study both the participants in the control group and experimental group expressed that math in general was not an exciting or fun subject to study. Both groups described math as dull and monotonous. The first week of my research, I witnessed both groups not enjoying math. I observed in both groups that the participants had low spirit and moral. They came to class late without any class materials. In class, they put their heads down on their desk, repeatedly asked to leave class, or asked for restroom passes. Throughout the process of the research the experimental group's attitude changed their perspective on math. I observed the participants were more engaged in each math lessons from the NCCMC. The innovative math lessons based on Navajo culture traditions math curriculum assisted the participants to identify math as enjoyable, exciting, and fun. For the experimental group participants, the math lessons from the NCCMC impacted their math achievement and learning experiences.

The cultural math lessons in the NCCMC improved the experimental group math performance and learning experiences. The participants bonded with the math activities through hands-on activities, visual aids, cultural symbols, narrations, and group work. Participants reported feeling more confident about math and appreciative that math standards were connected to their culture. Participants also indicated they might now consider going to college and enter a math related career.

The control group participants also improved their math performance using the traditional model of teaching and learning in learning the 11 Arizona math standards. However, the results of their scores from their pre-test and post-test were lower than the experimental group.

The experimental group validated the assumption that Navajo cultural traditions math curriculum impacted the Navajo students in improving their mathematical achievement and learning experiences.

This teacher action research study demonstrated that Navajo students using the Navajo Cultural Component Math Curriculum (NCCMC) based on using the Navajo cultural tradition heritage math curriculum increased academic achievement and reported improved learning experiences. I have developed NCCMC using my experience of 14 years teaching as a high school math teacher on the Navajo reservation. This NCCMC was developed particularly for the Navajo high school students who were preparing to take the Arizona math standards assessment. Another purpose of this study was for NCCMC to serve as a model to educators, leaders, communities, and parents to improve the quality of educational math program for Navajo high school students so that every student has access to successfully study mathematics. This study is the first based on a Navajo perspective in improving the quality of Navajo math programs for Navajo high school students.

Culture in Mathematics

The beacon of this research is grounded in the research question "How does integrating Navajo cultural tradition in the math curriculum impact student achievement and students' learning experiences?" This study indicated that Navajo cultural traditions in math curriculum increased the participants' math achievement. The National Council of Teacher of Mathematics (NCTM, 2000) argued that the central goals for schools and schools instructional programs are high expectations for students and achievement in mathematics. The participants in this study indicated that Navajo cultural component math curriculum (NCCMC) made a positive impact and experience in learning the 11 Arizona math benchmark standards. The initiative of the (NCCMC) is the catalyst agent in reforming the math education for Navajo high school students. NCCMC is an innovative educational math program that includes the Navajo cultural tradition to help the Navajo high school students amplify their understanding of the Arizona math representations and to gain an appreciation of mathematics in general. The NCTM (2000) argued that all students with all backgrounds need a nurturing environment that supports an equal opportunity to learn math. The NCTM stated that the educational program should be responsive to the students' personal interests, intellectual strengths, and prior knowledge (p. 13). The NCCMC harnesses the participants' natural curiosity in building the intricate web of the inter-relationships of mathematical ideas and representations. This study showed that the cultural notations of the NCCMC helped and impacted the participants to capture the connections and relationships of math. As a result it improved the participants learning experience and achievement on the Arizona math standards.

The cultural representation supported different math abilities of the participants and increased their understanding of the new math concepts through engaging with familiar cultural connections and representations. Vygotsky (1986) claimed that cognitive development of individuals is derived from the individual's origin of sociocultural. The sociocultural approach to learning and teaching bridges culture with the individual's learning orientations (Vygotsky, 1986). Gollnick and Chinn (1986) added that the view of multicultural education is to support the students' background with a positive meaningful purpose. This plays an important role in creating instructional lessons and is needed for the school environment. The data showed that the percent of change for the experimental group ranged from 1.34 to 4.56 and the percent of change for the control group ranged from 1.19 to 3.03. The mean for the pre-test for the control group was 34 percent and the mean for the experimental group was 36 percent. The mean for the post-test for the control group was 59 percent while the mean for the experimental was 87 percent. The pre-test and post-test data revealed that the experimental group significantly improved their mathematical achievement. The data showed that the NCCMC provided an innovative math program for the Navajo high school students. NCTM (2000) indicated that all students with different cultural backgrounds need access to high quality innovative mathematical education.

The participants in the NCCMC educational program study indicated that they appreciated the math lessons connected to their culture and it was the culture that helped them remember and understand math facts. How much one knows mathematics determines the opportunities for an individual and gauges an individual success in life and career choices (Spelling, 2006). NCTM (2000) claimed that for the stake of the future in technological advancement, mathematics should be learned and taught with understanding the complexity of mathematical representations. The participants indicated that the lessons in the NCCMC were understandable and made sense. The NCCMC followed the vision of NCTM (2000) that math concepts should be learned with understanding. Heibert, Carpenter, Fennima, Fuson, Wearne, Murray, Oliver, & Human (1997) stated that learning math by understanding is to connect or relate to things we know. The more connections and relationships are established the better we understand mathematical phenomena.

The data suggested that the NCCMC incorporated the local knowledge of the Navajos into the mainstream math curriculum which enabled the participants to see a network of relationships of mathematical ideas. For example, participant F stated that "My previous math classes the teacher explained math problems on the board and we did problems in the math textbook only, but this math class used our culture to help me understand math problems and it was cool doing math problems this way." Lipka, Mohatt, & Ciulistet Group (1997) claimed that understanding a situation includes the relationship of using local knowledge of people that consist of their social discourse, values, social organization, and instructions (p. 141). The data showed that NCCMC provided the network of enrichment of mathematical understanding through the cultural component of the

Navajo way of life. Lipka et al. (1997) argued that local knowledge can co-evolves with the school academic contents.

This study showed that NCCMC helped the participants to realize the importance of mathematics by linking their identity and cultural practices into the traditional frame of pedagogy. Culture and mathematics can coexist. Mathematics is created from the diversity of people's background (D'Ambrosio, 2001). D'Ambrosio (2001) stated that "we can help students realize their full mathematical potential by acknowledging the importance of culture to the identity of the child" (p. 3).

The participants in this study strongly agreed that the NCCMC helped them improve their understanding of solving difficult math problems and remembering the steps in problem solving the Arizona math standards. Cajete (1994), May (1999) and Banks (2002) suggested that school curricular should reflect the community and reforming the school curricula should be based on local perspectives. This study indicated that the NCCMC reflected the social culture of the Navajo way of life and practice and a local Navajo perspective aimed at improving the participants understanding of math concepts through exploration. The data showed that there is a strong desire for cultural math curricular based on local knowledge of the Navajo cultural traditions.

Mathematical Careers and the Future

The findings indicate that participants in this study developed a positive view about mathematics. The data showed that at the beginning of the study, the participants had no interest and did not enjoy mathematical computations, because math was not considered a priority and was too difficult to understand. At the conclusion of the study, the participants indicated that they had more interest in studying mathematics. Some of the participants stated that they might now consider going to college, studying engineering, becoming a nurse assistant, becoming a nurse, and entering a career that has math involved. NCTM (2000) claimed that with the individual's appropriate skills in mathematics, the individual would have more opportunities and success in manipulating math problems that "enables them to fulfill personal ambitions and career goals in an ever-changing world" (p.4.). NCTM (2000) and Spelling (2006) stated that students who amplify their mathematical understand have more opportunities and volitions in dovetailing their future ambition goals. The goal of multicultural education is to restructure the school system so that students of all backgrounds develop the attitude, skills, and knowledge to participate successfully in mainstream society and the mainstream workforce in the twenty-first century (Banks, 2002).

The participants in this study stated that they would continue taking math classes. They indicated that the NCCMC had influenced them to take more math and science classes in the future and it also helped them gain an understanding of the basic math facts. Multicultural education stands on reforming the structure of school to enable students of color, linguistic ethnicity, and social class to experience equality in education and the empowerment it will bring them (Banks, 2002). For the United States to maintain the competitive edge economically and technologically more science and math is desired for students (Spelling, 2006).

Action Research

I used teacher action research to determine the impact and the effects of NCCMC. The action research also allowed me to investigate the problematic issue that I face daily in my teaching practice as a researcher and math educator, and to create a solution for that issue. The problematic issue is that Navajo high school students are not meeting or exceeding the Arizona standardized math test. When teachers inquire into their own practice they ask meaningful questions that will allow them to systemically improve their teaching strategies, student learning, and/or the operation of the school system (Corey, 1953). In my situation, it was my responsibility to create an alternative educational program that would improve the Navajo high school students' achievement in mathematics and improve their learning experiences in mathematics. Mills (2003) stated that when teachers carry out their own teacher action research without influence from an outside force, the teachers are more willing to reflect on their teaching practice.

I have spent countless hours in my class pondering educational programs that will enhance my teaching practice and deliver a quality math educational program that will specifically work for Navajo high school students. Fowler (personal communication, May 1, 2010) stated that solutions of problems are located in the individual's hands. I realized what Fowler meant that solutions are situated in our own life experiences and our own effort to create solutions that will work best for our local situations. Stringer (1999) stated that action research allows the participants to study their own problems and create a meaningful solution to solve their problems.

I decided to create an innovative educational program that would address the concern of the disturbing report on the declining mathematical achievement of the Navajo high school students and their learning experiences in mathematics. To address these reports, I looked into my own culture for solutions that would improve the quality of learning for the Navajo high school student in mathematics specifically on the Arizona math standards. Ethnomathematics helped me recognize that culture and mathematics coexist. Ethnomathematics consists of social learning experiences that connect cultural experiences to mathematics (Zaslavsky, 1998). The activities of Native American and Alaskan Natives (NAAN) are not recognized as useful in the Western paradigm of education. The lack of educational relevancy puts the NAAN at odds with the Western formal education and at "risk" (Taylor, 1991). Taylor stated that to improve the quality of the academic education for NAAN the school system "must begin where they are, using materials and teaching methods relevant to their culture" (p. 15).

Using the action research model, I formulated the Navajo Cultural Component Math Curriculum (NCCMC), an educational program that was based on the Navajo perspective. The intention of NCCMC was to improve the quality of academic learning in math and to increase the Navajo high school students' math achievement. The NCCMC contains (a) learning the Arizona math content standards from the perspective of Western and Navajo knowledge; (b) teaching the Arizona math content standard from school based teaching and Navajo based teaching; and (c) context knowledge using the students' prior knowledge and combining it with local knowledge. Stringer (1999) stated that action research is participants' research. The focus of the research is to improve the practice of the participants by changing their current practice toward desirable practice.

The data showed that the implementation of NCCMC was an affective educational strategy that supported the participants in learning mathematics through active cultural engagement in learning the 11 Arizona math benchmark standards. The participants showed high interest in learning math concepts using the cultural perspective math curriculum that I created. They felt that there should be more culture based math material. The participants also indicated that the overall experiences with cultural traditions math curriculum was exciting and meaningful. Some participants said that when class was over that they did not want to leave because the math lessons were fun and exciting. Teacher action research improves the quality practice in a school system by trying or testing educational theory or implementing and evaluating an educational model (McNiff, 1988).

Additional Findings of Activities

Additional findings of activities emerged from this study. The participants strongly felt that hands-on activity, visual learning, group work, and cultural narrations were an exciting part of the math lessons in the NCCMC. Using these teaching and learning strategies, the participants stated that they enjoyed and learned math with understanding. The participants also indicated that NCCMC lessons were interesting, relevant, and linked to their experiences. Davison (1994) indicated key components of cultural relevant math curriculum as follows: a) multisensory experiences and relevant to the situation; b) concepts taught are embedded with local situations, home, community or within contexts; c) it has energy that is exciting and interesting to the students that incorporates hands-on construction and drawing, group work and practical; and d) instruction is based on students seeing the whole picture, link to culture and rich relationships (p.40).

Hands-on Activity

The participants in the study indicated that the math lessons in the NCCMC contained hands-on activities that were fun and exciting. Some of the participants stated that the hands-on activities assisted them to learn math facts quickly and they enjoyed making specific activities such as the Navajo headdress, Concho buckles, ketoh, Navajo cradleboard, and Navajo Hogan. Also the participants mentioned that the hands-on activities motivated them to learn more math problems. Piaget (1980) claimed that knowledge is constructed by individual acts on the objects within an environment and it is this activity of dialogue and action with the objects that creates knowledge. Cremin (1961) suggested that knowledge is acquired through the impulse of freedom of natural curiosity and that learning is favored through games, genuine objects, hands-on projects, play, and with interaction and acquaintance with objects and nature through discovery and observation.

Visual Learning Activity

The participants stated that the math lessons in the NCCMC provided visual learning. The visual aids were based on the Navajo cultural symbol images, colors, and diagrams. The participants reported that the cultural symbols related to their local knowledge, and the cultural visual image helped them learn and understand the Arizona math benchmark standards on transformations, order of operations, quadrilaterals, complementary and supplementary angles, scale model, and real numbers. Some of the participants described that the NCCMC contained variations of colorful diagrams that can help Navajo students in general pass the Arizona Instrument Math Standards (AIMS). The participants also stated that familiar cultural symbols such as Hogan Colors, Navajo Rug, and Hozho Models facilitated their learning the 11 Arizona math benchmark standards. They described that diagrams and cultural visual images contributed in building their confidence in math. Visual image can assist students to organize and analyze math information and assist with accuracy and efficiency in mathematical problem solving (NCTM, 2000). Bandura (1977) stated that "from observing others one forms an idea of how new behaviors are performed, and on later occasions this coded information serves as a guide for action." (p. 22).

Group Work Activity

Some of the participants indicated that they enjoyed working in groups. The participants described group work as fun, and that they learned more math problems by talking with their group members. The participants reported that working in groups helped them solve math problems. During their group work they shared ideas, drew diagrams, and used the cultural symbols to discuss the aim of the math problems. NCTM (2000) described communication as the key element in understanding mathematics. Communication allows for a clear consolidation of understanding of objects through sharing. Ideas about objects are open to group discussions. During this discussion the ideas of communication provide opportunities for the learner to refine modify or improve their understanding about their relationship of mathematical ideas (NCTM, 2000). Dewey (1916) claimed that democracy is more than the government - it is a cooperative learning in the classroom. Cooperative learning in the classroom brings an experience of mutual and conjoins a genuine sense of communication (Dewey, 1916).

Narrations Activity

Some of the participants were appreciative that the NCCMC contained Navajo cultural narration stories. They reported that the narration stories were fun to read. It also helped them visualize and think about the math lesson's objectives. The participants stated that cultural narration stories consisted of key math terms and concepts, and related to the Navajo way of life and to math problems. They said that they enjoyed reading the narrations. Also the participants felt that the traditional math text book lacks Navajo perspective and they appreciated that NCCMC contained narrations that related to their culture and math. Vygotsky (1978) believed that cognitive development is supported by home life experiences which should be infused with school curriculum to help students with school learning. Vygotsky (1978) referred this as cultural tools such as symbols and language that support cognitive development with understanding. Communication by language negotiates meanings of the higher order of thinking such as with problem solving.

Implications of the Study

For many years the educational math program for the Navajo high school students has been supported by the Western mainstream math curricular. This is the only form of math education the Navajo students have been exposed to since the Navajos started their formal Western education. Students had to comprehend mathematical notions ranging from basic math facts to abstract math and now the Arizona math standards. This form of math education is supported with many additional teaching resources on learning math such as enrichment activities, technology, real life applications, open-ended problem solving, group work, and assessments. Despite these additional resources that support the classroom math textbook, the Navajo high school students have been struggling and lagging behind in meeting or exceeding the state mandate math benchmarks test. The intention of this study was to determine if alternative educational math programs based on Navajo cultural traditions math curriculum would impact Navajo high school students' achievement and their learning experiences in a math class.

With this notion in mind, the development of the Navajo Cultural Component Math Curriculum indicated that it could be a model for other minority groups. The aim of NCCMC is to increase and impact the Navajo high school students' math performance on standardized math tests and learning experiences. The NCCMC could establish the foundation for other minority groups to examine their culture and use their local knowledge to bridge home life with school's standardized math curriculum, in particular for high schools students. Other minorities could adapt the model by placing into it their traditions, culture, stories and activities. Math educational posters, math textbooks, and other educational materials could be devised using the NCCMC model as a guide. There is a need to expand and amplify educational resources materials for high school minority students. School leaders should examine their math curricular and initiate the development of culturally relevant math activities specifically for their minority students. The NCCMC provides the base for other high volume minority schools to consider developing their own unique enrichment math activities for their students. The culturally related activities should be flexible and adaptable to deliver an equitable math education for all students.

The NCCMC also has implications for instruction. It provided teaching strategies that could work for all minority students. Teaching based on hands-on activities, visual aids, culture narrations, and group work could be incorporated into school wide reform to improve the quality of mathematical learning and teaching. Likewise, in language arts and science it could enrich their content activities with culturally relevant educational materials. The implication of culturally relevant materials is a school wide effort. Through teaching with culturally relevant materials the learner understands values, and acknowledges cultural differences of ethnicity, race, gender, social class, and language (Manning and Burah, 2000).

Recommendations

The research related to the multicultural education, ethnomathematics, National Council Teacher of Mathematics paradigm's view that all students should have an equal opportunity and success in the 21st century education. The American society is becoming more diversified linguistically and demographically (Banks, 2002, NCTM, 2000, D'Ambrosio, 2001). Ethnic groups like Latinos, Asians, and Blacks are planting their cultural roots in the American academic classes. How are the Navajos preparing their children for the 21st century education? This research is a small illumination on a Navajo perspective in improving the Navajo high school math achievement and learning experiences through Navajo cultural tradition math curriculum. The study was conducted on a small Navajo Reservation high school with enrollment of approximately 160 students. The participants were relatively small with the control group of nine participants and the experimental group of six participants. This study could represent the start of the creating ethnomathematic curricula for Navajo high school students in general.

The recommendation for this study is to expand the research across the Navajo Nation high schools using the Navajo Cultural Component Math Curriculum (NCCMC) with larger number of participants so statistical comparison can be made. The other recommendation is to conduct the research longer with more time allocated in using the NCCMC and to track the participants in their progress of their math achievement and success, and determine whether the NCCMC study would encourage the participants to take more math courses, go to college, or improve their overall math performance and attitude.

This study adds collections to the perspective of multicultural education and ethnomathemics based on Navajo perspective math educator. The result of the study can be used to increase the volume of ethnomathematics materials for Navajo students in general. It also can be used for professional development for teachers, principals, superintendents, school board members, parents, leaders, and communities. This research also can reform the Navajo education in mathematics and it opens opportunity to extend the research for other indigenous people in improving their math education for their children.

Navajo Model for Math Education

I developed a Navajo educational model for math education specifically for Navajo high school students. The model is a replica of a Navajo basket. I selected this Navajo cultural symbol because the Navajo basket is important to Navajo life. The Navajos have created the Navajo basket for a variety of purposes. The popular purposes are for the Beauty Way and Navajo Wedding ceremony. The basket is made from sumac, a native scrub to the Southwest. The branch of the sumac is coiled and the split sumac is wrapped around to create the circular Navajo basket. There are three colors arrangements that give design to the basket. These colors are white maroon, and black. The diameter and depth of basket can be any size.

The center of the basket, which is the starting point for weaving a basket, represents where the Navajos emerge into this world. Weaving in a clockwise direction, the inner white represents the stages of human development or birth; the inner congruent black triangles represent the sacred-mountains of the Navajos: East is Mount Blanca; South is Mount Taylor; West is San Francisco Peaks; and North is Mount Hesperus; the maroon path way represents the sun ray or rainbow. The sunray and the rainbow signify growth of Life and expansion of one's knowledge. The outside black congruent triangles represent darkness, moisture and black clouds. The whole basket represents the universe and a cycle of one's life.

The circular ring is a replica of the Navajo basket. The eight circles represent eight sacred mountains consisting of different teaching strategies that can be implemented in a math class or other content subjects. The first mount is Mount Blanca associated with cultural relevant learning. Teaching should be connected to the student's prior knowledge and their cultural familiarity context. This includes ethnomathematics from the perspective of the Navajos. The second mount is the Mount Taylor associated with visual aid learning. Math lessons should be supported with colorful visual aids. Visual aids help students to reinforce what they already understand about the mathematical structure and use this prior knowledge to promote more learning by connecting a rich relationship of mathematical ideas and representations. The third mountain is San Francisco Peaks. This mountain is associated with hands-on activities which engage students to explore math concepts by manipulating math objects. Hands-on activities assist in building math knowledge and should start with concrete examples. Such examples will assist the students in understanding the abstract math concepts. The fourth mountain is the Mount Hesperus. Mount Hesperus is associated with group learning which encourages students to share their ideas by bouncing ideas off each other to hypothesize and test their solutions. The fifth mountain is Huerfano Mesa. This mountain is associated with homework. Homework enhances student understanding of mathematical objectives. Students use their class notes to extend their learning. The sixth mountain is Governador Knob. This mountain is associated with goal setting and math objectives. Math objectives should be clearly defined for students and provide what students must learn and perform. Goal helps the students stay on task with their work.

The seventh mountain is Black Mesa. This mountain is associated with comparing and contrasting ideas. This instruction allows the students to see the picture or concept as a whole. The whole is then broken into small pieces for students to see the similarities and differences of a concept to further understand the rich relationship of it

The eighth mountain is the Navajo Mountain. This mountain is associated with narrations. Math is learned through language. Language provides a way the students can communicate math through math vocabularies and narration stories.

Not mentioned in these teaching strategies is technology. Technology should be considered in teaching and learning math concepts and principles. Similar to the Navajo basket story, this model represents growth and expansion of one's knowledge in math. The cycle represents the journey of a teacher and student working together in harmony and balance to learn from one another and to learn mathematics together.

Conclusion

Mathematics is portrayed as a gatekeeper for more opportunities and options for students in their future careers. Mathematics also is a symbol of the economic and technological strength of the United States, and as such, should be considered an important academic content to study. For the Navajo students, it is assumed that they are gaining the necessary math skills through math curricular that is comfortable for them in preparing for the modern technological world. However, the reality for Navajo students is that math is not considered as a priority subject to engage in studying. The art of learning math is presented to Navajo students through the mainstream traditional math curricula based on the view of Eurocentric. The Navajo students refer to this model of math education as mathematics. Their way of knowing mathematics and local knowledge of Navajos is excluded in the modern math curricula. When Navajos see their way of doing math at home, they do not consider these activities as mathematics.

Bridging local Navajo knowledge with school content math knowledge, the Navajo students realized that they also come from a background rich in mathematics. Culturally relevant based math curricula will help the Navajo students see that they are systemically a part of the development of mathematics. The result of this effort may turn around the Navajo students' attitude about mathematics to the point where they appreciate the beauty in the structure of math. When the Navajo students feel more at ease doing math, they are more likely to increase their mathematical achievement and learning experiences in a math class.

NCCMC has planted the seed for educators, leaders, parents, and communities that Navajo cultural traditions math curriculum is possible. This goal has tackled the issue in improving the low math test scores of Navajo students. The NCCMC introduced that culturally relevant math lessons helped students increase their math test scores and instilled that mathematics is an important subject to study. Providing Navajo students with cultural based math curriculum will assist the students to build their confidence in learning math and create a future with more opportunities and options. The Navajo student needs equity in math education that is the Navajo perspective. This provides them with more access to a coherent challenging math curriculum (NCTM, 2000).

References

Ascher, M. (1991). *Ethnomathematics: A multicultural view of mathematical ideas.* New York: Chapman & Hall/CRC. This is the format, without tabs, except for the lines after the first. If you click on your paragraph symbol, you will see that all of the other references have tab or paragraph returns in them, and they should not have these.

Anderson, G. L., Herr, K., & Nihlen, A. N. (1994). *Studying your own school: An educator's guide to qualitative practitioner research.* Thousand Oaks, CA: Corwin Press, Inc.

Arizona Department of Education. (2002). AIMS result. Retrieved December 1, 2003 from http://www.ade.state.az.us/ResearchPolicy/AIMResult

Arizona Department of Education. (2007). 2006 and 2007 State Report Card. Retrieved June 23, 2007 from http://www.ade.state.az.us/srcs/ statereport-cards/StateReportCard06-07.pdf

Arizona Department of Education. (2008). 2007 and 2008 State Report Card. Retrieved March 11, 2008 from http://www.ade.state.az.us/srcs/state report-cards/StateReportCard07-08.pdf

Arizona Department of Education. (2008).AIMS result. Retrieved November 15, 2008 from http://www10.ade.az.gov/ReportCard/Default.aspx?Report Level=1

Arizona Department of Education. (2009). State of Arizona consolidated state application accountability workbook. Retrieved May 12, 2009 from http://www.ade.az.gov/azlearns/conappaypwb_09_05_01.pdf

Bandura, A. (1977). *Social Learning Theory.* New York: General Learning Press.

Baldi, S., Jin, Y., Skemer, M., Green, P. J., & Herget, D. (2007). Highlights from PISA 2006: Performance of U.S. 15-year-old students in science and mathematics literacy in an international context (NCES 2008-016). Washington DC: National Center for Education Statistics, Institute of Education Sciences & U.S. Department of Education.

Banks, J. A. (1995). Multicultural education: Historical development, dimensions, and practice. In J. A. Banks & C.A.M Banks (Ed.), *Handbook of research on multicultural education* (pp. 3-24). New York: Simon & Schuster Macmillan.

Banks, J. A. (1996). *Multicultural education, transformative knowledge, and action: Historical and contemporary perspective.* New York: Teachers College Press.

Banks, J. A. (2002). *An introduction to multicultural education.* Boston, MA: Allyn and Bacon.

Banks, J. A., & Banks, C. M. A., (1995). *Handbook of research on multicultural education.* New York: Simon & Schuster Macmillan.

Beaulieu, D. L. (2000). Comprehensive reform and American Indian education. *Journal of American Indian Education 39*(2), 29-38.

Bonar, E. H. (1996). *Woven by the grandmothers.* Washington, DC: Smithsonian Institution Press.

Bradley, C. (1983). The state of the art of Native American mathematics education. In H. N. Cheek (Ed.), *Handbook for conducting equity activities in mathematics education.* Reston, VA. National Council of Teachers of Mathematics.

Brooks, J. G., & Brooks, M. G. (1993). *In search of understanding: The case for constructivist classrooms.* Alexandria, VA: Association for Supervision and Curriculum Development.

Cajete, G. (2000). *Native science: Natural laws of interdependence.* Santa Fe, New Mexico: Clear Light Publishers.

Carnegie Foundation for the Advancement of Teaching. (1906). *First annual report.*

Cheek, H. N. (1984). A suggested research map for Native American mathematics education. *Journal of American Indian Education 23*(2), 1-9.

Cremin, L. A. (1961). *The transformation of the school.* New York: Random House, Inc.

Creswell, J. W. (1994). *Research design: Qualitative and quantitative approaches.* Thousand Oaks, CA: Sage Publications, Inc.

D'Ambrosio, U. (2001). What is ethnomathematics, and how can it help children school? *Teaching Children Mathematics, 7*(6), 308-310.

Davison, D. (1994). Mathematics. In J. Reyhner (Ed.), *Teaching American Indian Students: Mathematics* (pp. 241-250). Norman, OK: University of Oklahoma Press.

Dewey, J. (1916). *Democracy and education.* New York: Free.

Dewey, J. (1938). *Experience and education.* New York: Schribner.

Dewey, J. (1958). *Experience and nature.* New York: Dover Publications, Inc.

Draper, R. J. (2002). School mathematics reform, constructivism and literacy: A case for literacy instruction in the reform-oriented math classroom. *Journal of Adolescent & Adult Literacy, 45* (6), 520-529.

Fennema, E., & Romberg, T. A. (1999). *Mathematics classrooms that promote understanding.* Mahwah, New Jersey: Lawrence Erlbaum Associates, Inc.

Fine, J. (1997). School supervision for effective teaching in American 1910-1930. *High School Journal, 80,* 288-294.

Fowler, S. (2003). Personal communication, May 12, 2003.

Fowler, S. (2005). Personal communication, June 22, 2005.

Fowler, S. (2010). Personal communication, May 1, 2010.

Freem, C., & Fox, M. (2005). *Status and trends in the education of American Indians and Alaska natives* (NCES 2005-108). Washington, DC: National Center for Education Statistics, Institute of Education Science, and U.S. Department of Education.

Gay, G. (1995). Curriculum theory and multicultural education. In J. A. Banks & C.A.M Banks (Ed.), *Handbook of research on multicultural education* (pp. 25-43). New York: Simon & Schuster Macmillan.

George, B. W. (2006). President George W. Bush's address before a joint session of the Congress on the State of the Union. Retrieved May 16, 2007 from http://www.cspan.org/executive/transcript.asp?cat=current_event& code=bush_admin&year=2006

Goals 2000: Educate America Act. (1994). Public Law 103-227. H.R. 1804: One Hundred Third Congress of the United States of America. Retrieved April 4, 2008 from http://www.ed.gov/legislation/GOALS2000/TheAct/intro.html

Gonzales, P., Williams, T., Jocelyn, L., Roey, S., Kastberg, D., & Brenwals, S. (2008). *Highlights from TIMSS 2007: Mathematics and science achievement of U.S. fourth- and eighth-grade students in an international context* (NCES 2009-001 Revised). Washington, DC: National Center for Education Statistics, Institute of Education Science, and U.S. Department of Education.

Greene, J. C., Caracelli, V. J., & Graham, W. F. (1989). Toward a conceptual framework for mixed-method evaluation designs. *Educational Evaluation and Policy Analysis, 11*, 255-274.

Hayes, W. (2007). *The progressive education movement: Is it still a factor in today's schools?* Lanham, Maryland: Rowman & Littlefield Education.

Hernandez, H. (2001). *Multicultural education: A teacher's guide to linking context, process, and content* (2nd ed). Upper Saddle River, New Jersey: Prentice-Hall, Inc.

Hiebert, J., Carpenter, T. P., Fennema, E., Fuson, K. C., Wearne, D., Murray, H., Oliver, A., & Human, P. (1997). *Making sense: Teaching and learning mathematics with understanding.* NH: Heinemann.

Inch, S. (2002). The accidental constructivist. *College Teaching, 50*(3), 111-114.

Jackson, P. W. (1996). *Handbook of research on curriculum: A project of the American education research association.* New York: Simon & Schuster Macmillan.

Klein, D. (2003). *A brief history of American k-12 mathematics education in the 20th century.* Retrieved October 12, 2007 from http://www.csun.edu/~vcmth00m/AHistory.html

Lee, J., Grigg, W., & Dion, G. (2007). *The Nation's Report Card: Mathematics 2007* (NCES 2007-494). Washington, DC: National Center for Education Statistics, Institute of Education Sciences & U.S. Department of Education.

Lipka, J., Hogan, M. P., Webster, J. P., Yanez, E., Adams, B., Clark, S., & Lacy, D. (2005). Math in a cultural context: Two case studies of a successful cultural based math project. *Anthropology and Education Quarterly, 36*(4), 367-385.

Lipka, J., & Mohatt, G. V. (1998). *Transforming the culture of Schools: Yup'ik Eskimo Examples.* Mahwah, New Jersey: Lawrence Erlbaum Associates, Inc.

Linn, R. L. (2001). A century of standardizing testing: Controversies and pendulum swings. *Educational Assessment, 7*(1), 29-38.

Manning M. L., & Baruth L. G. (2000). *Multicultural education of children and adolescents* (3rd ed). Needham Heights, MA: Allyn & Bacon.

May, S. (1999). *Indigenous community-based education.* Philadelphia, PA: Multilingual Matters LTD.

McNiff, J. (1988). *Action research: Principles and practice.* Great Britain: Mackeys of Chatham PLC, Chatham, Kent.

Meriam, L. (1928). *The problem of Indian administration.* Baltimore, Maryland: Johns Hopkins Press.

Miles, M. B., & Huberman, A. M. (1984). *Qualitative data analysis.* Beverly Hills, CA: Sage Publications, Inc.

Mills, G. E. (2003). *Action research: A guide for the teacher research* (2nd ed). Upper Saddle River, New Jersey: Pearson Education, Inc.

National Assessment of Education Progress. (2007). *Status and trends in the education of racial and ethnic minorities* (NCES 2007-039). Washington DC: U.S. Department of Education.

National Commission on Excellent in Education. (1983). *A nation at risk: The imperative for education reform.* Washington DC: U.S. Department of Education.

National Council of Teachers of Mathematics. (1989). *Curriculum and evaluation standards for school mathematics.* Reston, VA: NCTM.

National Council of Teachers of Mathematics. (2000). *Principles and standard for school mathematics.* Reston. VA: NCTM.

National Mathematics Advisory Panel. (2008). *Foundation for success: The final report of the national mathematics advisory panel.* Washington, DC: U.S. Department of Education.

No Child Left Behind Act of 2001. (NCLB)-Public Law 107-110. Retrieved January 30, 2006 from http://www.ed.gov/legislation

Piaget, J. (1980). *Adaptation and intelligence : Organic selection and phenocopy.* Chicago: University of Chicago Press

ProEnglish. (2009). Official English Is Not "English Only" Retrieved March 5, 2009 from http://www.proenglish.org/notenglishonly.html

President Nixon, Special Message on Indian Affairs (1970). Indian self-determination. Retrieved March 12, 2008 from http://www.epa.gov/tribal/pdf/president-nixon70.pdf

Rampey, B. D., Dion, G. S., & Donahue, P. L. (2009) *NAEP 2009 trends in academic progress* (NCES 2009-479). Washington DC: National Center for Education Statistics, Institute of Education Sciences, & U.S. Department of Education.

Rampey, B. D., Lutkus, A. D., & Weiner, A. W. (2006). *National Indian education study, part I: The performance of American Indian and Alaska native fourth-and eighth grade students on NAEP 2005 reading and mathematics assessments* (NCES 2006-463). Washington DC: National Center for Education Statistics, Institute of Education Sciences, & U.S. Department of Education.

Rashool, J. A., & Curtis, C. (2000). *Multicultural education in middle and secondary classrooms: Meeting the challenge of diversity and change.* Belmont, CA: Wadsworth.

Reyhner, J. (1992). *Teaching American Indian students.* Norman: University of Oklahoma Press.

Romberg, T. (1992). Problematic features of the school mathematics curriculum. In P.W. Jackson (Ed.), *Handbook of Research on curriculum.* New York: Macmillan.

Spelling, M. (2006). *Math now: Advancing math education in elementary and middle school.* Washington, DC: U.S. Department of Education.

Szasz, M. C. (1999). Education and the American Indian: The road to self-determination since 1928 (3rd ed.). New Mexico: University of New Mexico Press.

Souviney, R. (1989). *Learning to teach mathematics* (2nd ed). New York: Macmillian.

Stringer, E. T. (1999). *Action research: A handbook for practioners* (2nd ed). Thousand Oaks, CA: Corwin Press, Inc.

Tayor, F., W. (1967). *The principles of scientific management.* New York: W. W. Norton& Company.

Tyack, D. R. (1974). *The one best system.* Cambridge: Harvard University Press.

U.S. Department of Education. (2008). *A nation accountable: Twenty-five years after a nation at risk.* Washington, DC: U.S. Department of Education.

Vygotsky, LS. (1978). *Mind in society: The development of higher psychological processes.* Cambridge, Massachusetts: Harvard University Press.

Zaslavsky, C. (1996). *The multicultural math classroom: Bringing in the world.* Portsmouth, NH: Heinemann.

Generosity, Fortitude, Respect, Wisdom: Using Popular Culture to Teach Traditional Culture

Carol R. Rempp, M.S.

> Education should consist of a series of enhancements, each raising the individual to a higher level of awareness, understanding, and kinship with all living things. *Author Unknown*

Introduction

"What makes otherwise average teachers, good teachers and turns good teachers into great teachers is their ability to connect with students effectively and often." (Bergstrom, Cleary, & Peacock, 2003, p. 161) When working with Native American students, this process of connection is at times difficult, but when done increases student achievement. However, as Bobby Ann Starnes states in her 2006 *Phi Delta Kappan* article "What We Don't Know Can Hurt Them: White Teachers, Indian Children," even an award-winning, veteran teacher with advanced degrees and a love for American history, who had studied the works of and about Native Americans and had rejected the mythical representation of Native Americans in history, teaching on a reservation was difficult, although not impossible work. When educators are willing to learn about the students, they are serving the rewards are endless.

In order to do this, Starnes states that there are two important facts teachers must learn. First, they need to accept how little they know about the ways that Native American children learn. "We don't recognize the chasm that exists between their needs and our traditionally accepted curricula and methods" (Starnes, 2006, p. 385). Second, even for very skilled and dedicated white teachers, it is difficult to teach well when they do not have an understanding of the history, culture, or communities in which they are teaching, and when their experience is based on white Eurocentric education. "In such cases, solid teaching skills, good intentions, hard work, and loving the kids, just aren't enough. There is too much we don't know about teaching Native American children and what we don't know, definitely hurts them" (Starnes, 2006, p. 385).

How then do non-Native educators connect with Native American students in meaningful ways that promote student achievement? In their book, *The Seventh Generation*, Bergstrom, Cleary and Peacock (2003) share many characteristics of good teaching. Positive teaching characteristics, according to the students they interviewed, "include teachers having cultural knowledge, using encouragement, using explanation, using examples and analogies, having high expectations, being fair and demanding respect for all learners, being flexible, being helpful, being interested in students, listening and trying to understand and using multiple approaches" (pgs. 160-161). These ideas are supported by the work of other researchers. According to the Indian Nations at Risk Task Force (1991), there is a direct correlation between student success in school and the students' understanding of their culture. The Task Force also indicated that schools that demonstrate respect and support of a student's language and culture are significantly more successful in educating students in their care. They recommend that schools take responsibility for promoting students' tribal language. The integration of contemporary, historical, and cultural perspectives of Native Americans, while providing a multicultural focus that works to promote understanding among all races, is also recommended. (1991)

Among the approaches that work best with students is demonstrating an understanding of the tribal people they are teaching. One Navajo student summed up how students enjoy class more by stating:

> Last year, I had one teacher, Mr. S_____. He was a history teacher, and I like, usually don't like my history teachers 'cause they never teach anything about Native Americans. I walked into the room, and all I saw on his walls were pictures of Native American people. And I think, 'Okay, I'm going to like this guy.' And then, when we got to Native American subjects, I think he spent about four weeks . . . I like that guy, he was pretty nice. And the weird thing about it was, he'd always ask me after he said something, if that was right. (Bergstrom, Cleary, & Peacock, 2003, (p. 162).

Another approach is the use of explanation, so that students understand the concepts. Teachers are facilitating in-depth knowledge of subjects by accessing the students' prior knowledge, and helping students connect that knowledge with new knowledge. "The best teachers would encourage or require them to practice what they had learned by thinking, writing, or speaking about it." (Bergstrom, Cleary, & Peacock, 2003, p. 161) Other strategies the students reported working for them included classes where they felt teachers had high expectations for them and challenged them. "Students really appreciated it when teachers were imaginative in them beyond stuck places . . . (and), students thrived when teachers used multiple approaches," (p. 164). Most students said, "Good teachers don't sit there and talk all the time," (p. 166). An Ojibwe student further explained, "Sometimes, I wish that the teachers would teach differently, instead of being in the classroom and lecturing. I wish there were more activities . . . I like to visualize things, like when a teacher says something, but I like hands-on more, because I learn more from it" (Bergstrom, Cleary, & Peacock, 2003, p. 166).

Indian education in the United States is often a tragic story. It is full of oppression and unsuccessful policies of the federal government, to force assimilation on the American Indian tribes. In 1871 federal policy determined that Indians should be eradicated or isolated in Indian Territory, and if that did not occur, they would have to be civilized. In fact, of the nearly 400 treaties negotiated between the government and tribes, 120 contained educational provisions calling for Indians to be civilized (Reyhner, 2006). The government did not acknowledge the education system of the American Indian that was actually complex and thorough.

> "Before Columbus and the invasion of Europeans, North American Indian education was geared to teaching children how to survive. Social education taught children their responsibilities to their extended family and the group, the clan, band, or tribe. Vocational education taught children about child rearing, home management, farming, hunting, gathering, fishing, and so forth. Each tribe had its own religion that told the children their place in the cosmos through stories and ceremonies. Members of the extend family taught their children by example, and children copies adult activities as they played" (Reyhner, 2006, p. 2).

Over time, laws and government policies have changed. The naïve policies that Indian youth would be best educated and assimilated if they were removed from their families and placed in boarding schools have changed. Also, the idea that there was no need for educators in Bureau of Indian Education or BIE, (formerly known as Bureau of Indian Affairs) and religious boarding schools, to have any understanding of or knowledge of Indian life, has been proved to be false. What has been found to be true is that these policies left most Indian children ill-prepared to return to the homes on reservations, or to be productive in white society (Reyhner, 2006).

Reviewing the research that includes a brief history of government policy, along with teaching strategies that have proven to be effective provides the groundwork for this paper. The strategies expressed in this paper are designed to share with educators, ideas for how they can integrate Native American culture into their classrooms in a unique way that will engage their students in the learning process. Both teachers and students will discover new and interesting ideas about Native culture, while bringing prior knowledge to their learning and developing a deeper understanding of American Indian people, from both an historical and contemporary viewpoint.

Define Popular Culture

One of the challenges in today's educational system is to find ways to connect
with youth in order to engage them in the learning process. Today's youth are
surrounded by a fast paced world that appears to focus on the use of technology
for communication, entertainment, exploration and education. Traditional
"teacher lecture—student learn" methods are no longer engaging students in
their own learning, if they ever truly did. A unique challenge facing educators
working with American Indian students is how to teach accurate and authentic
information about identity that also presents both an historical and contemporary
viewpoint, while meeting the state standards of literature or social science. Educators can use popular culture texts, such as books and movies with Native
themes to engage students, while helping them better understand tribal history
and culture.

In *Cultural Theory and Popular Culture: An Introduction*, John Storey
states that in order to define popular culture, we must first define the term 'culture.' He goes on to suggest three possible ways to understand the term, based
on the work of Raymond Williams. First, culture could refer to the intellectual,
spiritual, and aesthetic development of a group, in terms of their understanding
of philosophy, art or poetry. Second, culture could refer to a particular group of
people's way of life, for a period of time. This could include such things as traditions, religious festivals, or literacy development. Finally culture can be the
signifying practices that produce intellectual and artistic meaning. All of these
meanings support what is often referred to as "high culture," that is ballet, opera,
novels, fine art, or poetry (Storey, 2006). This is in direct contradiction to the
definition of popular culture. In other words, high culture is exclusive, and
popular culture is for the masses.

According to Storey, again based on the work of Williams, popular culture
could take on several definitions. These include the concept that popular culture
is well liked by many people and made by the people, for the people. More explicitly, popular culture is widely favored by many people. It can also include all
that is left over, after high culture is excluded. This idea, however, leads one to
think of popular culture as an inferior culture, because it is not exclusive. Popular culture is mass produced and available to all, instead of the individual creation of high culture. Popular culture has therefore, been seen as less valuable.
This leads to another discussion point that defines popular culture as mass produced and commercial, suggesting that it loses something authentic, that high
culture has (Storey, 2006).

Another definition that expands the idea of popular culture is that it is a culture of the people; originated by the people and used by the people. Often "the
people" are equated with the working class, which alone separates it from the

exclusivity of high culture, because one of a kind, also interprets to expensive and unattainable the by working class, simply because of cost. The postmodernism definition of culture would also support the idea of a culture by the people, because it does not recognize a distinction between high and popular culture, in that it blurs the lines between "authentic" and "commercial" culture (Storey, 2006).

Finally, Storey refers to Marxist Antonio Gramsci's term "hegemony" to describe popular culture. Hegemony is defined as "the way in which dominant groups in society, through a process of intellectual and moral leadership, seek to win the consent of subordinate groups in society" (Storey, 2006, p. 8). This approach to popular culture suggests there is a resistance between subordinate groups and the interests of dominant groups. Those who would use this definition, would not see popular culture as emerging from the people, but rather being orchestrated by the dominant culture to manipulate the masses. This definition is referred to here because of the implications the hegemony theory can highlight, in terms of both exploring and explaining conflicts involving ethnicity or race, among others, and their struggles over time with "homogenizing forces of incorporation of the official or dominant culture" (Storey, 2006, p. 8).

Interestingly, the common thread between all of the ideas presented on popular culture is that they all have emerged since industrialization and urbanization. Industrialization created several shifts in society as a whole, but in particular, a shift in relations between employers and employees. Through urbanization there was a shift in the residential settings, where for the first time, there were entire neighborhoods of working class folks. This created a climate where the common culture of the dominant class was no longer the controlling influence of society, thus a space for popular culture was created (Storey, 2006).

Define Traditional culture

Traditional Culture will be defined as "the ideas, customs, skills, arts, etc. or a people or group, that are transferred, communicated, or passed along, as in or to succeeding generations" (Agnes, 2000, p. 353 [5a]). There was no single definition of 'traditional culture' that reflected the ideas the author had been taught or read about. Therefore, the definition presented here represents one the author has chosen to use in the context of these materials. It may not fit with everyone's idea of traditional culture, and may not apply to all or other cultures beyond the scope of this work. That is both acceptable and understandable.

Part of understanding traditional culture, in particular to this work, Lakota culture, is to understand the virtues of traditional people. There are many lists of Lakota virtues; some containing as many as twelve or more. Generally, the four discussed in this work, respect, generosity, bravery and wisdom, are the central or most often spoken about (Marshall, 2001). Each of these virtues provides guiding principles for Lakota people to live by. They are taught through example and storytelling. In historical times they were not taught with books or papers. In modern times, they are still taught through example and storytelling, however, educators are also attempting to teach them in our schools. This is both admirable and problematic, supporting the idea of why works such as this are so valuable to educators. It is recommended that educators of tribal students, other than Lakota or Dakota, search out the traditional virtues taught by the tribal people they are working with, in order to make the ideas presented here most relevant to the local population.

Working with the standards

The academic standards that support the work of this project are the American Indian Content Standards, rather than any state's standards. The American Indian content standards were developed through the Goals 2000 efforts of the Bureau of Indian Affairs in an effort to assist schools in developing local standards, with an emphasis on American Indian/Alaska Native students. They are designed to be used by both non-Indian schools to better understand contributions of American Indians and Alaska Natives, and by schools serving American Indian/Alaska Native students to increase student achievement by better integrating traditional culture into the curriculum. These standards were developed through the integration of Indian content into national content standards. They are not complete in and of themselves, and are intended to be used as an enhancement of national or state standards (http://www.ldoe.org/cetia/aics.htm). As used in this chapter, they can be a model for cultural integration into the curriculum. The specific standards selected for this work, relate to the middle and high school curriculum, and are in most agreement to the argument for using popular culture to teach traditional culture. They also support the use of the texts that are selected to be part of this chapter.

Language & Literacy—Grade Level: 5-12

Standard 8: Reading popular and classical literature from diverse cultures and times, especially American Indian literature, for a variety of purposes and in a variety of genres, and becoming aware of the ways readers and writers are influenced by personal, social, cultural, and historical contexts

Standard 9: Developing multiple strategies to appreciate, interpret, and critique various types of literature and of the print and non print text, including student work—e.g., evaluating literature with Indian themes by non-Indian writers in contrast with literature by Indian writers.

Standard 14: Using a range of technological forms of communications, and in understanding and evaluating critically the conventions, opportunities, and responsibilities of technologically based discourse.

Standard 15: Exploring ideas & feeling imaginatively through a variety of creative modes, e.g. journals, storytelling, drama & media projects (http://www .ldoe.org/cetia/aics.htm).

The Center for Research on Education, Diversity & Excellence (CREDE) focuses on improving education for all students, especially those whose ability to reach their potential may be challenged by language or cultural barriers, race, geographic location, or poverty. Between 1996 and 2001, CREDE funded 31 research projects around the country. These projects gathered data and tested curriculum models in a wide-range of settings, with diverse student populations both on and off reservations, including predominately native speaking students. From 2001 to 2003, synthesis teams produced authoritative reports based on the key findings and practices from the field. From these reports, the CREDE developed Five Standards of Effective Pedagogy and Learning (http://crede.berkeley .edu/research/crede/index.html).

The Five Standards of Effective Pedagogy have been proven to be effective in educating all students. They do not support a specific curriculum. They are the best teaching practices that can be used in any classroom environment with any grade level or group of students. The Five Standards of Effective Pedagogy are: 1)Teachers and students producing together; 2) Developing language and literacy across the curriculum; 3) Making lessons meaningful; 4) Teaching complex thinking; and 5) Teaching through conversation. These standards are supported by CREDE's philosophy, which among other things states that "language and cultural diversity can be assets for teaching and learning" and that "teaching and learning must accommodate individuals" (p. 1) (http://crede.berkeley.edu/ research/crede/index.html).

By further examining the Five Standards of Effective Pedagogy, educators of Native American students can implement teaching strategies that work with the Native American Content Standards to support their Native American students. The CREDE website offers various tools for what effective learning looks like, and a rubric to assist educators in self- assessing their implementation of the Five Standards of Effective Pedagogy. The rubric can be located at: http://gse.berkeley.edu/research/credearchive/standards/spac.shtml. The complete list of standards and indicators can be found at: http://gse.berkeley .edu/research/credearchive/standards/stand_indic.shtml. The "What Effective Teaching Looks Like: Comparing a CREDE classroom to a traditional classroom" chart can be found at: http://crede.berkeley.edu/products/profdev/classroom.html.

Making a case for popular culture

In *Linking Literacy and Popular Culture: Finding Connections for Lifelong Learning*, Ernest Morrell makes the case for the use of popular culture in the educational setting. Morrell focuses primarily on the concepts of popular culture relating to how youth use experience and consume popular culture. He states that the growing diversity of our classrooms is a challenge, because students are bringing an array of experiences into our classrooms. These experiences, he asserts, should enrich the literacy-learning environments, but too often they fail to do so because the experiences that are rewarded are those that most closely mirror academic literacy. "What can happen, what needs to happen, is that teachers create environments in which students can learn from each other's diverse language and literacy experiences, how to see the world differently and how to participate more fully as critical citizens in a multicultural democracy" (Morrell, 2004, p. 4).

When specifically relating popular culture to youth culture, Morrell (2004) states "American teens are saturated with popular culture as they are major producers and consumers . . . " , p. 38). He also states that "Much of popular cultural production through mainstream media is a reflection of youth experience and an inspiration for it" (Morrell, 2004, p. 38). While these may seem like opposing views, Morrell (2004) states that "The two sides are not exclusive of one another and do not detract from the argument that whether they are the producers or consumers, popular culture plays a central role in dictating how youth define themselves in relation to the larger world as well as framing their practices (i.e., dress, speech, or recreational activities) within that larger world,"(p. 39).

The media and major corporations have been criticized because of the often negative stereotypes they reinforce in relation to youth. These include everything from body image, to behaviors, to gender and ethnic compartmentalizing. They also include feelings of low self worth, for not consuming 'popular' products, or having enough material possessions. By teaching critically, popular culture, educators can help control some of these negative images by creating informed and engaged youth, who are able to "more carefully discern and interact with the messages that bombard them on a daily basis" (Morrell, 2004, pgs 44-45)

Morrell also discusses the idea of critical pedagogy by referencing McLaren's 1994 book *Life in Schools,* which supports the idea that "critical pedagogy attempts to provide teachers and researchers with a better means of understanding the role that schools actually play within a race-, class-, and gender-divided society" (p. 46). Darder's 1991 book, *Culture and Power in the Classroom: A Critical Foundation for Bicultural Education* asserts that "the core tenants of critical pedagogy are also conducive to the needs of bicultural students—students who must learn to function in two distinct socio-cultural environments: their primary culture and that of the dominant mainstream culture in the society in which they live" (p. 47). Bicultural pedagogy can "create conditions for bicultural students to develop the courage to question the structures of domination that control their lives" (p. 47). They can become actively involved in both their education and overcoming attitudes in education that continue to oppress (Morrell, 2004).

Instructional materials and strategies

When beginning a unit on popular culture and traditional culture, the teacher may elect to use Robert Pergoodoff's lesson plans that are available at: http://www.media-awareness.ca/english/teachers/lesson_search_results.cfm. These lessons include, "Defining Pop Culture" and "Individuality vs. Conformity."

The Native American curriculum ideas presented here along with the suggested texts, provide a framework for using both literature and film to teach both historically accurate content and contemporary content. These texts are only suggestions based on the experience of the author. It is highly recommended that educators from various regions select literature texts that represent their own region, keeping in mind the selection criteria used for these texts. For example, by using *Waterlily* by Ella Clara Deloria (1988) and *The Absolutely True Diary of a Part-Time Indian* by Sherman Alexie (2007), students are offered two works in terms of the authors themselves, the times in which each book is written and depicts, the differences between boys and girls, how times have changed and how they have stayed the same. Both books reflect youth culture at different points in history and both books represent traditional culture at different points in history.

Some examples of teacher activities would be to do a character analysis of *Waterlily* and *Junior*. Define each character in relation to his/her parents or family, using the ideas of kinship rules presented in *Waterlily*. Compare and contrast the characters, in terms of the point in history in which they are living. How is each time in history defined as easy or difficult for a teenager? Looking specifically at reservation life, is life on the Spokane reservation different than life on the Rosebud or any other reservation? What makes reservation life challenging? What makes it less challenging? The way of life Waterlily knows is ending. How does *Dances with Wolves* visualize this ending? What scenes from *Dances with Wolves* are particularly relevant to scenes from *Waterlily*? *Smoke Signals* and *The Absolutely True Diary of a Part-Time Indian* are both based on the work of Sherman Alexie. How is this noticeable? Thinking through the script and the book, where do you see similarities in his writing?

In addition, because *Smoke Signals* and *The Absolutely True Diary of a Part-Time Indian* are both based on the work of Sherman Alexie, there are many other options for discussion available to the educator. Jim Charles's 2001 article "Contemporary American Indian Life in *The Owl's Song* and *Smoke Signals*," was written before Alexie's *The Absolutely True Diary of a Part-Time Indian*. In his introduction, he states that the two works parallel each other in form and content and that they both "feature young adult American Indian protagonists of the Coeur d'Alene tribe" (p. 54). This statement would also be true of the two works by Alexie. The author of this paper has not read *The Owl's Song*, however, Charles offers a thorough summary of this book in his paper. It is suggested that teachers who are selecting materials to use, review both works and decide for themselves which would best fit their student population and curricular goals. Several teaching variations for these works could be used. Students could be divided into two groups with one group reading *The Owl's Song,* and one group reading *The Absolutely True Diary of a Part-Time Indian.* Then students could compare the two authors' writing styles, interpretation of life on the Coeur d'Alene reservation, or life experiences of the primary characters and how each learns or grows from these experiences. Following the reading of the novels, students can conduct a critical review of the film in comparison to the novels.

Using these texts to teach *Generosity, Respect, Fortitude, and Wisdom,* identify specific passages from each text (literature and film) where these are demonstrated. Have a chart or journal for students, while reading to make notes of these virtues. Why do they think this particular passage or scene teaches one of these virtues? How does it relate to the student?

A different way to teach generosity, respect, fortitude and wisdom is to teach about the Native Americans who have served in the armed forces throughout the history of the United States. The United States military has enjoyed the active participation of Native Americans in every war at home and abroad. Furthermore, the proportion of Native Americans in the armed forces, are greater than any other ethnic group in the nation (Viola, 2008) *Warriors in Uniform* (2008) a National Geographic book by Herman J. Viola chronicles the powerful history of Native soldiers who have served the armed forces of the United States from the 1770s to the present. The stories presented in this book are of real people, real Native American heroes. To introduce the concepts of using popular culture films and novels, the teacher can use the 2002 MGM film *Windtalkers,* and the 2005 Joseph Bruchac novel, *Code Talker: A Novel about the Navajo Marines of World War Two.* Additionally, the National Museum of the American Indian website includes an on-line resource *Native Words, Native Warriors.* Additionally, the National Museum of the interactive American Indian website includes an on-line resource to understand the use of code-talkers to pass secret message past the enemy during WWI and WWII. (*Native Words, Native Warriors.*[http://www.nmai.si.edu/education/codetalkers][http://www. nmai.si.edu/education/codetalkers]) In addition to the ideas mentioned above, the website includes lesson plans, standards alignment and objectives, and technology integration. Also included is an extensive list of additional resources.

An additional resource that can be brought into the classroom is the art of interviewing. Whether students live in reservation communities or urban communities, there are many Native American veterans who are willing to speak with students about their time of service. Should teachers be willing to take the necessary steps students may also take part in the Veterans History Project, which is a project of the American Folklife Center of the Library of Congress. Details can be found at: (http://www.loc.gov/vets/vets-home.html).

Conclusion

In presenting the case for popular culture, Morrill states that American teens are saturated with popular culture through mainstream media, which is at once a reflection of the youth experience, while also being an inspiration for popular culture. He also goes on to discuss how popular culture plays an important role in how youth define themselves within the larger world. This is manifested in their dress, speech, recreational activities as well as the texts they bring into their lives.

This leads to a discussion about youth identity within the realm of popular culture and especially tribal youth identity. Morrell (2004) quotes from Antonia Darder's book *Culture and Power in the Classroom: A Critical Foundation for Bicultural Education,* when he states that educators need to better understand the role of schools in a race-, class-and gender-divided society. He discusses the concepts of bicultural pedagogy that can create environments in which bicultural students can learn critical skills needed to function in their primary culture and the dominant mainstream culture in which most live. Tribal youth, especially those who live off or away from reservations, have distinct challenges in nurturing their tribal identity. By using the curriculum ideas presented in this project, educators can help students become engaged in defining for themselves their identities as both young adults and tribal members.

When considering whether or not to use popular culture in instruction, there are key concepts to remember. American Indian Youth are as involved in popular culture as any other youth. American Indian Youth have unique identity issues. Educators can use popular culture to connect with the students they are teaching, while confidently teaching them traditional culture. Because so many teachers of American Indian youth are not American Indian themselves, this last point is particularly important.

This project is not intended to be a complete guide to teaching traditional cultural ideas to American Indian youth. It is intended to assist educators in connecting with the students they teach through text that is relevant and interesting to them in both contemporary and historical contexts. It is also intended to remind teachers that popular culture is a major player in identity development, and that popular culture is the source from which youth receive information about themselves. This can be both positive and negative. Critical instruction of popular culture can create youth who are able to think critically about the information bombarding them, while using it to assist them in developing their contemporary identities and connect to their traditional culture.

References

Agnes, M. (2000). *Webster's New World College Dictionary,* 4th ed. IDG Books World-wide: Foster City, CA.

Alexie, S. ((2007). *The Absolutely True Diary of a Part-Time Indian.* New York, NY: Little, Brown and Company.

American Indian Content Standards. *http://www.ldoe.org/cetia/aics.htm.*

Bergstrom, A., Cleary, L.M., & Peacock, T.D. (2003). Lessons for educators: Teaching, curriculum, and research. In *The seventh generation* (pp. 155-182). Charleston, West Virginia: AEL.

Bruchac, J. (2005). *Code Talker: A novel about the Navajo Marines of World War Two.* New York, NY: The Penguin Group.

Center for Research on Education, Diversity & Excellence. http://crede.berkeley.edu/.

Chang, T. (Producer), & Woo, J. (Director). (2002). *Windtalkers.* [Motion Picture]. United States: MGM.

Charles, J. (2001, Jan). Contemporary American Indian life in *The Owl's Song* and *Smoke Signals. English Journal*, 9(3): 54-59.

Costner, K. (Producer), & Costner, K. (Director). (1990). *Dances with wolves.* [Motion Picture]. United States: MGM.

Deloria, E. C. (1988). *Waterlily.* Lincoln, NE: University of Nebraska Press.

Eyre, C., (Producer), & Eyre, C. (Director). (1999). *Smoke signals* [Motion Picture]. United States: Miramax Films.

Hale, J.C. (1998). *The Owl's Song.* Albuquerque, NM: University of New Mexico Press.

Indian Nations at Risk Task Force. (1991). Final Report. Washington, DC: U.S. Department of Education. (ERIC Document Reproduction Service No. ED 3399587)

Marshall, J. M., III. (2001). *The Lakota way: Stories and lessons for living.* New York, NY: Penguin Compass.

Morrell, E. (2004). *Linking literacy and popular culture: Finding connections for lifelong learning.* Norwood, MA: Christopher-Gordon Publishers, Inc. *Native Words Native Warriors.* National Museum of the American Indian. http://www.nmai.si.edu/ education/codetalkers/

Reyhner, J. (2006). American Indian/Alaska Native education: an overview. Retrieved from http://jan.ucc.nau.edu/~jar/AIE/Ind_Ed.html.

Starnes, B.A. (2006, Jan). What we don't know can hurt them: White teachers, Indian children. *Phi Delta Kappan, 87*(5), 384-392.

Storey, J. (2006). *Cultural theory and popular culture: An introduction* (4th ed.). Athens, GA: University of Georgia Press.

Veteran's History Project, American Folklife Center of the Library of Congress. http://www.loc.gov/vets/vets-home.html.

Viola, H. J. (2008). *Warriors in uniform: The legacy of American Indian heroism.* Washington, D.C.: National Geographic Society.

FIGURE 1

Guided Viewing Chart

Film Title: _____

Characters (names, roles)	Characteristics (physical, emotional, personality)

Relationship between films or film and literature
(setting, plot, theme, cultural aspects, dialogue, symbolism, historical references, characters, etc.)

Similarities	Differences

Cinematography

(camera angles, shots, movement; sound—dialogue & music score)

How does the cinematography enhance or detract from the story/message?
What dimension or visuals can you relate to the literature?

What elements of literature can you relate to the film?

Additional Resources

Benard, B. (2004). *Resiliency: What we have learned.* San Francisco: WestEd.

Brendtro, L., Brokenleg, M., Van Bockern, S. (1990). *Reclaiming youth at risk: Our hope for the future* (revised edition, 2002). Bloomington, Indiana: Solution Tree (formerly National Education Service).

Deloria, V. Jr. & Wildcat, D. R. (2001). *Power and place: Indian education in America.* Golden, CO: Fulcrum Resources.

Doble, J. & Yarrow, A. L. (2007). *Walking a mile: A first step toward mutual under-standing—a qualitative study exploring how Indians and non-Indians think about each other.* New York, NY: Public Agenda.

Erdrich, L. (1999). *The birchbark house.* New York, NY: Hyperion Paperbacks for Children.

Fox, S.J. (2002). *Creating a sacred place to support young American Indian and other learners in grades K-3* (2nd ed.). Polson, MT: National Indian School Board Association.

Goble, P. ((2005). *All our relatives: Traditional Native American thoughts about nature.* Bloomington, IN: World Wisdom, Inc.

HeavyRunner, I. & Marshall, K. (2003). "Miracle survivors" promoting resilience in Indian students. *Tribal College Journal, 14*(4), 14-17.

Keoke, E.D. & Porterfield, K.M. ((2003). *American Indian contribution to the world: 15,000 years of inventions and innovations.* New York, NY: Checkmark Books.

Marshall, J. M., III. (2005). *Walking with grandfather: The wisdom of Lakota elders.* Boulder, CO: Sounds True, Inc.

Peacock, T. & Wisuri, M. (2006). *The four hills of life: Ojibwe wisdom.* Afton, MN: Afton Historical Society Press.

Reyhner, J. & Eder, J. (2006). *American Indian education: A history.* Norman, OK: University of Oklahoma Press.

Sprague, D. A. (2004). *Images of America: Pine Ridge Reservation.* Charleston, SC: Arcadia Publishing.

Strutin, M. (1999). *A guide to contemporary plains Indians.* Tucson, AZ: Southwest Parks and Monuments Association.

When Numbers Dance for Mathematics Students: Culturally Responsive Mathematics Instruction for Native Youth

Jim Barta, Ph.D., Marilyn Cuch, M.S., and Virginia Norris Exton, Ed.D.

> American Indian children may struggle with math because for some, the numbers don't dance! (Personal conversation with Elmer Ghostkeeper, Metis educator, March 17, 1998.)

"I cannot do math because I am Indian," lamented Shirley, a former student at my university. When I regained my composure, I asked who told her that. Shirley replied:

> My people (Kiowa/Dine) were never discussed by my teachers and certainly not in math class, even though most of my classmates were also American Indian. I grew up thinking that there must be something wrong with me and my people. I thought my people didn't know anything about mathematics, and never used it.

While this interaction occurred a number of years ago, the profound impact of that interaction forever changed my perception of mathematics and culture. Shirley was studying to become a teacher, and ultimately she was able to succeed. Her educational career was nearly ended by the fact that after four attempts, she was still unable to pass the required college algebra course. An advisor, knowing of my work in Native American mathematics, asked if I would be willing to help a most persistent student struggling with math, and I agreed.

I wanted to meet this student who wanted so tenaciously to become a teacher, that she was willing to take a class repeatedly in an attempt to earn a passing grade. The day I met Shirley, I noticed that she was carrying her books and other study materials in a leather backpack, decorated with beadwork strips she had created and stitched. I asked her if she used any math when she did her beadwork. Shirley smiled and began a lengthy explanation of how she had to rely on math constantly, to complete the beadwork and have it look nice.

Shirley and I had many future discussions about her mathematical history. She grew to realize that mathematics was something she counted on regularly, and that math was more than what she learned in school. She began to see mathematics as an integral aspect of her life: her beadwork, the dance outfits she designed and sewed, and the calculations critical to her family's pow-wow travels. The last time I visited with Shirley, she informed me that she remained dedicated to helping her students enhance their mathematical potential. She does this by connecting their cultures and mathematics in her classroom.

This chapter describes the development of a model of mathematics instruction, specifically designed to focus on culturally relevant curriculum and instruction for American Indian teachers and students. Our purpose is to help teachers learn and implement these strategies, to enhance their own instruction, and hopefully get the numbers 'dancing' for their students. The chapter concludes with examples of teachers implementing culturally responsive mathematics instruction, and the voices of students and teachers describing the new insights they have gained.

Refocusing Math Education

Pre-service teachers must critically reflect on their own cultural and educational backgrounds, and the role of culture in teaching and learning. This foundation provides the basis for assimilating and accommodating their newly gained knowledge and insights. Just like the students they will teach, they must establish a home for their new learning, as they consciously integrate prior and new knowledge and experience.

Marilyn (Hunkpapa Lakota), a teacher-educator, faced many challenges as she pursued a new focus on the instruction she provided her Native American students. She stated:

> While teaching at one of the oldest Tribal colleges in the United States, I was asked to teach pre-service elementary education majors in a math course equivalent to a college algebra course. One of my main challenges in designing the class was how to teach students the abstract procedural routines expected by my administrators, while empowering my students with an integrated conceptual understanding using process-based, project-oriented, instructional strategies.

She further explained that the course began with building a collaborative classroom atmosphere, with intra and interpersonal reflection time at the end of each class. Students were required to talk about how they processed mathematical questions to one another, while maintaining a mathematical journal for lectures, homework questions, defining mathematical language, and outlining their progress towards becoming successful problem-solvers. Students were also taught how to read their mathematics text books, learn the symbols of the mathematics language, and understand academic writing structure.

Together, Marilyn and her students traversed new territory from what they had previously encountered. Marilyn had her students write mathematical auto-biographies, where they uncovered personal revelations about their past mathematical classes, and interactions behind successful or non-successful course-work. Many students began to see that the source of their mathematical disempowerment could be found in the disenfranchising stories they were told as students. In earlier classes, mathematics was seldom taught within a familiar context, and often the students' sole interactions were between themselves and their teachers. Collaborative dialogue and problem-solving were seldom experienced.

By revisiting their past histories through a new lens of understanding, some could now see that their previous mathematical challenges were also related to instructional techniques that were not well-aligned to their individual learning needs. Students were empowered with a new realization of their mathematical potential, and began to heal from their previous educational misconceptions, as they reshaped their educational destiny.

They uncovered misconceptions about their own mathematical understandings, through writing about them. They shared insights about the ways they solved their problems, and learned from their peers. Together they began to see that a number of solutions all lead to the right answer, and they began to trust that they, too, could be successful in mathematics.

The students began to perceive that by learning about mathematics in familiar contexts, they could experience the relevance of mathematics in their lives, and in the lives of their people. Marilyn integrated culturally responsive lessons whenever possible.

One lesson involved students studying traditional indigenous home construction that focused on the teepee. Using simple items found in most classrooms, such as unsharpened pencils, brown construction paper, and empty coffee cans (small and large), they investigated mathematical relationships between the length of teepee poles, the angle at which they were positioned, and the circle on the ground that resulted. Students investigated variables affecting the required pole length and teepee circle, as Marilyn challenged students to consider the average height of adult women who historically set up the teepees, and lived and worked inside. The height of a teepee and the length of poles needed for construction was a function of the height of women! Students measured, and then graphed the number of times a diameter could encircle its circle. Students discovered the universal relationship (π) between a circle and its diameter, through Marilyn's facilitation of their learning.

As Marilyn read the students' math journals, denoting their reflections on the activity, she was amazed to discover her students were starting to realize how the successful construction of a teepee was so dependent on the use of math concepts they were now learning. Students came away excited to share their new knowledge with others. They grew confident that their histories and cultures reflected a strong reliance on math knowledge and application. Their increased cultural awareness guided their growing realization that they were American Indian, and therefore, mathematically competent.

Theory and Context for Change

Historically, Americans have been slow to accept the need for culturally-relevant curricula for any student, much less Native students. As early as 1928, the exhaustively-researched Merriam Report acknowledged the importance of multicultural influences in Native education, challenging the assumption that American Indian education should be oriented towards assimilation. The Report recommended providing bicultural and bilingual education in reservation schools—a radical suggestion at the time—and ultimately led to the gradual closure of many American Indian boarding schools, as well as, to changes in curricular content at those which remained.

Twelve years later, the American linguist, Whorf (1956, 1940), suggested that as human beings, we are enculturated by the codes, language, and values of those around us. This research validates that our community affiliations shapes who we are as individuals, and in turn our participation in these communities helps to maintain the cultural influences surrounding us. Landmark federal legislation during the 1970s, including the *Indian Self-Determination and Education Act of 1975*, continued to influence American Indian education. One important provision acknowledged the unique educational needs of Native students, by recommending the adoption of culturally relevant curriculum materials and Native language components.

Systems of education involving American Indian children existed long before the forced intervention by outsiders wishing to civilize and improve on Native culture. Education from a traditional perspective meant knowing oneself and one's place in the world. The classroom was the place where one lived, and one's teachers were those around them. What was learned was done within a context provided by ongoing interaction with the environment, with respect for the multiple dimensions of being—spiritual, mental, social, physical (Cajete, 1994).

Early Western educational practices attempted to remove students from their traditional practices. Rather than learn about one's people and tribal ways of life from an elder, Native children were forced to learn about the ways of others in an alien context, from teachers knowing little about the Native culture or its influence on the teaching and learning of children. Reyhner and Eder (1994) argue, "Had the goal of coercive assimilation been reached, there would be no recognizable Indian people today" (p. 33).

The importance of understanding and acknowledging one's own cultural identity, is closely linked to teaching effectiveness. A teacher must first come to understand his or her identity as a member of various cultural communities, in order to become capable of understanding the necessity of teaching students to identify their own place, purpose, and position as cultural members. Teachers who do not consider their own cultural identities, run the risk of not accepting or not respecting the diversity in cultures displayed by their students.

Native people remain; many continue to raise their children embracing traditional indigenous perspectives and practices, despite ongoing challenges. In spite of all we know, the mathematics curriculum taught in most public schools rarely includes overt connections with culture. Consequently, many students view mathematics as a spectator sport, rather than one in which they can participate. Perso (2002) contends that the mathematics taught in schools, exclusively reflects a 'Western-techno mathematics.' Its roots lie in the creation of a thought pattern, resulting from a Cartesian (Rene Descartes) worldview developed in the 17th century. This worldview has been accepted as the standard for not only mathematical and scientific endeavors, but also has been infused into virtually every aspect of modern society around the world (Barta, Jette', & Wiseman 2003). This perspective includes a perception of linear deductive logic and separate objectification of the world and things found in it.

For the Native American student, this cultural perceptual disconnection, can pose additional obstacles for achievement. it is as if the child were being asked to see through two different pairs of glasses; one which includes a perception of 'reality-based' on a reliance of the traditional (Western) worldview and the other, the subject, whose concepts, content, and information are all encased in the cloak of western impression and definition. because "their own culture of everyday life and meaning continues to intrude on every side" Native American students, who may already feel separated from the culture of school, may feel doubly removed from the subculture of math and science classes, and may find it even more difficult to negotiate "meaning from one domain to another" (Cajete (1999, p. 97).

Connecting mathematics and the particular cultures of the Native American student can have beneficial effects on their ability to learn mathematics, and the way they value the acquisition of this knowledge (Aajete, 1994). In "culturally negotiated schooling: toward a Yup'ik mathematics," Lipka (1994) discussed the process and effects of constructing curricula, with those who are likely to be most affected by it (incorporating language, culture, and daily living practices). Rauff (1996) maintained that if indigenous people are to successfully participate in today's technological society, and still survive as a culture, then educators must realize the role of culture, in both teaching and the learning. Culturally relevant curricula connect the student with his or her heritage. It is the bridge between his or her world on the reservation or in the community, with the world of school academics created at school. Such curricula provide a basis for exploring and learning how many of the same mathematical and scientific principles of Native people are applied and understood in different ways today by mainstream society. The development of such curricula is incumbent upon the inclusion of indigenous ways of knowing.

Overcoming Obstructed Identities

The importance of understanding and acknowledging one's own cultural identity is closely linked to teaching effectiveness (Lipka, Webster, & Yanez, 2005). A teacher must first come to understand his or her identity as a member of various cultural communities, in order to become capable of understanding the necessity of teaching students to identify their own place, purpose, and position as cultural members. Teachers who do not consider their own cultural identities, run the risk of not seeing, not accepting, or not appreciating the diversity in cultures displayed by their students.

The concept of teacher, as well as cultural identity, is a crucial factor in student learning. According to Hammerness et al. (2005), teachers who develop a core sense of professional purpose, become more effective and more reliable teachers: "The identities teachers develop, shape their dispositions where they place their effort, whether and how they seek out professional development opportunities, and what obligations they see as intrinsic to their role" (p. 384). Another way to look at teacher identity, is to examine what Palmer (1998) called "the teacher within" (p. 31). Palmer advocated peeling away layers of expectations, in a conscious process of personal and professional self-discovery: "The teacher within is not the voice of conscience, but of identity and integrity. It speaks not of what ought to be but of what is real for us, of what is true . . . . We can speak to the teacher within our students only when we are on speaking terms with the teacher within ourselves" (p. 31).

Teacher training designed to examine self-concept, perception, and motivation may generate more receptive attitudes toward multicultural awareness and sensitivities (Lehman, 1993). Banks (1995) argues that such inquiry must include a study of individual history, and how this relates to one's current beliefs and values. In studies of teacher education students entering multicultural foundations courses, Brown (1998) and Lehman (1993) found that students project various stages of resistance. The stages of resistance were predicated on the degree of cross-cultural experiences that pre-service teachers had been exposed to, and on their current worldviews. The teacher of a multicultural foundations course—often the only course in a teacher education program devoted to the study of diversity—can also affect how information about culturally appropriate attitudes and instruction are transferred to classroom practice.

One American Indian teacher shared in an email about her teacher education courses at a large state university: "Probably having a competent professor teach the one multi-cultural class might be a start [to improving the program]. The last professor was nice and all, but she was all about loving the Indians and not teaching the subject" (Arlene, Personal correspondence, May 14, 2006).

Native as well as non-Native teachers need to be aware of the role culture plays in their professional identities, and that 'loving the Indians' is not a substitute for effective, culturally relevant instruction.

The following anecdotal narratives excerpted from Exton (2008), illustrate some of the challenges and solutions experienced by classroom teachers (some of them Native American, as noted), who instruct Native American students. Maria (Northern Ute) faced a disconnect during student teaching, between the ways she had been taught, and the strategies that worked best for her Native math students at a reservation high school in Utah. She had successfully negotiated a Eurocentric, non-Native educational system, and felt comfortable in the lecture mode. However, Maria knew that the way she learned and retained information did not fit with what she had been taught in her teacher education classes, about how Native children learn. She said,

> I would love a math teacher to get up and say, 'These are the steps, and this is how you do it. Now do it!' That's me. I would love that. Give me those visuals and stuff, and I get confused. Direct instruction would be fine for me.

Maria's dilemma illustrates the need for Native, as well as non-Native teachers, to align theory and practice about teaching mathematics to Native students. In this way, teachers are able to strengthen a surface philosophy, into an educational conviction. Sergiovanni and Starratt (2006) used the terms espoused theory (assumptions and beliefs of educators) and "theory in use" (educator behaviors which actually occur) to explain how teachers can operate, simultaneously, on two educational platforms (p. 231). For example, teachers may espouse the concept of a culturally relevant curriculum because cultural relevancy is an educational buzz phrase which has positive connotations to most teachers and administrators."

Culturally relevant mathematical tactile or visual experiences have been shown to help Native students become more successful (Lipka & Yanez, 1998) Teachers may refrain from using practices because the math curriculum is too demanding to allow time for using student-centered strategies, or that manipulative materials are simply not available in the classroom. Resolving this dilemma to better align research and practice is the responsibility of the teacher, as well as his or her peers and administrators.

The importance of collegiality in effective math teaching, is addressed in the National Council of Teachers of Mathematics (NCTM, 2000) Principles and Standards for teaching mathematics: "Collaborating with others . . . to observe, analyze, and discuss teaching and students' thinking is a powerful, yet neglected, form of professional development. Teachers need ample opportunity to engage in this kind of continual learning" (Overview: Principles, p. 3). Maria was aware of the disconnect between her past experiences and the needs of her

Native students. However, she found limited resources in her reservation classroom to alleviate the curriculum gap. Maria said:

> I wasn't given the best supply of manipulatives and hands-on math materials, so using a variety of teaching styles was a struggle for me.

To counteract the dearth of classroom materials and broaden her own teaching approaches, Maria collaborated with her Native and non-Native colleagues to share culturally relevant resources and strategies.

In addition to ongoing professional collaboration, the NCTM Principles and Standards, also address the importance of formative assessment in math classrooms: "Assessment should be more than merely a test at the end of instruction to gauge learning. . . Teachers should be continually gathering information about their students through questions, interviews, writing tasks, and other means" (Overview: Principles, p. 3). Another new teacher, Arlene (Navajo), shows how she interacted with her students to provide more effective curricular experiences. Like Maria, Arlene began her first year of teaching Native students, by modeling her own classroom on the 'by-the-book' academic experiences, which had worked for her as an adolescent in a non-Native classroom. Her students were not happy, and neither was she. But rather than become frustrated with her students' discontent, Arlene listened. The students from her reservation charter school classroom, turned out to be some of her best teachers. She replied:

> That's been kind of neat to have some of my students come up and say, 'When I was in junior high, we did this, we did that, and it was really fun.' And so I've been trying to do a lot more hands-on, but it's been really hard to step away from my own learning style.

Successful implementation of culturally relevant activities within the math classroom is a function of classroom design, as well as, teacher preparation and collaboration. To illustrate how an experienced teacher sets up his math classroom, we'll visit Pete in his algebra classroom at a large regional high school in Utah. Pete describes himself as:

> Right-brained enough, that I don't make a really good mathematician, but I can visualize patterns in ways that appeal to kids who have problems learning abstract concepts.

His students have failed one or more math classes in the past, and are not academically ready for high school algebra classes. His students, some of them American Indians, come into Pete's classes with low academic self-esteem, and he has to help them fill in the knowledge gaps and overcome math phobia.

Pete's classroom is colorful and non-linear. Prime numbers cut out of colored paper dangle from the ceiling, and a bulletin board lists hand-lettered, positively stated, "Goals for this Class" on cloud-shaped poster board. Pete's classroom has no individual desks. Instead, 6 rectangular tables (4 to 6 students at each one) are arranged at different angles around the room. This is a room designed for hands-on experiments, and Pete acknowledges that setting up math labs with manipulative materials, was much easier with students sitting around a table. Another advantage to the table set-up, he says, is that the face-to-face contact encourages kids to articulate their understandings. He says:

> If kids can verbalize the math problems and experiments, they're more apt to write it down because they can organize ideas and check out their impressions with other kids, before committing their ideas to paper. Students can see the beauty of math, without getting bogged down in the number crunching.

Vince (Ute/Navajo), just beginning his teaching career at a reservation school in Arizona, provided another example of how the classroom-learning environment can complement a culturally relevant curriculum. The large size of Vince's classroom was particularly suited for his use of kinetic activities with Navajo students. He states:

> What I did to it was I plastered my walls with Velcro because I like to use word walls and so I hooked Velcro all over my room. I also use a lot of pictures, drawings, and do a lot of Total Physical Response storytelling with them. It's a lot of work, but it's effective and makes learning a lot of fun.

The Total Physical Response strategies that Vince uses combine body movements, with audio stimuli, including drum rhythms. Students watch and then they perform, learning vocabulary kinetically. Like many first year teachers, Vince had originally thought of himself as a content area teacher:

> I thought . . . the teacher had all this information and they were supposed to disperse that to the students . . . although that's not really what good teaching is about. It's more of taking a journey alongside your students and learning something with them, rather than just pouring out the information that you know.

Vince gradually learned that his classroom audience, Navajo children, would learn more effectively, if they physically participated in their own education.

Unfortunately for Vince and other teachers, who have discovered the power of culturally-relevant instruction, the proliferation of high stakes standardized tests and the practice of direct instruction for low performing students, gives credence to the idea that mathematics is something to be put into students' heads, apart from their lived experiences and daily lives. In fact, a national trend to improve student test scores to the 'basic,' rather than the 'proficient' competency level in math using National Assessment of Educational Progress (NAEP) scores as measurement, emphasizes the calculation of routine problems, rather than a conceptual understanding of mathematics (Ellis, 2008).

The challenge remains, as it has since the Merriam Report in 1928, recommending bicultural and bilingual education in reservation schools. Research has long existed, pressing for teachers to educate Native American students, by presenting mathematics as both personally and culturally meaningful. We describe in the next section, an indigenous paradigm of culturally responsive teaching, that educators may consider when creating an appropriate educational environment long considered.

An Indigenous Paradigm of Culturally Responsive Mathematics Teaching

Can numbers tell stories? Do shapes sing songs? Can blocks teach us important mathematical concepts as we patiently listen to them? Our model of indigenous mathematical education, 'Dancing Numbers,' is to design and provide culturally sensitive and pedagogically responsive mathematics instruction for American Indian students. Dancing Numbers illustrates relationships involving American Indian cultures, their ways of knowing, beliefs and values, and mathematics. Dancing Numbers enables students to see themselves as bright and capable math learners, in relation to their cultural identities. Students do not have to forget who they are as Native people, when they dance with numbers. Providing educational opportunities is part of the government's trust responsibility to American Indian tribes, under the principles of tribal sovereignty. In over 400 treaties between 1778 and 1871, American Indians gave up land to the federal government, in return for promises of goods and services, including the provision of education (Pavel, 1999). American Indian education has endured almost 200 years of varying quality, with more poor quality than good, under this trust responsibility. DeJong (1993) commented, "The history of education among American Indians, in many respects, constitutes miseducation" (p. 263).

Jolly (2003) suggested that some Native children are penalized in our schools, for not being privy to the cultural nuances of westernized teachers and their curricula. Jolly spoke of 'missing bricks' in the foundation of the child's education. These are areas of knowledge many people erroneously presume we all see and similarly experience.

Christensen (2003) described the necessity of the "3 Rs" or principle behaviors that fit successful tribal education. These include respect, reciprocity, and relationships. Respect involves humility in the learner and the teacher, a gratitude for what is to be learned, and an honoring of the knowledge and of those who are willing share it. Respect involves the importance of building a classroom climate, that is non-competitive and supportive of collaborative ways of learning. Reciprocity includes flexibility and spontaneity between the teacher, the learners, and the understanding that is being individually and collectively constructed. Relationships describe the connections situated within what is being taught, and its purpose and place in the lives of our children. If Native children are indeed confronted with missing bricks of knowledge, and if their education is lacking in respect, reciprocity, and relationships, then the curriculum they are provided, is toxic to teacher and learner alike.

It is apparent that students can learn as much from what teachers do not tell them, as they do from what is expressed. Students who see their stories included in the curriculum, are often better able to understand the usefulness of what they are learning. While the inclusion of these culturally relevant examples, appear to be conducive to enhancing mathematics education for Native children, it is only a part of what is necessary to make our instruction more appropriate and effective for students. Native students can struggle in our public educational programs, because of the cultural mismatches that may occur between the worldview of the teacher and his or her curriculum, and the worldview held by the student, his or her family, community and/or Nation.

Not only may few pertinent cultural examples be presented, but these examples may typically carry with them a western influence or paradigm. Students' exposure to a 'cultural event' in school too frequently is framed within a sporadic celebration of a particular holiday or a specific food specialty rather than situated in a deeper and broader social context. Culture, when it is included in the school curriculum, is typically found in social studies, reading, or perhaps music, but seldom in mathematics.

While many consider mathematics to be a 'universal language,' few realize the variety of dialects spoken. Mathematics is in reality, shaped by the culture of those using it, and reciprocally influences those through its use. Inherently, any mathematics instruction cannot be separated from the worldview from which it has evolved. Its application is also imbued with its worldview impression and solidified as active validation by those who use it. This impression is typically invisible to the teacher or the learner, and often goes unquestioned.

The worldview perception is an expression of how students and teachers have learned to 'see their world' as a result of the enculturation process. Each community and every society functions under this set of rules for how one functions socially and psychologically, as a successful member in that community or society (Barta & Brenner, 2009).

While it is not our intention within the scope of this chapter, to provide a detailed description of either a Western or an indigenous worldview paradigm, we will share an explanation of each as germane to this discussion. Our understandings of each comes from our collective studies, experiences on reservations, time spent with Native teachers and their students, and lengthy discussions with Native elders, friends, other Indigenous educational scholars.

The Western worldview:
1. Teaches us to think in straight lines, where discreet points matter most;

2. Emphasizes knowing the world, mainly through the mind in a setting organized in time and space; and
3. Describes the world, in terms of dualities of either/or, and where only human beings are "really" alive.

In comparison, an Indigenous worldview:
4. Has us thinking in circles, rather than lines, where interactions create meaning;
5. Emphasizes us knowing the world through the mind and our heart in time, space, place, and spirit; and
6. Describes the world, in terms of relationships where *everything* has life.

The student who functions from an indigenous paradigm, benefits from a curriculum that fosters the web of multiple relationships within the learning, while embracing the development of a cognitive and spiritual understanding what is being studied. From this perspective, it is not only possible, but also useful to consider that the objects with which the student interacts in the mathematics classroom, have their own stories to tell.

When numbers dance, the objects or models tell us their stories, if we have the ears to hear and the eyes to see. Teachers may be able to enhance their mathematics instruction for American Indian students, by purposefully acknowledging the life of the objects they use when they teach.

Consider a Base 10 model completed with commercially produced base blocks. Once built, there are many stories it can relate. Our model 'tells' us of its quantity, both total and distributed. It sings of its perimeter and area, its volume, its color, texture, weight, and density. Models which are seen as inanimate can become teachers for Native American students as these children learn to interact with them in the ways just described.

Joe Aragon (Acoma Pueblo) is a math and physics teacher who considers himself to be a Native person that goes between the two worlds (Western and indigenous). In conversation, he giggled at his self-description that such a blend has caused him to be a *controlled-Schizophrenic*. Joe was asked what Dancing Numbers meant to him, and if he thought it were possible to hear the stories told by objects and entities we come across in our daily activities. Joe explained that the responses he provided were not his personal thoughts, but rather thoughts he expressed for the Elders who have taught him during his life about such things.

> There are some old ones of my people who live entirely in the world just described. To them, all things have a story. Dancing Numbers are ways that students can make meaning of the math that they are taught. With my people, the Acoma, dance is often sacred. Through a dance, people can connect to the deeper spiritual understandings of what being a member of our people means.

In speaking of the life of objects, Joe explained:

Objects already know their names, their purpose, and their culture. I am not sure that they (the objects) are obligated to tell us their stories, but some do. At one time, we all spoke the same language and even though now there are many languages spoken, we can still communicate with each other at some level. We are all part of the same thing; we all come from the same place. We are no different. Human beings are the only beings that have to go to school to know who they are. Plants, animals, rocks, etc. know what they are from the beginning. Human beings must constantly search for who they are and work hard to stay right with who they were meant to be. It is becoming harder for our students to know who they are, as they are pulled to what contemporary society prizes; Things like big houses and nice cars. It is easy for our young ones to forget the ways of their people, which have sustained our people through centuries of hardship and challenge (Personal communication, November 20, 1997).

The concept of Dancing Numbers offers teachers opportunities for adapting their instruction to align with a Native way of knowing. As such, students learn important mathematical concepts and principles, while also learning critical aspects of what it means to be a member of a Native community. Native Elders must play a significant role in this education process as they share their wisdom concerning traditional activities, beliefs, and values.

Culturally situated instruction connects not only with the activities and traditions of the people for whom it is designed, but also reflects community values and beliefs. Dancing Numbers focus on allowing us to see the math that lives within an activity or action. It illustrates multiple connections and meanings, between math and the world in which the child lives. These meanings are embedded in instruction that includes connections to who they are as Native people. We must seek to build bridges of understanding that connect from the students' worlds, to the concepts we teach. Native cultures and traditions provide countless opportunities.

A Framework for Creating Culturally Responsive Mathematics Teaching

The following is one model that we have developed (Barta & Brenner, 2009) and used successfully in accessing cultural information that can then be reshaped for our instructional benefit. It is dependent on developing a relationship with a cultural expert, often a person who is recognized as an Elder within the community. The Elder ensures what is learned and presented, is correct and appropriate for those for whom it is intended. Teaching and learning are situated within the community context. New vocabulary, knowledge, and application reflects contemporary use, while maintaining connections of what was known and how such knowledge was used in the past.

Teachers can:

1. Interview experts/elders/cultural representatives who will describe a particular activity important to the cultural community, and share not only content knowledge, but also related beliefs, values, and traditions related to the doing of the activity. Such experts often maintain a special respect in the community and their words and presence can establish motivation, as well as credibility for what will be taught.

2. Examine the knowledge gained for curricular connections to the core mathematical objectives or expected curricular standards. A list of possibilities are made, and one or more mathematical principles/concepts to teach are selected.

3. Design a lesson or series of lessons around the selected principle or concept. The lesson, while focused on the mathematics to be learned, can also include objectives to inform students of important cultural knowledge and practices. Information is presented using a variety of techniques, but the main instructional emphasis should be on cooperative problem-solving using materials/models and hands-on interaction. The context of the culturally relevant application, provides additional opportunities to share and discuss the values, beliefs, and traditions inherent in application. Students should be encouraged to establish a personal understanding of what is studied, and offer their newly gained knowledge/wisdom in circles of sharing during the activity.

4. Assess using performance-based techniques. Attitudinal, as well as cognitive evaluations can be established. The process a student has exhibited in the completion of an activity, will often be as good, if not a better demonstration of learning as that of the final product. Primary in the learning is the degree to which the learner establishes personal meaning for use in ones life, and for the benefit of the community.

Can teachers really emulate the vision of Dancing Numbers and implement it successfully in classroom? Do educators help students develop habits of the heart and of the mind, so that they successfully participate in an expanding mathematical dialogue, learn deeply the necessary mathematical concepts and content, and understand their responsibility to work hard and learn well, so that they may give back to their communities who have supported them? We know it is possible, because we ourselves have been involved in this work for more than a decade. You do not need to simply believe us. Rather, the growing evidence that this work is taking place is illustrated in the growing number of books, scholarly articles, conferences, organizations, and curricular materials involving mathematics and indigenous cultures. We share four vignettes to demonstrate briefly that not only is this work possible but it is taking place in a variety of locations, in a range of classrooms, impacting a number of students and their communities. We hope you will look for the commonalities amidst the differences, and define for yourself how you will reorient your instruction to get the numbers dancing for your students. Notice that each lesson is situated in a meaningful context involving active learning. Sophisticated mathematical understandings are developed as students learn of math's relationship to other subjects and contexts, themselves, and real life applications.

Authentic Examples of Application

Mathematics in a Mayan Village

Mayan children in the village of Santa Avelina, located in the highlands of Guatemala, are reconnecting with their ancestral heritage through mathematics and the farming of corn. For the children and their families corn was historically and remains today the single most important staple beyond air and water in their community. Corn provides food for the people and their animals. Young and old alike enjoy a corn mush drink. The husks are used as wrappers in the preparation of certain favorite foods, and husks, when burned, provide heat with which to cook and warm the home, or as ash to enrich the soils. What is not used personally helps feed the chickens, pigs, and animals. Finally, excess corn is sold at the market, so that families may purchase other necessary commodities required for life.

Growing corn requires significant time and care, as it is estimated that upwards of 40% of what farmers produce, becomes diseased, rotted, or eaten by local rodents competing for food. Traditional Mayan practices of growing corn have farmers planting three to five corn kernels in mounds dispersed approximately one meter apart. The *cuerda* or corn plot is traditionally 20 meters by 20 meters, with rows also spaced one meter distant.

Volunteer consultants are working with local teachers to develop communities of effective practice support education at a village school. School administration favors culturally situated learning opportunities for the students, who learn at school to speak, read, and write the home language first, before they learn the national language of Spanish.

HELPS mathematics consultant's work with local experts and teachers to design lessons after selecting a cultural context, thus providing the rationale and foundation for the teaching. A recent example illustrates this connection. Fourth grade students were studying double-digit multiplication, which traditionally was taught procedurally without any real application. Lucas, the community's Mayan agricultural expert, had been discussing research indicating the corn could be planted in mounds much closer, thereby significantly increasing corn production.

In one project, Lucas, a youngster working with the children's teacher and the consultant, partnered to design a multiplication lesson where students would calculate the number of kernels needed for planting, and the overall estimated crop production when comparing the two different measures (one meter vs. 40 centimeters). Students working in small groups collaborating on a calculation were asked to explain their thinking in writing or in diagrams. One team shared their thinking using "Ixil" their home language. This written description was perhaps, the first time a Mayan student in a contemporary classroom, responded in this Mayan dialect. Students further enhanced their mathematical proficiency while communicating with peers as they realized the utility and necessity of what they were learning. Juana exclaimed, "Now I can go home and tell my father how to grow more corn!"

Math and Maple Sugar

Ziinzibaakwad is the Ojibwe word for maple sugar. Maple sugar was made by American Indians from the Carolinas northward into Canada, and westward into Minnesota, and everywhere that sugar maple trees were found. The mathematics in the process of making maple syrup and sugar and Woodland Indians, lends itself to integrating science, technology, and mathematics in grades K-12.

In another project, Educator Rich Sgarlotti was working at Hannahville Indian School (Michigan) dedicating himself to providing his students optimal mathematical experiences and by connecting his culture throughout his instruction. He shares tribal legends of how maple sugar came to the people, and its collection and use. Much of the learning takes place outdoors, where math can be observed in nature. The following are just a few of the lessons he has developed:

Kindergarten to early elementary classes

Earlier in the morning, when the sap is just dripping, students count the drips per minute. Students can compute the approximate number of drips in a given time period, or the number of drips in a tablespoon or other measure. Students will also see the process of boiling sap, and understand the changing states of matter.

Early elementary to late elementary

Students can find the relationship between temperature and sap flow. They can compute the time necessary to fill a one gallon container with sap. Later, elementary students can also look at the temperature of boiling sap, and syrup, and perhaps relate that to the specific density of the sap or syrup, using a hydrometer.

Late elementary to middle school

In addition to previous activities, students can assist in the selection of trees, by measuring circumference and crown spread. Students can assist in the tapping of trees, by finding the cardinal directions and locating the places on trees to be tapped. Students can assist in the collection of sap, and estimating the gallons collected, and relating that with the measurements taken earlier. They can find the amount of sugar in the sap from various trees using a hydrometer, and relate that to circumference, location (amount of sunlight), and crown spread. Students can also relate the barometric pressure to the amount of sap flowing from the trees. Data can be put into tables or charts, by hand, or on computer spreadsheets.

Middle school to high school

Students can assist in boiling the sap to make syrup, by use of a hydrometer to find the specific density (sugar content) of the sap, or the changing boiling point as the sap becomes thicker. Students can determine the number of gallons of sap needed to make one gallon of syrup, and relate that to the specific density. Students can assist in boiling the syrup to make sugar, also checking the temperature. Students can also examine the crystal structure of the sugar. Students can bottle the syrup and sell it, keeping records of costs and profits. They can also make sugar or other candies which can be sold. They can also give it to elders or others in the community.

The Verbification of Math

The Mi'kmaq are the Aboriginal inhabitants of Atlantic Canada. Mi'kmaw communities in Nova Scotia have a unique jurisdictional agreement with the Government of Canada that gives them control over their education system and collective bargaining power. Disengagement from mathematics and science is a concern for many teachers in these schools, as they grapple with the tensions between school-based mathematics and Mi'kmaw ways of reasoning about things seen as mathematical.

In one project, Lisa Lunny Borden had experienced these tensions herself, having taught for ten years in one of these schools. In this brief summary, she shares how her students unexpectedly articulated 'life' in the math activities and objects she presented. This was in contrast to Lisa's personal previous experiences with teaching and learning. Lisa discovered her students 'verbified' mathematics in their classroom discussions. Objects typically seen as having to life were described as being animated. Apparently, students, most of who were from Mi'kmaw families and enculturated in Mi'kmaw language and tradition, were transferring their interactions in the culture, to events taking place in the classroom. Lisa, being responsive to these cultural nuances and learning needs of her students, not only allowed them, but also encouraged them. As a result Lisa's style of instruction began to shift, as she realized the importance of re-framing her instructional voice, to include the student's cultural/linguistic per-ception, that math was action *best* denoted by verbs, rather than as an object known through its nominalization.

Lisa, working with a fluent Mi'kmaw language expert, learned that move-ment and motion was a critical component of the language. She began to under-stand that there was a sense of motion embedded in many words. *Paktaqtek* is a word to describe something that is straight, such as a fence. It was explained that there "is a sense of motion from here to the other end – *pektaqtek* [it goes straight]."

Similarly, when learning similarities between prisms and pyramids, she heard her student's state, for example that prisms could sit still, they had faces that could see you, and that pyramids could not stand on their heads.

Lisa believes that using action-oriented language when teaching mathemat-ics, could be effective in better educating her students. Certainly, such practice acknowledges Mi'kmaw language, and its role in shaping the paradigm of those who have been enculturated in this linguistic community.

Anishinaabe Arcs

Native Americans who lived in the Great Lakes region, spoke a family of lan-guages called Anishinaabe. Many of their structures were built with arcs, created by bending wood: practical dwellings, such as the wiigwaam and longhouse, and religious architecture, such as the sweat lodge and mide lodge. Canoes were built with arcs, as were bows for arrows, snowshoes, lacrosse sticks, basket rims, dreamcatchers, and cradleboards. Anishinaabe Arcs (http://csdt.rpi.edu/ na/arcs/) is one website on the suite of Culturally Situated Design Tools (http://csdt.rpi.edu) developed by university educator and ethnomathematician, Ron Eglash. The Arcs website allows students to create 3D virtual models of these indigenous structures using parabolic arcs.

The website is divided into three main sections and includes a brief history of the Anishinaabe, reviews the many structures made from arcs, and the physics of wood held in tension, which makes arcs an ideal basis for these structures. An interactive Java applet allows students to explore various parameters for creating 3D parabolic arcs, by specifying the arc center, height, width (where the arc in-tersections the Cartesian plane representing the ground), and rotation. A 2009 STEM summer workshop for Native American students (mostly from Anishi-naabe communities), gave the students the opportunity to review the cultural background sections, train on the software, and produce their own creative forms.

In his reflections on the workshop, Ron reported the following: "One of the striking aspects of this experience was to see how each student brings their own sensibility, perspective, and motivations to the design. For example, one student was interested in a sort of cultural authenticity: she wanted a precise intersection of arcs, that reflected her vision of what a traditional wigwaam might embody. This caused her a lot of frustration, but in the end, the degree of control she had over the forms—specifying parameters past the decimal point—showed that it was an effective way for her to climb the learning curve" (Personal conversation with Ron Eglash, May 23, 1997)

Often, figures can help students understand concepts. One student told me a particular figure helped confirm her interest in architecture and produced forms that looked nothing like traditional structures.

For a third child in the project, this was all about using mathematics to express her creativity with a fluid play of forms. Yet she too mastered the software. Rather than searching for the one optimal lesson, we can enhance student learning by helping them appropriate mathematics (and culture) as tools for their own agency.

Conclusion and Final Thoughts

A number of voices have been involved in the writing and in telling of the Dancing Numbers story. It is through these collective thoughts, ideas, and examples that one can begin to understands the opportunity, purpose, and direction of our suggestions for getting students more involved, and successful in their mathematical interactions.

We hope readers come away with ideas for enhancing their mathematical instruction for American Indian students. We caution that we believe there exists no single, perfect model of instruction that will be optimal for all learners. Rather, each teacher must take what has been presented, and discover useful ways to access the cultures and voices of those they teach. Only then can the dialogue continue to not only mark what has taken place, but define a new educational vision of success, purpose, and promise for American Indian students in mathematics. Long may you dance with the numbers!

References

Banks, J. A. (1995). Multicultural education: Historical development, dimensions, and practice. In J.A. Banks & C.A. McGee Banks (Eds.), *Handbook of research on multicultural education* (pp. 3-24). New York: Simon & Schuster.

Barta, J. & Brenner, B. (2009). Seeing With Many Eyes: Connections Between Anthropology and Mathematics. In B. Greer, S. Mukhopadhyay, A. Powell, & S. Nelson-

Barber (Eds.), *Culturally Responsive Mathematics Education* (pp. 85–110). Oxford, UK: Routledge Publishing.

Barta, J., Jette', C., & Wiseman, D. (2003). Dancing numbers: Cultural, cognitive, and technical instructional perspectives on the development of Native American mathematical and scientific pedagogy. Educational Technology Research and Development, 51(2), 87-97.

Brown, E. L. (1998). The relevance of self-concept and instructional design in transforming Caucasian preservice teachers' monocultured world-views to multicultural perceptions and behaviors (Doctoral dissertation, The University of Akron, 1998). *Dissertation abstracts international, 59*(7), A2450.

Cajete, G. A. (2005). American Indian Epistemologies. *New Directions for Student Services, 109,* 35-44.

Cajete, G. A. (1994). *Look to the mountain: An ecology of indigenous education.* Durango, CO: Kivaki Press.

Cajete, G. A. (1999). *Igniting the sparkle: An indigenous science education model.* Durango, CO: Kivaki Press.

Christensen, R. (2003). Cultural Context and Evaluation: A Balance of Form and Function. www.nsf.gov/pubs/2003/nsf03032/session1.pdf. 14-22.

Clarke, A. (1994). *American Indian Youth at Risk Study. Office of Educational Research and Improvement* (ED), Washington, DC. R117E10215. 23-33.

Demmert, W. G., Jr. (2001). Improving academic performance among Native American students: A review of the research literature [Electronic version]. Charleston, WV: ERIC Clearinghouse on Rural Education and Small Schools.

Exton, Virginia (2008). *A qualitative case study of developing teacher identity among American Indian secondary teachers from the Ute Teacher Training Program.* Doctoral thesis. University Archives, Merrill-Cazier Library. Utah State University, Logan, Utah.

Ellis, (2008). Leaving no child behind yet allowing none too far ahead: Ensuring (in)equity in mathematics education through the science of measurement and instruction. *Teachers College Record 110.* 1330-1356 http://www.tcrecord.org ID Number: 14757, Date Accessed: 3/12/2010.

Fried, J. (1993). Bridging emotion and intellect: Classroom diversity in process. *College Teaching, 41*(4), 123-128.

Hammerness, K., Darling-Hammond, L., & Barnsford, J. with Berliner, D., Cochran-Smith, M., McDonald, M, & Zeichner, K. (2005). How teachers learn and develop. In L. Darling-Hammond & J. Bransford (Eds.), *Preparing teachers for a changing world: What teachers should learn and be able to do* (pp. 358-389). San Francisco, CA: Jossey-Bass.

Jolly, E. (2003). On the Quest for Cultural Context in Evaluation: Non Ceteris Paribus – C!XZ. www.nsf.gov/pubs/2003/nsf03032/session1.pdf. 14-22.

Lehman, P.R. (1993). The emotional challenge of ethnic studies classes. *College teaching, 40*(4), 134-137.

Lipka, J. Webster, J. & Yanez, E. (2005) Factors that affect Alaska native students' mathematical performance. *Journal of American Indian Education*, 44(3), 1-8.

Lipka, J.& Yanez, E. (1998) Identifying and understanding cultural differences: toward culturally-based pedagogy. *In Transforming the Culture of Schools: Yup'ik Eskimo Examples.* Jerry Lipka, with Gerald Mohatt and the Ciulistet Group. Pp. 111–137. Mahwah, NJ: Lawrence Erlbaum Associates.

Lipka, J. (1994). Culturally negotiated schooling: Toward a Yup'ik mathematics. *Journal of American Indian Education*, 33, 14-30.

NCTM, (2000). *Principles and standards*. Reston, VA: National Council of Teachers of Mathematics. *http://standards.nctm.org/document/chapter2/index.htm*

Palmer, P.J. (1998). *The courage to teach: Exploring the inner landscape of a teacher's life*. San Francisco: Jossey-Bass.

Pavel, D. M., Larimore, C., & VanAlstine, M. J. (2003). A gift to all children: Native teacher preparation. In M. K. P. Ahnee-Benham & W. J. Stein (Eds.), *The renaissance of American Indian higher education: Capturing the dream* (pp. 193-211). Mahwah, NJ: Lawrence Erlbaum Associates, Inc.

Perso, T. (2002). *Investigating current research and systemic approaches to improving the numeracy of indigenous children*. Churchill Fellowship Report. 1-38. West Perth, AU: Churchhill Fellowship Trust.

Rauff, J. (1996). My brother does not have a pickup: Ethnomathematics and mathematics education. *Mathematics and Computer Education*, 30(1), 42-50.

Sergiovani, T. J. & Starratt, R. J. (2006). *Supervision: A redefinition* (8th ed). New York: McGraw-Hill.

Whorf, B. (1956): *Language, thought and reality*. J. B. Carroll's (Ed.). Cambridge, MA: MIT Press.

Whorf, B. L. (1940). Science and Linguistics. *Technology Review, 42*(6), 229-31.

'Olu'olu i ka pä a ke Kaiäulu: Community and Place as a Textbook for Learning

Kay L. Fukuda, Ph.D. and ku'ualoha ho'omanawanui, Ph.D.

Introduction

Schools have never adequately supported Native Hawaiian children. One indicator is that in the State of Hawai'i, fifty-one schools (twenty percent of public schools) have failed to meet adequate yearly progress (AYP) on standardized tests in reading and/or mathematics over the last four years. The majority of those schools are in high poverty communities serving Native Hawaiian students. Native Hawaiian children are twice as likely to attend schools involved in restructuring, than non-native children, with approximately one in eight Native Hawaiian students (13%) attending restructuring schools, compared with approximately one in seventeen non-Hawaiian students (6%) (Kana'iaupuni, Malone, & Ishibashi, 2005) attending such schools. Furthermore, Native Hawaiian children, along with other Pacific Island groups, were the only group which did not show a decline in dropout rates during the 1990's (U.S. Census Bureau, 2003). Overall, Native Hawaiian children as a group score in the bottom quartile on standardized tests of reading and mathematics, are overrepresented in special education, and have the highest school dropout rate of any group in Hawai'i (State of Hawai'i, 2007, SB 1784). It's clear to Hawaiian community members, educational leaders, and teachers that education, as it is currently constructed, is not serving the needs of Native Hawaiian children and that alternatives need to be sought (Kana'iaupuni, 2005; Kawakami, 1999; 2004; Meyer, 1998).

In particular, alternatives are needed that are better aligned with the multiple cultural contexts in which Hawaiian children live, and that embrace and support positive identity development, intellectual growth and a sense of community engagement and responsibility.

This chapter explores a place-based cultural project curricular framework that is based on the multiple cultural ecologies of children and which guides the work of an after-school program for children and describes the impact the program has upon children's identity development, school engagement, academic achievement, and environmental stewardship. We begin with an introduction to the Program for Afterschool Literacy Support (PALS) and the context in which the program operates. We will then explain the theoretical foundation of the PALS framework and describe the way in which this theoretical approach is enacted in a place-based, cultural project curriculum. Finally, preliminary data will be shared that communicates the impact of PALS on children's school engagement, environmental stewardship, identity development, and motivation for reading and academic achievement.

History and Context of PALS

PALS is a program initially funded by the United States Department of Education (US ED), Native Hawaiian Education Program in 2006. It currently serves over 120 fourth, fifth and sixth graders in Native Hawaiian communities on the Wai'anae coast of the island of O'ahu, Hawai'i. PALS is currently in the first year of its second three-year funding cycle; and in its third year operating in schools. The first year of funding was a planning year devoted to the conceptualization of program operations and recruitment of schools, teachers and students.

The community of Wai'anae, while rich in history, spiritual traditions, geographic resources and family strength, has also been faced with long-term economic challenges. While the median income in Hawai'i is actually above the National median income (Hawai'i $66,413–National $50,046) this does not show the trends that occur across ethnicity and when annual income is adjusted for larger family patterns and higher cost of living. In fact, using Census 2000 data, Kana'iaupuni, Malone, & Ishibashi (2005) describe Native Hawaiians as the most socioeconomically disadvantaged ethnic group both within the state of Hawai'i and at the national level when accounting for household size and cost of living. These economic trends are well-represented within the community of Wai'anae and in the schools as can be seen by the fact that Free and Reduced Lunch rate in the schools in the project are almost double that of the state average (see Table 1).

Table 1
Demographic and Academic Performance Indicators in Participating Schools

	Native Hawaiian	Average Daily Absences	Free/Reduced Lunch Program	5[th]grade HSA Reading[1]
State DOE Average	28%	9	39%	60%
Kamaile Academy	60%	19	85%	33%
Makaha Elementary	67%	19	75%	38%
Waianae Elementary	70%	16	77%	21%

[1] Proportion of 5th graders **proficient** on the Hawai'i State Assessment in Reading

Source: Hawai'i Department of Education, 2009

While income is not the sole representation of well-being, long term economic stress has a significant impact on children and families (Chevalier, & Lanot, 2002; Conger, et.al, 1992; Kana'iaupuni, Malone, & Ishibashi, 2005), as children from economically unstable families may struggle with health problems, high rates of depression and suicide, and live in communities with high levels of substance abuse, fewer social and economic resources (Kana'iaupuni, Malone & Ishibashi, 2005), and in families where there are strained parental interactions, given the stress of poverty and of working low-income jobs (Conger, et al., 1992).

PALS operates three days each week during the regular school year, for an average of 67 program days. The program typically begins with a 30 minute homework block, followed by 90 minutes of program time. Across the three PALS school sites, there are 19 tutors who work with the 120 children. PALS ensures a low tutor to student ratio of no more than 1:8. The tutors are paid for their time with the children, and are additionally, paid for 30 minutes of prep time for each program day. The majority of the PALS tutors are certified classroom teachers in the schools in which PALS operates, but only a small minority shares the children's ethnic, cultural history. This cultural incongruence between teachers and students is not uncommon in schools throughout Hawai'i—but are particularly prevalent in rural Native Hawaiian communities. Approximately six in ten students at the schools on the Wai'anae Coast are Native Hawaiian, including those participating in PALS, compared to only one in ten teachers (Hawai'i Department of Education, 2008).

Place-based Cultural Project Curriculum

The PALS program is committed to providing a culturally relevant and responsive education for the children in PALS. However, given that only a small percentage of PALS tutors in the target schools were familiar with the history and culture of the communities, and a significant proportion were also new to Hawai'i and unfamiliar with its multicultural history, they struggled to understand how to take up heritage culture in respectful and authentic ways. Consequently, there was a turn toward the concept of 'place' as a starting point within a place-based approach to learning, which utilizes the community and its natural resources as the springboard for learning. Place has occupied an important place in indigenous epistemology (Goodyear-Ka'ōpua, 2009). Learning from and with the land or place, has been shown to be critical to indigenous communities (Hermes, 2000; Lipka, 1991), and particularly for Native Hawaiians (Kana'iaupuni & Malone, 2006; Meyer, 1998). 'Ike 'Aina, a form of place-based learning (Ho'omanawanui, 2009) can be seen as an approach to, "cultivating culturally based literacy learning" (p. 1) for Hawaiian and non-native children alike.

Using place as a starting point allows the tutors and children, who come from many ethnic and geographical cultural locations, to learn about the rich history and strengths of the local context, as well as develop commitments of stewardship and preservation for the land and culture. Tutors are not expected to be cultural experts; instead the program reaches out in culturally respectful ways to the school or community kūpuna (or "elders"), who are able to speak and teach about local and island culture from a culturally embedded position. The invitation to explore 'place' was welcomed by both new teachers to school communities, and veteran teachers who are connected to both the culture and community. However, for the newer teachers, who were not from the community and/or unfamiliar with Hawai'i, the exploration of school communities connects them to their students more quickly and deeply. This is consistent with findings by Lieberman and Hoody (1998) that indicate place-based learning results in better working relationship between teachers and their students and colleagues, and helps them become a "learning-teaching team focused on the same objectives" (p 17). In pursuing a place-based cultural project curriculum, tutor activity interests and talents were also incorporated into the program. This was important in motivating both tutors and students during after school hours, after long school days and being under the constant pressures of *No Child Left Behind* (NCLB). Literacy activities were then woven throughout the activities. Examples of the activities (i.e., tutor interests) included performing arts, health and nutrition, media and technology, and outdoors activities.

The PALS curriculum is constructed around a cultural ecological framework that draws upon the multiple cultural locations in which children live and that influence the educational and social well-being of children. Thus, the theoretical framework of PALS (see Figure 1) places children's traditional, local, and contemporary culture/s within a place-based approach to curriculum; supports multiple literacies; and actively develops assets that contribute to the assets already existing within the children's families and communities in a way that creates a stronger foundation for them. The multiple cultural ecologies approach to culture taken up by PALS is able to more fully account for children's various strengths and needs, than attention to any one of these approaches alone.

In the next sections, we describe the way in which culture is understood and used to situate children within the multiple cultural ecologies that shape and influence their experiences and identities. Additionally, we will explore the way in which this understanding is enacted through the dimensions of a place-based, cultural project approach to teaching and learning within PALS. Examples from actual curriculum within PALS will then be used to more fully flesh out this understanding.

Multiple Cultural Ecologies of Learning

> Place-based pedagogies . . . explicitly root the learning experience in the loca-
> tion of the learner—the home, the backyard, the school grounds, the commu-
> nity the bioregion—the place the learner inhabits. A place based pedagogy ap-
> proaches the individual as part of a cultural, social and biological context—an
> ecology, Jan Woodhouse (2001, p. 04)

As a curricular approach, PALS attempts to embed children in a culturally relevant and individually responsive curriculum. The PALS theoretical framework,
however, does not equate culture with ethnicity or heritage culture exclusively.
In education ethnicity and culture have typically been closely linked, and these
terms have been conflated (Quintana et al., 2006). As a result, rather than focusing on children's multiple cultural locations, efforts to create culturally relevant
curriculum have often focused on attempts to define and learn about ethnic cultures as monolithic sets of stable traits. Within the PALS theoretical framework,
culture is understood as fluid and in process (Hermes, 2000; Mahoney & Galis,
2006) not monolithic or unchangeable. Additionally, there are no 'fixed and
tangible boundaries' between cultures that are impermeable, there are rather
"ongoing relationships that are always affected by the larger systems and structures of which they are a part" (Levinson & Holland, 1996). Culture, then, is not
solely a product of history nor an encapsulated system separate from other social
networks. Culture exists in a dynamic suspension among past, present and future
social networks of influence. Thus, three dimensions of time and culture are
taken into consideration in the PALS approach—history, present and future.

Though these temporal constructs are themselves theoretical and do not represent discrete and separate cultural locations, as constructs they provide a way
of thinking about how to situate children within a more complete and complex
accounting of the multiple cultural contexts, in which they are shaped and influenced. Place (Kemp, 2006; Sobel, 2004; Woodhouse, 2001) is additionally used
as an organizational point for the curriculum as the geographical and concrete
temporal location of place represents the intersection of the multiple temporal
locations of history, present, and future. Place as an organizational starting
point, prevents the curriculum from becoming too focused on any one cultural
context. Accordingly, PALS activities bring together heritage cultures and contemporary youth and popular cultures in curriculum that draws from the cultural
backgrounds of the children, while providing them with many opportunities to
learn through and express new learning, using heritage cultural forms of expression, as well as technological, popular, and youth cultural symbols and tools.

Figure 1: Cultural Ecologies of Learning

Cultural Ecologies of Learning		
History Heritage Culture	Present Community Culture Socioeconomic Cultural Context Youth Culture	Future Hawai'i Community Citizenship

⇓

Culture-based Project Curriculum					
Nurtures a Caring Commu- nity	Develops Internal/ External Assets	Draws on Community Resources	Builds on Cultures of Place Com- munity, Youth, etc.)	Emphasizes Doing/ Hands-on	Supports Multiple Literacies

⇓

Outcomes				
Positive Community Identity	Environmental Stewardship	Increased Moti- vation/ Engage- ment	Positive Identity as Learners	Improved Aca- demic Achievement

In the following sections we more fully describe how culture is used as a curricular and theoretical construct to help plan educational experiences for the children in PALS. Again, we want to emphasize that attention to multiple temporal locations described below, does not mean that we see these as separate, distinct cultural locations. Indeed, traditional heritage cultures that are historically rooted, are continually passed through succeeding generations and both co-exist with, and are changed by the other, even while these same cultural locations are projected into a rapidly changing and ever-shifting context for the future. The reason that we find it helpful to consider these temporal cultural locations separately and together is that it helps avoid a fixation on any one, and instead, allows for a more complete and complex accounting of children's cultural lives.

Historical Dimension: Heritage Culture

Even as we begin to talk about the way in which PALS situates children within heritage culture, we are aware of the fact that, Hawaiian culture, like any culture, is not monolithic, but is enacted and understood differently across Hawaiian cultural communities (Meyer, 1998). However, there are also shared cultural stories and shared cultural patterns, as well as common epistemological perspectives and values that unite many contemporary Hawaiians (Meyer, 1998). Since

PALS uses place and community as a starting point for heritage cultural inquiry and learning, the Wai'anae community and to some extent, the larger community of O'ahu frame the context for this learning.

Hawaiian culture is rooted in an epistemological relationship with the land and the natural world. In fact, indigenous Hawaiian scholars point out that within a Hawaiian epistemology, Hawaiians are not in relationship with the land, but are actually relatives of the land and that "nature, in its totality, and all the parts separately apprehended [are] sensed as personal. The-Sky-that-is-Bright-and-Wide (Wakea), the level Earth (Papa) were primordial Father and Mother" (Handy & Pukui, 1972, p. 24). According to Malo (1898/1951) Haloa, the first man, was born of Wakea (Sky) and Papa (earth):

> The first-born son of Wakea was a premature birth [keiki alualu] and was given the name of Haloanaka. The little thing died, however, and its body was buried in the ground at the end of the house. After a while, from the child's body, shot up a taro plant, the leaf of which was named lau-kapalili, quivering leaf; but the stem was given the name of Haloa. After that, another child was born to them whom they called Haloa, from the stalk of the taro. He is the progenitor of all peoples of the earth (Malo, 1898/1951)

Hawaiian culture evolved in close relationship with the *'äina* or land and with island geography (Kame'eleihiwa, 1992) and the strong connection to the *'äina* that many Native Hawaiians have is a result of centuries of living, cultivating, learning, stewarding, and dying on the same land (Kana'iaupuni, Malone, and Ishibashi, 2005). Thus, indigenous Hawaiian scholars emphasize the particular significance of place and identity (Kame'eleihiwa, 1992; Kana'iaupuni & Malone, 2006) arguing that, because indigenous knowledge systems view people and place as overlapping and interacting, people carry the energy of places as part of their being (Memmott and Long, 2002)

The *'äina* (land) is closely linked with 'ohana (family) in Hawaiian culture and history. According to Kana'iaupuni (2005):

> Hawaiian culture promotes interdependence and strong families, the backbone of our people. The strengths of families include the connection and relationships borne through genealogy; treasured spiritual and practical links to the 'äina (land) as resource and kin; and commitment to 'ohana and to the ideals of reciprocity and inclusion that 'ohana implies (p.36).

Relationship to 'äina is not just ancient and mythic, it is a contemporary cultural value as well, succinctly expressed by educator and kumu hula (hula master) Pualani Kanaka'ole Kanahele as "I am this land and this land is me" (2005). As a result of the connections between spirit, 'ohana, (family) and 'äina (land), Meyer (1998) maintains that, learning involves a continual "exchange among the environment, the gods, and people. Indeed, the very image of 'ohana (family) stems from the psychic and spiritual link the staple food (taro or poi) that Hawaiians shared with the progenitor of the race, Haloa" (p. 23).

Given the deep and spiritual connection of 'ohana (family) and 'äina (land) in Hawaiian culture and epistemology, the land and the community becomes a natural starting point for the PALS curriculum and the expertise of küpuna (elders) is a critical link within this learning process (Kana'iaupuni, 2005). For example, learning about and recovering traditional Hawaiian relationships with the land are focal points within PALS. This includes issues of land and water reclamation, preservation, and stewardship as well as traditional and contemporary methods of subsistence or sustainable living. The first part of the title of this chapter, "'Olu 'olu i ka pä a ke Kaiäulu" (refreshed by the touch of the Kaiäulu breeze) reflects this 'äina-centered perspective. Kaiäulu literally means community; it is also the name of a "pleasant, gentle wind" of Wai'anae, O'ahu (Pukui and Elbert 1986). Reflecting the Hawaiian preference for kaona or metaphoric and multiply-layered meaning, it thus references both a specific feature of the 'äina PALS is based on, as well as the life-giving element of community in such an endeavor. While the hot dry Wai'anae lands are indeed refreshed by the touch of the gentle Kaiäulu breeze, the PALS students are refreshed, revived, and supported by the guiding touch of the kaiäulu—their home communities along the Wai'anae coast.

This sentiment also reflects how the PALS curriculum is embedded within the spirit of 'ohana. Children learn, practice, and use Hawaiian reconciliation practices (ho'oponopono), cultural art forms, songs (mele), chants (oli) and dance (hula) as they investigate the way in which traditional Hawaiian cultural practices connected families and communities.

The Present: Contemporary Socioeconomic, Popular, and Youth Culture

Providing educational opportunities that draw from the ethnic or heritage cultural strengths and epistemologies that children bring certainly enhances the chances that children will succeed in school (Foster, 1997; Heath, 1983; Irvine, 1990; 2003; Ladson-Billings, 1994; Noordhoff & Kleinfeld, 1993; Siddle-Walker, 1996) as decades of culturally congruent education for White, middle-class children has shown. However, as discussed earlier, cultural-based curriculum is often equated with ethnic or heritage culture to the exclusion of other significant and influential cultural contexts in children's lives (McCarthy, 1998). The PALS curricular framework embeds children within ethnic and heritage culture, however, it simultaneously accounts for the contemporary cultural contexts of which they are a part and the ways in which these multiple cultural temporal influences intersect and impact the other. This means taking into account the ways in which Hawaiian heritage culture has been and continues to be influenced by contemporary cultures as socioeconomic class-based cultures and local community culture as well as the way in which youth and contemporary, popular cultures influence our children.

Native American scholar and teacher, Mary Hermes (2000) maintains that in many indigenous communities, "culture-based curriculum has become the catch phrase for success [. . .]. Often, 'culture' in education is expected to remedy complex and deep-seated social problems" (p. 9). Hermes states that explaining the failure to adequately support and educate indigenous children and other children of color who live in generational poverty as a problem with cultural incongruity alone, ignores the impact of structural inequality, such as generational poverty, on children's lives and communities.

Cultural incongruity explanations contrast with structural explanations of social inequality offered by critical theorists who point to a history of structural conditions such as institutional racism and classism that operate to marginalize and oppress communities (Noguero, 2003). This history also influences the 'cultural context' of children's communities and families in ways that are rarely addressed in the current literature on multicultural, culture-based or culturally responsive curriculum. Structural racism and classist institutional structures operate to limit opportunities for indigenous communities and other communities of color in ways that affect their economic viability and financial security. Long-term poverty is the most damaging effect of structural racism and classism and yet there is a strange silence around the real effects of poverty on communities and children within current academic literature (Hermes, 2000; Rothstein, 2008). Even though teachers and administrators are anxious to talk about the effects of poverty on children's lives and go so far as to say that the culture that their children bring is not traditional Hawaiian culture, but rather a poverty culture (Personal Correspondence), educational scholars remain focused on ethnic culture and identity to the exclusion of socioeconomic, class-based cultural impact on children's lives (Hermes, 2000) Given the prominence of deficit theories that rationalize inequality as the outcomes of dysfunctional culture, this is not surprising. Theorists and scholars intent on avoiding the 'blame the victim, cultural deficit explanations' for failure have steered clear of naming poverty as negative influence at all in children's lives (Rothstein, 2008). But attending to the real conditions of poverty as outcomes of long term oppression and social inequality does not have to result in an individual deficit theory. In fact, maintaining an understanding that such poverty is a result of ongoing social inequality situates the problem, not in individuals or their traditional cultural contexts, but as a result of social conditions that rob communities of the resources and opportunities needed for health, opportunity, and well-being.

Statistics clearly indicate that many children whose families struggle with poverty do not get the support that they need (Kana'iaupuni, Malone, & Ishibashi 2005). For instance in a short summary of the effects of poverty on children and families, Wood (2003) maintains that:

1. Many of our poorest families are struggling to survive in communities that often exacerbate rather than mitigate the disadvantages of poverty— communities where a lack of public resources, economic investment, and political power sometimes serve to separate and isolate families from main-stream society.
2. Families are isolated further by the violence and crime that are concentrated in neighborhoods of families with low income.
3. Kids who live in neighborhoods that are poor are less likely to participate in sports or after-school activities and/or the quality of those programs differ widely.
4. Economic, social, health, and other factors converge in high poverty settings to produce more severe, persistent poverty and deprivation that has a detrimental impact on the intellectual, emotional, and physical development of children (pp. 708 – 710).

While the PALS curricular approach is based on a strengths-based understanding of children and communities (Kana'iaupuni, 2005) that recognizes and builds from heritage cultural strengths and resources within the community, it also recognizes the effects of long-term economic poverty in the lives of many of the children in PALS. In doing so, the curricular framework includes attention to the environmental factors and risks that children face when their families and communities contend with long term poverty. Toward these ends, the curriculum draws upon a Developmental Asset approach (Benson, 2006) to deliberately provide assets that might otherwise be missing in a child's life. Instead of an individual deficit approach, a developmental asset approach focuses on "transforming the developmental contexts in which young people are embedded" (Benson, 2006, p.10) through the intentional and sustained development and delivery of a framework of assets connected to healthy behaviors in children and adolescents. This framework of assets is divided into external and internal assets and is the result of a synthesis of more than eight hundred studies related to the kinds of assets important for children's healthy development (Benson, 2006; Scales & Leffert, 2004).

In the PALS program it is recognized that the poverty level in the community of Wai'anae is one of the highest in the state of Hawaii and that the percentage of children on free and reduced lunch in the schools that PALS serves are almost double that of the state average (see Table 1), and many of the children in PALS come from economically stressed family where resources are stretched thin and where family health and viability are compromised. In response to the challenges that children and families may face, the PALS curriculum intentionally works to provide certain developmental assets that may be missing in children's lives. For example, several important developmental assets include access to after-school programming as well as weekly participation in activities related to the arts or sports. Similarly, assets such as ongoing homework support and access to caring relationships with two or more adults outside of the family are routinely provided within PALS. Finally, perhaps one of the more important subsets of internal assets that PALS focuses on has to do with the development of competency and achievement identity in children.

In addition to socioeconomic cultural influences, popular and youth cultures also influence and shape children's identity, imagination, and engagement in school. The prominent cultural icons, values, and behaviors in popular media and text, hip hop culture, music, and technological genres are just some of the contemporary cultural symbols and artifacts that make their way into the cultural worlds of children and impact and shape children's identities, aspirations, abilities, and literacy practices. Popular and youth cultural literacy practices are often especially important in the lives of children historically marginalized by schooled, academic literacy practices (McCarthy, 1998). For example, Mahiri's (1998) work with children in diverse urban contexts suggests that popular culture can be a starting point for making academic culture and literacies relevant to children from diverse cultural communities. And for critical educators such as Morrell (2002) popular culture "provides a logical connection between lived experiences and the school culture for urban youth" (73). He argues for the "need to examine nonschool literacy practices to find connections between local literacies and the dominant, academic literacies" (72) maintaining that critical-literacy educators should envision teaching popular culture as [. . .] culturally and socially relevant" (76).

Because popular and youth culture are compelling social and cultural locations for children, the PALS curriculum draws from these cultural locations and introduces children to the symbols and tools important within contemporary culture. Children study and produce visual media such as photography and film, write poems and perform slam poetry and learn to use various technologies as tools to acquire new knowledge and express and learn about contemporary as well as heritage cultures. For instance, children use online resources to investigate historical and contemporary local issues of stream restoration, determine nutritional value in popular fast food items and create survey tools for restaurant reviews. PALS children love the incorporation of technology into the program. Throughout the school year, students produce video and/or photographic documentation of their community and PALS activities. As the kids learn about the history and stories of their community, they document the events with video and still cameras. Part of the video documentation is narration and interviewing. The children learn interviewing techniques and conduct additional research to contribute to the video and/or pictures they produce.

Future

Hawaiian people like many others in colonized societies, find themselves in a struggle to reclaim place, identity, and epistemological legitimacy as well as control over their own destinies (Kana'iaupuni , 2005; Meyer, 2001; Goodyear-Ka'ōpua , 2009).

Despite the consequence of over 100 years of non indigenous influence, the Native Hawaiian people are determined to preserve, develop, and transmit to future generations their ancestral territory, and their cultural identity in accordance with their own spiritual and traditional beliefs, customs, practices, language, and social institutions. (Native Hawaiian Education Act of 1994).

If these goals are to be accomplished, Hawaiian children must be provided with educational and social experiences that prepare them with a sense of cultural identity, integrity and power, and the competencies and talents they need to be political citizens in a quickly changing world. As Senator Danial Inouye (1994) further maintained, "Without a means of assuring that our Native Hawaiian children develop a confidence of spirit and intellect, sovereignty and self-governance may never be realized (Native Hawaiian Education Act of 1994, p. 1).

The cultural ecological framework assumed in the PALS curricular model embraces the future as a temporal influence in children's lives and deliberately works to provide them with opportunities to develop strong cultural/political identities and to see themselves as competent learners both in and out of schools even while it uses heritage and contemporary culture.

Furthermore, Hawaiian children, like children everywhere need to be able to envision a productive and healthy future for themselves where they can pursue aspirations that are too often smothered under the weight of poverty. For many Native Hawaiian children this may be a challenge. For instance, "'opio 'Ōiwi Hawai'i, (Native Hawaiian youth), have among the highest rates of self-reported drug use, youth arrests, teen pregnancy and relationship violence" (Kana'iaupuni & Ishibashi, 2005).

Meyer (2001) reflected on the need to conceive of an education equal to these needs and to achieving these purposes.

> There it is. How do we educate our youth for the challenges of the next millennium? We surround them with our community, we give them meaningful experiences that highlight their ability to be responsible, intelligent, and kind. We watch for their gifts, we shape assessment to reflect mastery that is accomplished in real time, not false. We laugh more, plant everything, and harvest the hope of aloha (p.146).

The PALS curriculum provides meaningful experiences grounded in the children's community experiences and gifts as it supports them toward productive, self-sufficient futures and responsible citizenship. Toward these ends, Hawaiian culture and cultural tools and contemporary culture and cultural tools are combined in complimentary ways. For instance, activities in the PALS curriculum nurture the development of technological competencies and skills, and also provide children with supported opportunities to use these competencies in the service of community and environmental stewardship. Overall, the commitment in the PALS curriculum is to support children in projects, learning, and activities that help them to see themselves as powerful and capable of making their own life and pursuing their own dreams, of being entrepreneurs, of planning and carrying out important social and personal goals, of being involved in the care of their community and the environment, of having the ability to impact their own future as well as the world around them.

PALS Place-based Cultural Projects Curriculum as encountered by the Haumana (student)

In taking up the theoretical commitments above, PALS has adopted what we call a place-based cultural projects curriculum. As described above, with place as the foundation, this approach allows us to consider past, present, and future cultural contexts in a curricular framework that does the following: 1) nurtures a caring community; 2) develops internal and external assets; 3) draws on community resources; 4) builds on the multiple cultures of place; 5) emphasizes doing/hands-on in the learning process; and 6) supports multiple literacies. While the identified curricular elements are taken up separately in their description; in the actual implementation of the curriculum, they consistently overlap and are intertwined.

Nurtures a caring community

A strength of our curriculum is that PALS itself functions as a caring community. During the first year of implementation, the relationships between students and teachers grew close quickly, in part because of the place-based approach, which allowed teachers to engage with their students in renewed ways, such as inviting teachers to become co-learners along with their students. Such a shift in focus necessitates changes in the nature of the relationships between teacher and students, and as a result the relationships between them deepen, and conversations become more personal and caring. For example, a fifth grade student commented that she really liked her teachers in PALS because:

> . . . getting to talk to them and like they help us through . . . like when we talk to them they . . . they don't just like okay you "oughta" let it go, they talk to us about it and help us solve it . . . so, when our teachers talk us through stuff...and when I get to other problems I can think through it and . . . think about what they told me.

The importance of these relationships to students became apparent as the school year progressed, and are the foundation upon which PALS has developed. The nurturing relationships are further encouraged by the low tutor to student ratio; and, tutors bringing their own passions and interests to share with the students. PALS also incorporates Hawaiian cultural protocol to foster the sense of a community. For example, at the beginning and conclusion of each program day, students and teachers oli (chant) together. The oli signifies the coming together of everyone as a group and are student led. Typically, the students, teachers, and any visitors or guests stand together in a circle (or piko, center) holding hands while they chant. This reflects a common Hawaiian practice of such protocol in similar school and other community settings, such as with hula hälau (dance academies) or canoe club huis (groups). The purpose is to physically symbolize the spiritual and psychic connection between all members of the `ohana or group. Throughout the year, regular discussions about what it means to be part of a caring community are encouraged, which reinforces the importance of the discussions. The frequency and tone of such conversations varies, and is determined by students, teachers and program events.

For example, at one of the PALS school, some of the older students had gotten into trouble at the end of the regular school day, and were given office referrals: their behavior spilled over into PALS program time. This incident was preceded by a number of earlier behavior issues. The PALS teachers decided it was time for a community meeting. The original plans for program day were put aside as teachers engaged students in pono, a Hawaiian concept of 'rightness.' Teachers reminded students of the expectations for their behavior and the importance of being respectful and caring for each other. During the course of the discussion, some of the older students began to apologize to other students and teachers for past indiscretions. The community meeting was conducted in a loving and caring spirit and the students engaged in the same manner. As the discussion continued, the meeting turned into ho'oponopono, which is a Hawaiian process for conflict resolution. Another teacher then told the kids that ho'ponopono includes not only asking for forgiveness, but also forgiving and leaving the resolved problem in the past for good. What followed was a beautiful exchange of gentle discussions, apologies and forgiveness. Another of the teachers walked away from the circle with tears in her eyes; it overwhelmed her to witness the students so honestly engaging in and being pono. Teachers are mindful of the pulse of the students, and by taking the time to uncover the basis of problems, modeling expectations, and providing a safe environment, the students are enveloped by caring individuals and learn how to care in return.

Develops Internal/External Assets

The structure of PALS responds to important assets in children's lives such as providing constructive use of time through school or community activities, and constructive use of time through creative activities two or more times per week. Additionally, the low teacher to student ratio provides opportunities for students to be supported by adult relationships and within a caring school climate. PALS teachers recognize that there are many assets that they simply cannot impact; however, they identify and focus on those additional assets that can be impacted. For example, during the planning of projects, empowerment assets such as students feeling valued and appreciated by adults in their community, and opportunities to help others are explicitly tied to the project outcomes.

A popular activity at Makaha Elementary is health and nutrition. Adjacent to Makaha Elementary is a five-acre community farm. The caretaker of the farm is very supportive of the students learning on, and caring for the farm. During the first half of the year, the students in the outdoor group built and planted gardens. At the same time, students in the health and nutrition group researched their favorite recipes, and discussed the nutritional profile of the recipes based on the ingredients, offering possible ingredient substitutions in order to make the final product healthier. Midway through the school year, while the outdoor group was taking swimming lessons, the health and nutrition group harvested the garden. They then gathered in the kitchen and prepared a recipe each day while sitting around a table for talk story. The students were very enthusiastic, and clearly enjoyed the time they spent on this activity, as well as the time they spent together around the table for a meal. Once their time together was over, the students took the leftovers home to share with their families.

At one point, the health and nutrition group discovered that the farm's executive board was meeting the next week, and offered to prepare dinner for the board members. In preparation for the dinner, students surveyed the garden to identify the best available produce and pulled out their indexed recipe books for recipes appropriate for the board. Since the board meeting was taking place in the evening and the students would not be present, they also had to think of a meal that could be served cold. Students took great pride in their work, which included decorating the table with plants from the farm, and creating a restaurant review form so that board members could provide feedback on the quality of the meal, presentation and atmosphere, something inspired by their previous experience studying restaurant reviews. Needless to say, the students were very proud to contribute to the wellness of adults in their community; and to feel valued by them as well.

Community Resources

PALS students also benefit from many collaborations with community resources. The resources fall along a continuum of individuals and organizations within the immediate school community, to those along the Wai'anae coast but outside the school community, to individuals and organizations throughout the State of Hawai'i. Community resources range from local artists, writers, environmental activists, media productions companies, cultural preservation organizations, a horse rescue ranch, kumu hula, and organic farms. In our experience, the various community resources are eager to engage with the teachers and students, but not always certain how to best contribute to the education of the keiki in their community. Thus, PALS provides a setting and framework for such opportune engagements.

In one instance, a community kūpuna took the students from two schools on an excursion to one of the dried-up streams in Wai'anae. He is a member of local group dedicated to the restoration of Makaha stream and area lo'i, which had disappeared as a result of decades of well pumping and the diversion of water by the Board of Water Supply. The students were fascinated with the excursion, and at the end of the hike had the opportunity to swim in a pond that was filled with water running from the mountain. As a result of this activity and new-found knowledge of their community, the students stated they would like to engage in a letter writing campaign to the Board of Supply to have the stream restored. Issues around water have been addressed by a number of the community members, and as a result PALS students speak often about issues of water restoration and conservation, including their role in water conservation. Therefore, by focusing on places through the eyes of community members, students are provided the opportunity to gain valuable insights about their community, with the potential for bringing about change (Kana'iaupuni, 2005). As a Native Hawaiian teacher of 35 years participating in PALS observed, "They're (the students) starting to realize they have the power to make . . . they're the ones that's gonna change their community."

The kūpuna returned to the students to further discuss the issue of water restoration and strategies for approaching bureaucracies with tactics, such as letter writing campaigns. We know that this issue has been taken up by the students deeply enough, that it will continue as a theme in coming years. This project has evolved into a topic of considerable interest to the students, in part, because it is rooted in the history of their 'place,' made relevant to their lives today, and has spurred the student to advocate for their community's future environmental health. It has involved community resources, hands-on learning, literacy, a caring community, culture of place and a focus on developmental assts.

Culture of Place

As described earlier, PALS utilizes the land and the community as a focal point for its curriculum. The Makaha stream restoration project illustrates the learning about and recovering traditional of Hawaiian relationships with the land. The PALS curriculum incorporates contemporary forms of expression and technology that are important to students. A favorite activity of the blossoming PALS photographers is the documentation of their community and program activities. A well-known local slam poet conducts workshops for the students, to provide them with a venue of expressing how they feel about their place, and what is going on in their lives, and what is important to them. At the conclusion of the workshops, we set up a full audio system, and Kealoha (the slam poet) conducts the final workshop as if it is a full fledge performance. Before the last workshop, students from Wai'anae High School slam poetry team came to the school to talk about how they feel about performing, how they handle nervousness and how slam poetry affected their ideas about poetry. At the conclusion of the first series of workshops, the high school students performed before the PALS students. Initially, the majority of the PALS students were hesitant to perform on the stage, hooked up to the audio system. But, by the end of the period, the students were lining up for repeated opportunities – some creating and performing poems impromptu. Their energy was electric.

Hands-on Learning

A focus on place facilitates hands-on, authentic learning opportunities (Sobel, 2004), such as the Makaha stream excursion and helping students become better stewards of their land and water. Hands-on authentic learning experiences for students also more closely reflect the heritage learning style of Native Hawaiian students (Meyer, 1998). Kawakami and Aton (2001) show that best practices among successful teachers of Native Hawaiian students include experience-based, authentic activities. PALS projects consistently incorporate hands-on learning as part of the learning experience. The incorporation of tutor interests easily facilitates this experience. Hands-on activities are a part of every PALS activity. The media and technology group uses cameras and camcorders to document their community and PALS activities, which deepens students' understanding of the role of technology as a tool for learning. The health and nutrition group plants and harvests gardens and uses the produce for cooking. The performing arts group creates murals and props for the performances, learns the traditional practice of kapa making, and uses the community explorations as inspiration for scriptwriting. The outdoor groups build garden containers, plant gardens, and participate in swim lessons.

Supports Multiple Literacies

PALS takes up an expanded notion of literacy. Neuman and Rao (2004) note, "the value of literacy is realized not merely through the ability to read and write, but through an individual's ability to employ those skills in order to navigate, shape, and be an agent for his or her own life, as well as the ability to change one's knowledge, self, and situation" (p. 8).

Literacy, as a collection of cultural and communicative practices shared among members of particular groups, includes technological, oral, performance, visual, mathematical, scientific, and written. Because technology has increased the intensity and complexity of literate environments, the twenty-first century demands that a literate person possess a wide range of abilities and competencies—multiple literacies that are malleable and dynamic, and inextricably linked with particular histories, life possibilities and social trajectories of individuals and groups. As PALS takes up multiple literacies in its curriculum framework, it includes critical literacies whereby children become political actors in the future of Hawai'i; that they are able to understand and critique what has happened in their community, in Hawai'i, and expand their understanding to include a global community.

Following are examples of the manner in which multiple literacies are incorporated into the PALS place-based, cultural projects curriculum. With the study of place as a significant foundational building block, students with health and nutrition research favorite recipes and then discuss nutritional factors for the ingredients. They then alter the recipes for the purpose of creating healthier dishes; and prepare meals for each other using the alternative recipes. Prior to taste testing, the students explain the ingredients to the group and the substitutions made. Often the students have to adjust ingredient quantities in order to accommodate a larger group, requiring that they incorporate mathematical calculations. At the end of the school year, each student has created her/his own recipe book, which includes ingredient indexes.

Prior to beginning swimming lessons, the students watched a Red Cross approved water safety video. As part of the swimming experience, the students and teachers decided to write and tape their own water safety video; one that is more relevant to children in their community. Two days each week, the students swim and on the third day they work on the video development – scriptwriting, camera shots, and performance. Another outdoor group, built a garden to replicate the Hōkūle'a, a traditional double-hulled canoe, using wooden boards as the outline of the canoe. Prior to building, the students and teachers had to determine size and angles of the boards. Once the garden canoe borders were in place, the students discussed and researched the most appropriate produce to plant and harvest, based on the soil and weather conditions. They then created and posted signs indicating each of the garden produce.

The technology group incorporates interviewing kūpuna into their documentation of the PALS excursions. They practice interviewing each other. In the peer interviews, they describe PALS activities, and the significance of what they are learning. One of the technology groups created 'baseball cards' of each other. They took pictures of every PALS student in the school, interviewed each other to gather pertinent data about each, and then created cards for each student. Other peer interviews are conducted for the purpose of creating narrations of the PALS program. Technology is such a popular activity that we are in the process of creating a PALS website for students to use, in order to communicate with the community about what they are learning and doing with PALS. One teacher at each school will serve as website administrator.

Each year, the Honolulu Academy of Art, provides support for a project of the students' choice. One year, the students created a large mural to use as backdrop for the student-created play; another project was the study of kapa prints which were used to create note cards. The students then used their newly created stationary to write congratulation letters to the newly-elected President Obama. They were thrilled to receive thank you notes from the White House!

One of the authors of this chapter, a Professor of English with the University of Hawai'i, worked with students in creating poems describing 'where I'm from.' The exercise included reading two poems by Native Hawaiian writers about place, one from the Wai'anae area, the other written when the poet was in 5th grade, the same age as the PALS students. She went through each stanza of the Wai'anae poem (which does not mention the name Wai'anae at all), to see if the students could guess the place being written about by how the poet described it. She went over basic literary terms, such as different kinds of imagery, nouns, verbs, adjectives and adverbs, to show students how they could construct a poem about place as a "picture in words." She then brought in a Youtube video clip of another Native Hawaiian poet/musician, Höküle'a Haiku, with the words for his poem "Old School Toyota," sung over a video of young men four-wheeling and pig hunting on Ka'ala, the highest point of the Wai'anae mountain range that divides the coast from the rest of the island. She also showed still photos she took around the school campus and had students guess where they were taken, then describe them as vividly as possible. Students visibly reacted with enthusiasm when they recognized parts of Ka'ala or their school campus on the video and in the photos. Students were then invited to create their own "Where I'm from" poems, with illustrations if they wanted.

The most noticeable outcome of this activity was that some students who had not previously expressed much interest in activities such as writing, were more engaged with the theme of place as they experienced it—one boy wrote and illustrated a poem describing he and his uncles pig hunting on Ka'ala, and after sharing it with the class, told the Professor that he could not turn it in because he 'needed to take it home to give to his uncles.' This was a particularly positive moment, as this child was a Special Education student who had not previously engaged in writing or group sharing, and his teachers were ecstatic at this 'breakthrough.' Another was that teachers couldn't seem to help but sit down and write their own poems about place, right next to and alongside their students. This prompted much discussion between students and teachers, who shared memories, experiences, and laughter with each other, and who engaged in mutual support and encouragement for each others' writing. More often than not, the teachers had not had many opportunities to write on such topics of immediate interest—their own places and communities—and many shared a shyness or fear of writing based on their own school time experiences. Thus the activity of writing about their own experiences with their own places and communities created a sense of joy and fulfillment that was shared alongside their students, deepening their own relationships to their communities and each other.

Measure of Impact on Outcomes

The PALS curricular framework has evolved over a three year period. Our goal has and continues to be creating an educational experience for students, that is relevant to who they are today; that is founded upon their cultural history; that supports children as they envision a future that is hopeful and purposeful as stewards of their community. With that, we work toward the following outcomes: positive community identity, environmental stewardship, increased school engagement, increased motivation for reading, positive identity as learners, and improved academic achievement.

In order to measure progress towards these goals, PALS uses a mixed method approach that includes both qualitative and quantitative data. At this point, our data includes:

1. Student, parent and teacher interviews
2. Student artifacts,
3. School engagement and motivation for reading surveys,
4. Student progress surveys completed by both PALS tutors and PALS students' primary in-school classroom teacher, and parent surveys

Scores on the Hawai'i State Assessments (HSA)

While we do not attempt to provide a comprehensive accounting of the data concerning impact on outcomes, the following sections, broken down into qualitative evidence and quantitative evidence, explore preliminary data that demonstrates the way in which PALS is beginning to impact students positively.

Qualitative Evidence

Interviews have been used to gather data regarding students, teachers, and parents perceptions of PALS and the impact participation in PALS has on student motivation, achievement, positive identity development and commitments to community and environmental activism. In the following excerpts, two students describe the way in which they are beginning to connect with the history of their community, as well as develop a commitment to stewardship.

Makanani was in the fifth grade during her first year in PALS. One of the first field trips her group took was related to the importance of water in early Hawai'i. Students, teachers, and parents went to a dried up stream behind their school that was the source of water for all of the lo'i (taro patches) in their community in earlier years. At the end of the school year, Makanani commented:

We're gonna try get our waters back for our springs because Kikoo Springs—
we studied about that in PALS and we realized that it's gone and I talked to my
kumu (teacher). I talked to my class and I gave a little speech to my class and I
was like, "Oh yeah," they were encouraging me, my teachers were encouraging
me. So it was like yeah, I'm gonna do this.

In the following letter to the PALS Principal Investigator, a group of PALS students express a sense of community engagement and responsibility:

We've been thinking about volunteering so we can help out the community.
We want to make our community a better place. We have noticed graffiti in
parks and streets. We would like to ask PALS if they would want to make a
field trip volunteering to clean up the graffiti. Another thing we've noticed is
rubbish on the side of the road and along the ocean. We would like to help
clean up beaches by spending a whole day at Poka'i Bay. [. . .] Next, we
should clean up the parks for the little kids who like to play there. We could
pick up trash, sweep the rubbish, repaint the walls, and recycle bottles left
there. Some equipment might be broken and we could fix these by donating
new swings. [. . .] We are proud to be from Wai'anae and we want to make it
a safe, healthy and clean place to call home! So, please let us go on these field
trips to help our community.

There is also evidence that the children are developing a social connection to the
school and, as a result, a stronger achievement motivation. For instance, Paula,
who is the parent of a sixth grader in PALS, was notified that her son, Bryson,
had been accepted into a prestigious private school in Hawai'i. Bryson had been
in PALS for two years.

So it was a very humbling as a parent to say like, you know what, [PALS]
made me start to think like, okay, maybe it's not all about academics. I need to
feed other areas of his, I don't know his psyche, his being or whatever it's . . . .
whatever you call it . . . . but I think that [PALS] helped him socially and I
think by working on those relationships it just kind of elevated everything else.
[. . .] but really I think that if he hadn't been part of the PALS organization for
two years, honestly I don't think he'd be where he is or where he's going to go
today.

Overall, then, there is a robust set of interview data that indicates that students in
PALS are growing socially, academically and in their connection and responsibility to the community and the environment.

Quantitative Evidence

At the beginning and conclusion of each school year, all fourth, fifth and sixth
graders in the participating schools complete two surveys: a school engagement

and motivation for reading survey. The school engagement survey measures the following constructs: cognitive engagement; behavior engagement; emotional engagement, and voluntary literacy activity. Surveys were compared between both PALS and non-PALS students, and high-attendance and low-attendance PALS students. The preliminary data on the school engagement survey shows that while no statistically significant difference was found in any comparisons of the pre-survey results among the PALS students and non-PALS students, there were a number of significant results on the post-surveys between non-PALS students and high attending PALS students. A significant difference ($p < 0.005$) was found between these groups on cognitive engagement, behavior engagement, and voluntary literacy activity. The only comparison that was not significant in the post survey data was the comparison on 'emotional engagement.'

The motivation for reading survey includes the following constructs: self-efficacy, challenge, importance, curiosity, involvement, recognition, social purposes for reading, and reading for culture. The same pattern that occurred on the school engagement survey occurred on the motivation for reading survey. Students were, again, divided into three categories, non-PALS, low attendance PALS and high attendance PALS. The data show that while no statistical significance was found in any comparisons of the pre-survey results between the groups, statistically very significant differences ($p < 0.005$) were found in the post survey results between non-PALS students and high attendance PALS students on four of the eight constructs between the two groups (self-efficacy, importance, recognition, and social). Significant differences ($p < 0.05$) were also found for three constructs, challenge, curiosity, and culture. The only comparison that is not significant in the post survey data is the comparison on 'involvement.'

It is compelling that while we utilize a much broader and encompassing definition of literacy; statistically very significant differences were found on constructs that measure more traditional concepts of reading. Does this mean that the more encompassing, place-based, hands-on approach has a positive impact on the more traditional understanding of literacy which is taken up by school systems? We are encouraged by this data.

Conclusion

Initial PALS indicators support the research of scholars such as Kemp (2006) and Lieberman and Hoody (1998) who argue that utilizing a place-based pedagogical strategy has a positive effect on academic success. PALS place-based cultural projects curricular framework attempts to embrace the multiple cultural location, in which children exist and are influenced on a daily basis. In utilizing their community as the springboard for learning, children are provided the opportunity to connect, or reconnect, to the land; which in turn reconnects them to their heritage. Through these reconnections with the land, issues vital to the well-being of their community such as land and water reclamation, preservation and stewardship become significant to the children.

The exploration and inquiry into their communities has resulted in the children's interest in documenting the history of their communities, initiating letter writing campaigns regarding water restoration of ancient streams, and a call for community cleanup projects. They have reconnected to their land; they are becoming individuals who see themselves as possessing the power to influence their future and the future of their community; and in the process they carry on the energy of their ancestors.

Engaging students in learning that has relevance to their lives—in the exploration of their place and side-by-side with caring teachers and the guidance of respected community küpuna—supports them in reexamining who they are, where they come from. This curricular work is critical if they are to envision a future in which they are the creators of their own destiny and stewards of this place called Hawai'i. The place-based, cultural projects approach that PALS takes attempts to provide children with a vital connection, between where they live and who they are (Scott, 2002). History, present, and future come together in this "place" in which children live, play, and grow. It is a place surrounded by elders, by küpuna, and by the 'äina to which they are related. Opportunities to explore who they are within this specific cultural place is vital to the children's identity as Native Hawaiian and their ability to determine what it means in the future to be Native Hawaiian (Kana'iaupuni and Malone, 2006). As surely as the Kaiäulu breeze continues to revive and refresh the rugged Wai'anae coast, PALS participants and their 'ohana will be nourished and strengthened by and because of their community and 'äina.

References

Benson, P. (2006). *All kids are our kids*. San Francisco: Jossey Bass.

Chevalier, A., and G. Lanot. 2002. The relative effect of family characteristics and financial situation on educational achievement. *Education Economics* 10 (2):165–81.

Cole, M. & Engestrom, Y. (1993). A cultural-historical approach to distributed cognition. In G. Salomon (Ed.), Distributed cognition: Psychological and educational *considerations* (1-46). New York: Cambridge University Press.

Conger, R. D., K. J. Conger, G. H. Elder Jr., F. O. Lorenz, R. L. Simons, and L. B. Whitbeck. 1992. A family process model of economic hardship and adjustment of early adolescent boys. *Child Development* 63 (3): 526–41.

Engestrom, Y. (1993). Developmental studies of work as a test bench of activity theory: The case of primary care medical practice. In S. Chaiklin & J. Lave (eds.), Understanding practice: Perspective on activity and context (64-103). Cambridge, UK: Cambridge University Press.

Foster, M. (1997). *Black teachers in teaching*. New York: Free Press.

Foster, M. (1993). Educating for competence in community and culture: Exploring the views of exemplary African-American teachers. *Urban Education, 27*(4), 370-394.

Gay, G. (2000). *Culturally responsive teaching.* New York: Teachers College Press.

Goodyear-Ka'ōpua, N. (2009). Rebuilding the 'auwai: Connecting ecology, economy and education in Hawaiian schools. AlterNative: An International Journal of Indigenous *Scholarship* 5(2), 46-77.

Gutierrez, K. (2002). Studying cultural practices in urban learning communities. *Human Development, 45*(4), 312-321.

Handy, E.S.C. & Handy, E.G. (1972) *The Polynesian family system in Ka'u, Hawai'i.* Honolulu: Bishop Museum Press.

Hawai'i Department of Education. (2008). *School status and improvement reports: School years 2007-2008. http://arch.k12.hi.us/school/ssir/default.html.*

Hale, J.E. (2001). *Learning While Black.* Baltimore, MD: The John Hopkins University Press.

Heath, S.B. (1983). Ways with words: Language, life and work in communities and classrooms. London: Cambridge University Press.

Hermes, M. (2000). The scientific method, Nintendo, and Eagle feathers: Rethinking the meaning of "culture-based" curriculum at an Ojibwe tribal school. *Qualitative Studies in Education, 13*(4), 387-400.

Ho'omanawanui, Ku'ualoha (2009). 'Ike'Aina: Native Hawaiian culturally-based indigenous literacy. *Hūlili: Multidisciplinary Research on Hawaiian Well-Being.*

Irvine, J. J. (1990). *Black students and school failure.* Connecticut: Greenwood Press

Irvine, J. J. (2003). *Educating teachers for diversity: Seeing with a cultural eye.* New York: Teachers College Press.

Kana'iaupuni, S. M. (2004). Identity and diversity in contemporary Hawaiian families: Ho'i hou i ka iwi kuamo'o. *Hūlili: Multidisciplinary Research on Hawaiian Well-Being,* 1(1), 53-71.

Kana'iaupuni, S. M., & Ishibashi, K. (2005). "Hawai'i charter schools: Initial trends and select outcomes for Native Hawaiian students" (Policy Analysis & System Evaluation Rep. No. 04-5:22). Honolulu: Kamehameha Schools.

Kana'iaupuni, S. M. & Malone, (2006). This land is my land: The role of place in native Hawaiian identity. *Hūlili: Multidisciplinary Research on Hawaiian Well-Being,* 3(1), 282-307.

Kana'iaupuni, S. M. (2005). Ka'akalai ku kanaka: A call for strengths-based approaches from a native Hawaiian perspective. *Educational Researcher, 34(5),* 32-38.

Kana'iaupuni, S.K., N. Malone, and K. Ishibashi. (2005). *Ka huaka'i: 2005 Native Hawaiian educational assessment.* Honolulu, HI: Kamehameha Schools, Pauahi Publications.

Kanahele, Pualani Kanaka'ole. (2005). I am This Land and This Land is Me. *Hūlili:* Multidisciplinary Research on Hawaiian Well-Being, 2(1), 21-30.

Kawakami, A. J. (1999). Sense of place, culture and community: Bridging the gap between home and school for Hawaiian students. *Education and Urban Society,* 32(1), 18-40.

Kawakami, A. J. (2004). Issues central to the inclusion of Hawaiian culture in K-12 education. *Hūlili: Multidisciplinary Research on Hawaiian Well-Being,* 1(1), 111-130.

Kawakami, A. J. & Aton, K.K. (2001). Ke a'o Hawai'i/critical elements of Hawaiian

Kellner, D. (2004). Technological Transformation, Multiple Literacies, and the Revisioning *of Education 1*(1), 9-37. Retrieved from: *http://dx.doi.org/10.2304/elea.2004.1.1.8*

Kame'eleihiwa, L. (1992). Kula Kaiapuni: Hawaiian immersion schools. Repr., *The Kamehameha Journal of Education: Hana Hou*, 151-59. Honolulu, HI: Pauahi Publications,2003.
    http://www.ksbe.edu/pase/pdf/journal/Hana%20Hou/2003HanaHou15.pdf.
Kemp, A. T. (2006). Engaging the environment. *Curriculum & Teaching Dialogue, 8(1/2),* 125-142.
Ladson-Billings, G. (1994). *The dreamkeepers.* San Francisco: Jossey-Bass.
Lee, C. D. (2001). Is October Brown Chinese? A cultural modeling activity system for underachieving students. *American Educational Research Journal, 38*(1), 97-142.
Levinson, B. A. & Holland, D. C. (1996). The cultural production of the educated person: An introduction. In B. A. Levinson, D. E. Foley & D. C. Holland (eds.), *The cultural production of the educated person: Critical ethnographies of schooling and local practice.* Albany, NY: SUNY Press, p 1-54.
Lieberman, G. A, & Hoody L. L. (1998).Closing the achievement gap: Using the environment as an integrating context for learning. San Diego, CA: State Education and Environment Roundtable.
Lipka, J. (1991). Toward a culturally based pedagogy : A case study of one Yup'ik Eskimo teacher. *Anthropology and Education Quarterly, 22,* 203–223.
Mahiri, J. (1998). Shooting for excellence: African American and youth culture in new *Century schools.* New York: Teachers College Press.
Mahoney, C. & Galis, T. (2006). Redefining sudden contact. *Culture & Psychology, 12*(4), 435-442.
Malo, D. (1898/1951). *Hawaiian antiquities.* Trans. Nathaniel B. Emerson. Honolulu: Bishop Museum Press.
Memmott, P. & Long, S. (2002). Place theory and place maintenance in indigenous Australia. Urban Policy and Research 20, 39–56.
McCarthy, C. (1998). The uses of culture: Education and the limits of ethnic affiliation. New York: Routledge
McNeely, C. (2005). Connection to school. In, K.A. Moore & L.H. Lipmann, (Eds.), *What do children need to flourish?* (pp. 289-304). NY: Springer.
Meyer, M. A. (1998). Native Hawaiian epistemology: Sites of empowerment and resistance. *Equity & Excellence in Education, 31*(1), 22-28.
Morrell, E. (2002). Toward a critical pedagogy of popular culture: Literacy development among urban youth. Journal of Adolescent and Adult Literacy, 46(1) 72-77.
Neuman, M., & Rao, S. (2004). Adolescent Literacy:Beyond English class, beyond decoding text. *Voices in Urban Education, 3*(Winter/Spring), 6-13.
Nieto, S. (1999). The light in their eyes: Creating multicultural learning communities. New York: Teachers College Press.
Noguero, P. A. (2003). The trouble with Black boys: The role and influence of environmental and cultural factors on the academic performance of African American males. *Urban Education, 38*(4), 431-459.
Noordhoff, K., & Kleinfeld, J. (1993). Preparing teachers for multicultural classrooms. *Teaching and Teacher Education,* 9(1), 27-39.
Purkey, W., & Novak, J. (1996). Inviting school success: A self-concept approach to *teaching and learning* (3rd Ed.). Belmont, CA: Wadsworth.

Quintana, S. M., Chun, E., Gonsalves, S., Kaeo, W. D. K., & Lung, L. (2004). Hawaiian Children's Developmental Understanding of Race and Culture. *Hülili: Multidisciplinary* Research on Hawaiian Well-Being, 1(1), 173-195.
Rothstein, R. (2008). Whose problem is poverty? *Educational Leadership, 65(7),* p 8-13.
Scales, P. C. & Leffert, N. (2004). *Developmental assets: A synthesis of the scientific research on adolescent development* (2nd Edition). Minneapolis, MN: Search Institute Press.
Scott, I. (2002). Rebuilding the sense of place. *Taproot,* 13(3), 3-5.
Search Institute (2003). Boosting student achievement: New research on the power of developmental assets. *Insights & Evidence, 1*(1), 1-10
Siddle-Walker, V. (1996). Their highest potential: An African American school community in the segregated south. Chapel Hill: University of North Carolina Press.
Smith, G. A. (2002). Place-based education. *Phi Delta Kappan,* 83(8), 3-5.
Smith, G. P. (1998). Common sense about uncommon knowledge: The knowledge base *For diversity.* NY: AACTE Publications.
Sobel, D. (2004). Place-based education: Connecting classrooms and communities. The Orion Society.
Theobald, P. and Nachtigal, P. (1995). Culture, community and the promise of rural education. *Phi Delta Kappan, 77(2),* 132-136.
Villegas, A. M. & Lucas, T. (2002). Educating culturally responsive teachers: A coherent *approach.* Albany, NY: SUNY Press.
Woodhouse, J. (2001). Over the river and through the 'hood': Re-viewing 'place' as a focus of pedagogy. *Thresholds in Education, 27(3&4),* 1-5.
Yamauchi, L. A. (2003). Making school relevant for at-risk students: The Wai'anae High School Hawaiian Studies Program. *Journal of Education for Students Placed At Risk, 8*(4), 379–390.
Yamauchi, L. A., Wyatt, T. R., & Taum, A.H. (2005). Making meaning: Connecting school to Hawaiian students' lives. Hulili: Multidisciplinary Research on Hawaiian Well-Being, 2(1), 171–188.

Preparing American Indian Youth for the Transition from High School to College

By Jean E. Ness, Ed.D, and Dennis W. Olson, M.S.

Introduction

A transition is a passage from one place or time to another. American Indian students make many transitions in their educational settings: from home to Head Start, from Head Start to preschool and kindergarten, from kindergarten to first grade, from elementary school to middle school, from middle school to high schools, and from high school to postsecondary education. Although all of these transitions can be difficult for students and families, no transition quite compares to that of leaving the formal K-12 school setting and launching into adulthood. This period of transition requires particular attention because, unless prepared for, it can be an uncharted course full of challenges and changes (Ness & Huisken, 2002).

Many research studies support the need for transition strategies for American Indian students. The Editorial Projects in Education (EPE) Research Center (2007) reported that an estimated 30% of the class of 2007 would fail to graduate on time. American Indian students have some of the lowest high school graduation rates—54%, compared with a 72% rate for their White peers and a 79% rate for their Asian/Pacific Islander peers. Of 16-24 year olds, only Hispanic students had a higher status dropout rate (21%) than American Indian/Alaskan Natives (15%), based on 16-24 year-olds who were out of school and had not earned a diploma or General Educational Development (GED) credential (DeVoe, Darling-Churchill, & Snyder, 2008). In addition, American Indian and Alaskan Natives' SAT and ACT scores are lower than national norms (Swisher & Tippeconnic, 1999). Also, 66% of American Indian eighth graders had a serious number of absences as compared with any other race/ethnicity in 2007.

These statistics are of significant concern, considering that 80% of the fastest-growing jobs in the U.S. will require some postsecondary education (Carnevale & Desrochers, 2003). A smaller pool of minority high school graduates results in fewer students from some minority groups who go on to higher education, than White students. Additionally, schools serving the most minority students are five times more likely to have weak "promoting power." In other words, they promote 50% or fewer freshmen to senior status within four years (Balfanz & Legters, 2004).

A college-going culture within a high school increases the likelihood of both college degree attainment and students graduating from high school college-ready (Schramm & Sagawa, 2008). We are not building a college-going culture today for American Indian youth in high schools. College readiness, as well as college graduation rates are below average for American Indian college students. Not surprisingly, the college readiness rate for White students was 37%; for Asian students, 38%; and for American Indian students, 14 percent (National Center for Education Statistics,[NCES], 2003). In addition, the graduation rate of American Indian students from four-year colleges and universities was 38% in 2006, compared with 56% for all students (Greene & Forster, 2003). For both educational and societal reasons, these statistics are alarming, and there is an immediate need to address American Indian students' poor preparation for transition, which includes their low overall academic achievement. Despite a quarter century of tribal, state, and local efforts to implement special programs directed at needs of these students, overall retention in high school and achievement test performance have not improved (Peacock, 2001).

There are a multitude of reasons for these facts. First, American Indian student achievement has its roots in history. Historically, while there may have been collaboration in some communities, federal policies did not support cooperation on a national level. Federal policies for American Indian cultural assimilation were supported and implemented with federal and faith-based resources, targeting the children of American Indian nations, in particular (Ness & Huisken, 2002).

One particular historical occurrence that has had long lasting and far-reaching impact on the education of American Indian people was the creation of Indian boarding schools. The American Indian boarding school was designed to suppress the culture, language, and spirituality of American Indian Nations, throughout the U.S. During the late nineteenth and early twentieth century boarding school attendance was mandated. Thus, from the age of 5 through 18, American Indian children were removed from their families, for months or years at a time, and placed in boarding school, where harsh indoctrination occurred (Fixico, 2003; Swisher & Tippeconnic, 1999; Gilliland, 1995).

Boarding schools served as a means to assimilate American Indian children and train American Indian youth as laborers. For the most part, the level of education and training afforded American Indian students at boarding schools, prepared them for menial vocations. The remnants of the boarding school experience are still felt in the American Indian high school students throughout their school experience, but most especially, when they begin to prepare for their transition to life after high school. Most American Indian students today do not have generations of professionals—such as doctors, lawyers, or bankers—to emulate. Today, we are most likely to encounter a first or second generation American Indian professional, not because of cultural inferiority or academic indifference, but because of the historical lack of challenging educational opportunities (Ness & Huisken, 2002). This history adds to the challenges in the transition process that American Indian youth face (e.g., poverty, low self-esteem, lack of self-confidence, attendance, drug and alcohol use).

Focusing on the transition years (grades 9-12) is critical in keeping American Indian students academically engaged and motivated to complete high school. A review of literature on transition programs finds that students are less likely to drop out of high school if they participate in programs that promote successful transition (Mizelle, 1999). Any effort to increase college attendance for students of color should examine whether students participate in necessary activities that prepare them for college. For example, a decision that can lead to college attendance is whether a student takes the ACT/SAT exam. The process of exam preparation itself has the potential for creating higher aspirations to attend college among students of color. Postsecondary exploration must be an intentional act, one that includes the American Indian student, family, community, and school all working together.

In addition, during this critical time in high school, students need the support to acquire the skills to take rigorous and challenging high school coursework. According to the U.S. Department of Education study, "Answers in the Tool Box: Academic Intensity, Attendance Patterns, and Bachelor's Degree Attainment" (Adelman, 1999), the best predictor of persistence to *college* graduation is completing a rigorous *high school* curriculum, including math and science coursework. American Indian students tend to demonstrate lower achievement in math and science, than do members of other ethnic groups (Strang & von Glatz, 2001). For example, only 3% to 4% of American Indian high school seniors currently reach the 'proficient' level in math (defined as demonstrating an understanding of algebraic, statistical, and geometric and spatial reasoning).

In spite of the dismal formal education history of American Indians, increasing numbers of youth today are developing goals, educational aspirations, persistence, and skills to attend college. Clearly, communities want to support their youth. Therefore, it is extremely important that American Indian communities, including tribal leaders and community-based programs, play a proactive role in assisting families in that support. Family members need to be positive adult role models and participate in, and become actively involved in learning about the transition process. American Indian youth must participate in transition activities and have the opportunity to interact with successful American Indian adult role models and mentors in business and education, so that they can envision possibilities for their futures.

Background in the Development of Essential Transition Skills

Since 1995, the University of Minnesota's Institute on Community Integration (ICI) has maintained a collaborative relationship with American Indian communities and reservations, and the surrounding school districts in Minnesota to create culturally-based transition activities. These activities were developed in partnership with community elders, teachers, parents, reservation employees, tribal college faculty, and others to provide experiences for high school American Indian youth to prepare for life after high school. These working partnerships were created as a result of several federally-funded projects over the course of 15 years. These projects were 3 to 4 years in length and were funded by the U.S. Department of Education, Office of Elementary and Special Education, and the Office of Indian Education.

In most cases, funding was awarded to a local school district or tribe, and ICI was awarded a subcontract to work with the local site(s) on specific transition skill development. The transition-related activities were delivered to American Indian high school students in grades 9-12, in a variety of ways. In some instances, ICI staff went into high school classrooms and Indian Education resources settings and worked collaboratively with the on-site teacher, to deliver transition activity lessons with Indian youth. In other cases, on-site staff received training from ICI staff on transition-related activities which they, in turn, taught to students in their home sites with continued technical assistance from ICI staff.

On several occasions, weekend transition retreats were held in collaboration with other Organizations, such as the National Service Learning Council (NYLC; http://www.nylc.org) or Voyageur Outward Bound (VOB; http://www.vobs.org). On these occasions, ICI staff would collaborate with project sites and NYLC or VOB, to create weekend-long programming that incorporated cultural content, transition-related components, such as service learning and leadership related activities, and outdoor adventure training to build self-esteem. In these retreats, a small group of students (10-20) lived together for 48-72 hours, working intensely with staff from ICI, NYLC, and/or VOB to jump-start their attention and focus on exploring their interests for life after high school.

In other cases, ICI staff worked with on-site staff to develop summer transition programs for American Indian high school students. The summer programs were offered, whenever possible, at tribal colleges or other local colleges, so that students would have the experience of living on a college campus as part of the program. Still, other summer programs were attached to regular summer school programming in a school district, or even as part of summer youth work programs on reservations. The emphasis in organizing a summer program was to imbed the transition concepts and activities, as transparently as possible, within activities the district or reservation already had in place. This strategy, along with providing training in transition-related skills to local staff, was designed to promote sustainability of programming after federal funding ended.

Summer programs were generally one to two weeks in length. When at all possible, programs were designed as residential programs where students would live on a college campus for the duration of the program. The advantage of the residential model was twofold: to immerse students in the college experience, including dorm life, where students often lived with strangers for the first time; and the opportunity for staff to run programming from early morning to late at night, taking full advantage of the extended day with youth. An additional benefit of residential programming is that daily attendance becomes a non-issue.

Convening a transition conference was another format to engage American Indian youth in transition skill development. Project students from the 11 American Indian reservations and communities in Minnesota, converged on the University of Minnesota's Conference Center for this one-day conference. In this model, ICI staff organized 50-minute concurrent sessions throughout the day on topics such as: 'Interviewing for Your Dream Job;' 'What is Your Learning Style?;' 'What are Your Career Interests?;' 'Creating a Service Learning Project for Your Community or School;' and 'Problem-solving Exercises.' The value of this model was: (1) the ability to touch on a variety of 'teaser' topics in a short period of time, that on-site staff could then follow with additional activities; (2) parents, elders, and teachers who chaperoned simultaneously, attended sessions with students to gain exposure to transition skills; and (3) students from geographically diverse settings who had spent time in summer programs or weekend retreats together, had the opportunity to reconnect with their friends, encouraging attendance, participation, and continued interest in transition.

Over the course of 15 years, more than 2,500 students have participated in one or more of these transition-related activities. The table below illustrated the comparison in college and career readiness skills between students who had complete transition skill development activities, and those who had not as measured on a project based survey. The skill areas measured in the pre and post survey, were based on the curriculum, 'Expanding the Circle: Respecting the Past; Preparing for the Future,' which was the main resource used in transition skill development. The table indicates that those entering the new Outreach to Empower Project had lower scores, than the comparison students from previous projects in all areas.

Table 1: Comparison: Students Completing Transition Skill Development Training Transition Skill Development Areas							
	Commu-nication	Self-man-age-ment	Leader-ship & Advocacy	Com-munity	Col-lege Prep	Ca-reer Prep	Goals in Life
Out-reach to Em-power	3.64	3.06	2.54	2.66	2.30	2.47	3.30
Com-parison Group	3.82	3.45	3.92	4.08	3.65	3.58	4.09

Note: The highest possible scores for all categories was a five. The above table displays the averages for all students in each group. The comparison group had an N=29 and the Outreach had an N=30.

Essential Skills for Successful Transition

Based on extensive experience in transition skill expansion and the development of training formats described in this chapter, the authors have synthesized four essential skills and their sub-skills that have proven crucial in successful transition from high school to college. The remainder of this chapter will address these skills and sub-skills.

Self-Awareness

"All I can say is just remember where you came from," she said. "Even if you're far away from home, you still know you're Native" Tasha (2008).

The concept of self-awareness encompasses three essential areas commonly identified as protective factors in the resiliency literature: social supports, self-knowledge, and an ability to respond to change. Resiliency is defined as the presence of a caring adult in a young person's life to promote motivation, and foster the development of life skills needed to overcome obstacles (Masten & Coatsworth, 1998). The concept of resiliency used here, envisions resiliency not as an individual trait or characteristic, but as a dynamic process in the lives of people facing adversity or significant challenges (Luthar, Cicchetti, & Becker, 2000). It is essential to keep these core concepts of resilience in mind, when working with American Indian high school students in the transition process.

In order for students to be self-aware, possess self-knowledge, and be able to respond to change, they must first understand who the individuals are in their lives that support them and thus provide a sense of security and resilience. These individuals, known as social supports, provide a context for youth to move from what they know (e.g., home, supportive people, school, and neighborhood) to an unknown environment in college (e.g., dormitory life, cafeteria food, large classrooms, large numbers of students in classrooms, complicated textbooks). Assisting students in a detailed exploration of others' expectations (e.g., family, teachers, self) helps them begin framing and understanding the role these expectations have had and how these influences affect the way they define themselves.

Many young American Indians do not readily realize the identity of those who support them emotionally, physically, spiritually, or financially, because they may live with adults who are not nurturing. In these situations, it is helpful to ask students to remember times in their lives when a positive and significant event happened, and recall the adults who facilitated that experience—that is, the adults who are a part of their support system. Once students realize that adults who support them may not necessarily be family members, they are able to consider all adults in their lives as past or potential supporters (e.g., elders, teachers, social workers, and school staff). Youth will also realize that each adult in their lives has different strengths and as a result, can be helpful in different situations. For example, an elder may be the one to go to for spiritual advice, whereas a specific teacher may be the one to go to resolve an academic concern. This understanding allows youth to realize that they have a variety of reliable adults who support them and will continue to do so, as they make their transition from the known to the unknown. This awareness helps students to feel less alone as they move forward in their lives.

Many American Indian students today have become assimilated into a non-Indian community and know little about their heritage, spirituality, community, tribe, or reservation. However, understanding one's ancestry is an important aspect of self-awareness and can often open many doors of understanding for youth in the transition process. Interviewing family members and elders helps uncover this information. Some students may be averse to exploring their family tree, or may have no one to whom they can turn to glean this information. In such cases, it can be helpful for students to complete a family tree, comprised of those individuals who have raised the student. This may include grandparents, foster parents, siblings, aunts, or uncles. Those individuals named by the youth make up their family and should be acknowledged as such when describing their social supports.

Another important aspect of self-awareness, which is often a natural outgrowth of learning about social supports, is acknowledging personal accomplishments. Many American Indian high school students have low self-esteem, based on poor grades or attendance in school. However, they may be quite accomplished in activities in the community or other settings—for example, being a dancer or playing the drum at powwows, cooking for their family with a limited budget, or doing childcare or eldercare. Students need the opportunity to acknowledge all aspects of their lives and honor their achievements. Whether students create a 'picture book' about their lives, or are able to discuss how they live successfully in two worlds—the Native community and the surrounding community—all students need to acknowledge their skills and abilities. Native youth need to relate these strengths and special talents to the gifts that they bring to others and, as such, come to see themselves as valued members of society. Only with help in working through this process, can American Indian youth understand their own self-worth and thereby, build their self-esteem.

Once students have an understanding of their social supports and personal accomplishments, they will begin to see themselves as their own change agents. Students with strong self-esteem are better able to respond to change. They have an increased ability to recognize risk factors and stressors, and understand how they affect their ability to make decisions. Common risk factors for high school students in transition include drugs, alcohol, unprotected sex, smoking, and gang involvement. How students choose to address their personal risk factors, is part of their self-awareness process. The ways in which students deal with the inevitable risks in their lives are, in part, based upon their social network, ability to respond to change, and personal expectations for their future.

There are several ways American Indian students in transition can become their own change agents and learn to manage personal risks. Indian humor as revealed in stories about tricksters, jokes, or teasing has long been a method of managing difficulties in life such as poverty, loss, or disappointment. The ability to lighten a difficult situation with humor is an effective strategy for dealing with stresses brought on by many life situations.

Learning to recognize the origin of anger and effective and ineffective methods of responding to it is an essential skill in being able to respond to change. Whether students respond to their anger by withdrawing, internalizing the anger, making outbursts, or trying to the control the situation, recognizing the behavior and learning to modify the behavioral response is a necessary transition skill.

Part of responding to change effectively includes the ability to make decisions. Teaching a strategic process to formulate a decision provides youth with the ability to manage change. Specific decision-making steps can be taught: (a) defining the problem; (b) re-evaluating the situation and the options available to solve the problem; (c) gathering information needed to make a decision; (d) brainstorming solutions; (e) trying out alternatives; and (f) determining the which decision works to solve the problem. Essentially, decision-making and considering the consequences of the decision are the ultimate outcome in developing self-awareness. Youth in transition who can formulate good decisions, are those who know their social supports, are able to acknowledge their strengths and weaknesses, and can respond to change in a responsible manner.

Personal Responsibility

> My inner strength is my family . . . and my beliefs. I believe that we should leave the past behind us—grow from it, learn from it—but go on with your life and do the best you can. Why not try to make your life better for yourself and others? I've always felt that way. I guess that's why I try to do well in everything I do." (Davina Ruth in Garrod & Larimore, 1997, p. 63)

Increasing personal responsibility during the transition process encompasses five key skills: (1) goal setting; (2) self-advocacy; (3) problem solving; (4) organizational skills; and (5) communication skills. Each of these essential areas will be discussed in detail below.

An essential skill in learning to assume personal responsibility is the ability to set goals. Goal-setting theory suggests that, under certain conditions, setting specific difficult goals leads to higher performance when compared with no goals or vague goals, such as 'do your best' (Strecher, 1995). Because current American Indian high school students are often the first in their family to pursue postsecondary education, they have not grown up in an environment where adults are accustomed to setting the short- or long-range goals needed to attain a college degree. Therefore, students in transition need support to understand that goals are experiences one wants aim for and have. Goals should be positive in nature and moderately challenging, attainable, specific, and measurable so that the student can easily tell when the goal has been achieved. For example, a goal for a high school senior might be to take the ACT exam fall semester, and achieve a score of 22 or higher. This goal contains all the necessary elements to determine if it was attained, and it is moderately challenging, attainable, specific, and measurable. Students should practice goal setting, while still in the familiar environment of high school to become adept at this skill. Basic steps in goal setting are: (a) identify the goal; (b) form a plan of action; (c) develop step-by-step measurable objectives; (d) plan for obstacles that might occur; and (e) make the goal a reality by sharing it with others and asking for assistance when needed. Setting a small reward for completion can motivate the student to complete the goal.

A second essential skill in assuming personal responsibility is the ability to self-advocate. Self-advocacy allows students the self-knowledge to enter a new environment where others are unfamiliar with them, and to ask for help in an appropriate manner. Although sometimes misinterpreted as selfish, self-advocacy is quite the opposite. Individuals who know how to advocate for themselves know how to ask in an assertive and appropriate ways (rather than passively or aggressively), for the assistance they or others need. Self-advocates know their strengths and weaknesses, and know how to take the initiative to organize information to prove to another that their request is reasonable. The self-advocate state the request clearly, asks in a reasonable way, listens, is open minded, and has realistic expectations. Those who learn to self-advocate, can withstand the difficulty of adjusting to unknown surroundings, and establish an environment in which they can flourish. They are also on the path to develop the skills needed to be leaders in their communities: responsibility, listening skills, decision-making skills, creativity, and vision.

A third essential skill in assuming personal responsibility is the ability to problem solve. Like goal setting, problem solving requires the ability to analyze tasks, deconstruct a problem into nine steps, and tackle one step at a time. The problem solving steps are: (1) identify the problem; (2) identify possible causes; (3) list possible solutions; (4) consider the positive and negative outcomes of the possible solutions; (5) decide on a solution; (6) design a plan to try out the solution; (6) carry out the plan for solving the problem; (7) evaluate the results; (8) revise the strategy if necessary; and (9) try again. By integrating these strategies into real-life situations that naturally arise, American Indian role models can support American Indian students' learning of these proactive problem solving skills, which can then become a way of life in preparation for their transition. This allows the students a sense of mastery over difficult situations, and increases students' self-esteem and self-confidence.

A fourth essential skill in assuming personal responsibility is needed in a successful transition process—the ability to organize oneself. Organizational skills include learning how to prioritize tasks in a way that allows their completion in a manageable way. Students who live in chaotic settings, never learn to organize their lives. They are often unable to articulate their current responsibilities (e.g., homework, work schedule), and may not have skills to organize tasks and activities later in life. Organizational skills are essential in the learning process, because disorganization can exacerbate low grades and low achievement, and can cause students to appear academically unprepared even when they may not be. Teachers have noted that while some students knew the subject material, their grades did not reflect their knowledge because of their lack of organization. However, few educators have implemented a program for teaching organizational habits. It is often assumed that organizational skills will be taught at home with other life skills (Gambill, Moss, & Vescogni, 2008). However, if an American Indian child lives in a dysfunctional environment that does not provide the opportunity to learn from adults how to organize daily life they have difficulty finding ways to integrate organizational tools, methods, and skills into the transition process.

Examples of ways to teach organization skills can be as practical as providing students with yearly planners. Teachers can then use the planners to facilitate organization skills, by having students systematically record their assignment deadlines and test dates. In addition, students can be taught how to transfer syllabi due dates into their planner. This approach allows students to learn how to synthesize information from a variety of sources (in this case, course content) in one location, making the planner a readily accessible and useful resource. Students can also fill in other scheduled activities such as work, after school activities, and responsibilities at home. This approach leads naturally to another aspect of organization—time management. Once students have recorded important dates and deadlines in their planner, the next step is to determine how and when to complete the tasks in a timely manner. The planner allows students to visually locate the times in their schedules that are available, so they can begin to learn to prioritize their time, based on due dates copied from the syllabi.

Another example of an organizational skill that can be implemented in the classroom, is teaching students to budget. This includes teaching the difference between fixed expenses and variable expenses, and how to prioritize necessary spending before adjustable spending, in order to manage personal finances.

A fifth skill in the development of personal responsibility needed in transition is communication. Communication skills can be non-verbal (body language), verbal, or written. Once again, the American Indian high school student may be comfortable with the way he/she communicates in familiar surroundings; however, in an unfamiliar setting, the student can be misunderstood or misrepresent themselves to strangers. Because of this, it is important to deliberately teach communication skills to American Indian youth in transition. For example, when asked what emotions such as frustration, boredom, nervousness, or aggression look like when conveyed non-verbally, two students may illustrate them with entirely different body language, based on their own life experiences. When interacting in a familiar setting, body language is understood. However, in a new and unfamiliar setting, non-verbal behaviors can be interpreted in many different ways, depending upon individual experience and perspective.

Equally important is verbal and written communication. In an era when text messaging and tweeting are popular, it is easy for students to get into the habit of writing in abbreviated language. Creating an awareness of the importance of communication skills in different settings is essential to prepare students for life after high school in settings and groups that will be unfamiliar. It is vital that youth are prepared to alter their communication skills in a variety of situations.

Post High School Exploration

> For many American Indians, personal and cultural identity, as well as spirituality are inextricably intertwined with connections to family, community, tribe, and homeland. This intricate web of interrelationships and the sustaining power of the values with which we were raised pushed us toward higher learning while at the same time pulling us back to our home communities. (Garrod & Larimore, 1997, p. 3).

When graduating from high school, students are making a change in both their personal and academic lives. They may decide to move away from home, family, and community, or stay in their community and work. They may go directly into the workforce, become an apprentice in a field of interest, go into the military, or attend an institution of higher learning. Either way, the K-12 school system with all of its daily expectations (e.g., attendance, homework completion, social interaction with peers) is good preparation for the expectations of adult life. The skill development discussed thus far in the chapter helps in preparation for post-school options, but the actual decision can still be overwhelming. The skills students have attained apart from academics (e.g., development of a support system, self-knowledge, an ability to respond to change, goal setting, self-advocacy, problem solving, organizational skills, and communication skills), all play an intricate and vital role in the post high school exploration.

Preparing in high school for post high school experiences can be foreign to many American Indian high school students and their families. Because many American Indian adults in the student's life may have little or no knowledge of the college experience, those students are largely on their own to seek out the supports that will help them decipher the confusing and sometimes difficult path to postsecondary education, if that is the post high school path the student chooses to take. Because of this common lack of experience, it is helpful to make students and family members aware of the value of higher education. One of the many tasks necessary to assist students and their family members in understanding college is to first understand the many differences between high school and college, and then to create an awareness of all the types of postsecondary options.

These differences are vital in the transition process, and are usually very enlightening. The students begin to recognize that the overarching difference between success and failure in the postsecondary experience depends largely on the students' abilities to exercise personal responsibility. Discussing the differences between high school and college, allows for open communication to address the implications of these differences and to motivate students to address changes proactively. Examples of differences between the high school and college environment are addressed in Table Two.

Table 2: The Differences Between High School and College	
HIGH SCHOOL	COLLEGE
Most often you live at home.	Most often you live away from home and with strangers.
High school is paid by tax dollars.	You pay tuition or apply for scholarships and financial aid.
The same classes meet every day at the same time.	Classes meet on alternate days.
Attendance is required each day in each class.	Attendance is recommended but not monitored.
Someone wakes you up in the morning, and provides meals and a place to live.	No one is looking out for you. You are responsible for getting up for classes and finding food and a place to live.
Teachers repeat information over and over.	Teachers provide one lecture on a topic and it is your responsibility to take notes and read background information on the topic.
You are unique. You may influence many by the path you take to college.	You are one in the crowd. Your influence over your own actions is most important.
If you have special learning needs, assistance is provided for you.	If you need additional assistance in your studies, help exists, but you must seek out support on your own.
Everyone in your class is close in age.	Students in your classes may be younger, the same age, or much older than you.

In order to prepare for these and other differences in the learning and living environment and to be prepared for the rigors of college, Indian youth must stay on track with their high school coursework, taking rigorous classes, especially in math and science, so they will be prepared for the diversity, competence, and competition they will find in college courses. Many high schools offer a transition timeline of events, to help students stay on track for graduation. Such a timeline may include activities such as:

Table 3: Transition Timeline Grades 9-12	
Freshman Year (9th Grade)	Take a career/vocational assessment inventory.
	Join extracurricular activities such as cultural or academic related clubs.
Sophomore Year (10th Grade)	Attend college and career fairs.
	Meet with the high school counselor to make sure you're on track with earning the credits you need
Junior Year (11th Grade)	Make college site visits.
	Take college entrance exams (SAT or ACT) and the ASVAB if you are interested in the

	military.
	Apply for financial aid early.
Senior Year (12th Grade)	Apply to colleges (and their housing) early.

Once students have begun the process of thinking about life after high school, they will need the support of adult American Indian role models to take the next step; that of exploration of colleges and careers that are a good 'fit' for what they have learned about themselves, in the key skills areas outlined in this chapter. American Indian high school students must first reflect on who they are as community members, spiritual persons, and family members, and the importance of those life roles to them. Second, these students must council with those in their support circle who have supported them on their educational paths, and who will be there for them as they move forward to determine their best 'fit' for life after high school. Third, Indian youth should conduct research on the variety of postsecondary options available based on their personal interests, aptitudes, and values. School staff must work closely with these Indian students and members of their support network to explore the different types of postsecondary schools, their prerequisites, length of programs, size of schools, and availability of resources in difference schools (e.g., scholarships, American Indian Resource Center).

The variety of postsecondary options can be overwhelming, in light of the lack of exposure to postsecondary education of most Native youth. Many families unfamiliar with high education often perceive that all colleges are the same, except perhaps in cost. However, knowing the options available in postsecondary education can expand the possibilities and interest for many students.

For example, students who do not want to travel far from home and want to stay within their culture, may have the option of attending a tribal college nearby for two or four years. The tribal college provides a familiar environment with smaller classes, and has an open enrollment policy. Open enrollment refers to colleges that accept all students who have earned a high school diploma, and do not require entrance exams such as the ACT or SAT. Tribal colleges can also prepare students for transfer to a larger or distant college. Other options—also open enrollment alternatives—are community colleges and technical colleges. These colleges provide the option of receiving a certificate in a specialized technical skills (e.g., licensed practical nursing), or a two-year degree in a specific technical area (e.g., welding), or completion of an Associate of Arts degree that prepares students for transfer to a four-year institution entering as a junior. Any of these three options (tribal, community, or technical college) tend to be smaller environments with a smaller student body and average class size, and cost less than four-year colleges.

Other postsecondary options include public state universities, and universities or private colleges. Each of these options have more competitive admission requirements, as well as a wider array of programs and academic courses leading to bachelor's, master's and advanced degrees. These options also have more extensive opportunities for scholarships and extracurricular activities.

With so many options for postsecondary education, decision-making skills become important. In addition, support from experienced counselors, Indian education staff, mentors, and family members are crucial. Indian youth need to be able to rely on those trusted adults to act as guides, who will give advice based on their knowledge and understanding of the youth's individual interests, values, and aptitudes. Exposing them to as many opportunities in postsecondary settings as possible, no matter how short or seemingly insignificant has a large impact on the decisions made by Indian youth.

Career Development

American Indian high school students can discover their career interests in many of the same ways as they can explore postsecondary education options. Often, Indian youth live in remote areas and have little opportunity for employment, let alone exposure to a variety of employment options. If their reservation has an Indian gaming establishment, they may be familiar with some related employment options. However, finding out what really interests them based on a wide variety of first-hand experiences, is seldom possible. Therefore, exposure to career opportunities will most likely come from adults in the Indian youth's life, who proactively work to create those situations for them.

One way to help youth explore career interest areas is by having them complete a career interest inventory. There are many on the market and they are all useful in this process. These inventories focus on questions that elicit responses indicating interests that can be related to specific careers, such as: Do I like to work by myself or work with people?; Do I like working indoors or outdoors?; and Do I like structured settings or self-directed work settings? These types of questions can help frame likes and dislikes in early explorations of career interests. Students can take the results of these assessments and conduct an initial exploration of related careers online, to increase their basic awareness of career areas.

As part of the career search, it is helpful for students make a list of the factors they think will be important to make a job a good career for them, including factors such as availability and quality of health insurance and/or childcare, whether the working conditions are indoors or outdoors, opportunity for advancement, average starting wage, and frequency of pay raises. Such a list can determine the advantages and disadvantages of each career the student's research. Students can rate careers in order of 'best fit,' based on these factors. Students can also use the knowledge about careers of interest to investigate postsecondary schools where training/education exists for career entry.

Hands-on types of career exploration include activities such as taking students on tours of work sites, where employees demonstrate and describe the work they do, as well as the training they needed in their field. Even more in-depth methods of career exploration include job shadowing, in which the student literally shadows, or follows, the worker through one or several workdays to experience in real time what the workday is like. A more extended work experience is an apprenticeship that is most often designed for those who are ready to begin training for a career. Depending on availability, there are many more types of career exploration. The important factor, as with postsecondary preparation, is exposing youth to as many options as possible, to introduce them to the wide variety of opportunities available. These experiences not only prepare Indian youth for life after high school, but also encourage them to improve their academic skills in order to be prepared to access the opportunities of interest.

Too often, we only consider the *academic* successes of students when considering career or college choices. However, American Indian youth have many skills they have accrued, which should be valued in the college and career exploration process, including work skills, academic skills, extracurricular skills, and volunteer and community skills. Some of their greatest accomplishments may have taken place outside of school, and need to be considered in the student's life choices. Based upon students' experiences in and outside of school, they have skills that are transferable, adaptive, and job-related. Transferable skills are those that individuals take from job to job—for example, how to work with people. Adaptive skills refer to self-management skills, such as following directions. Job-related skills refer to those skills that are specific to a particular job, such as waitressing. All of these skills are worthy of consideration in the career exploration process.

Military Training as a Career/Training Option

Most American Indian youth have had exposure to the armed services, in one way or another. Many have a relative who is a veteran and who participates in the Veteran's Pow Wow on their reservation each year. Most high schools have military recruiters from all branches of the armed services who come to visit students. The uniform and the options the recruiter presents sometimes intrigue students, and the military may be a very good option for some students. It is important for students to explore the various branches of military service, based on what they have learned about themselves—their strengths, weaknesses, interests, aptitudes, and values—since each branch of the military has a different mission. Students should research the branches and their missions, and ask informed questions of the recruiters, as they would on a college or work site visit. Asking questions about jobs and training in the student's particular areas of interest available in that branch of the military, can help Indian youth determine if the military is a good option for them to pursue.

Knowledgeable Decision-making

The process of post-school exploration described in this chapter, is a coherent set of skills for Native high school youth that provides a framework to prepare for life after high school. By learning about themselves, youth will begin to see a logical path emerge as their next steps become clearer. Students will find a new sense of confidence and self-esteem as they begin to recognize the skills they have acquired. They have, in fact, made the transition from not having goals or knowing their individual gifts or how to put them to use, to having a direction based on their own personal style. When Native youth are able to come forward as confident young adults, they are creating opportunities for themselves as well as uplifting their communities. Complete with new-found knowledge and awareness, Indian youth are more capable of setting long-range goals and achieving them.

Conclusions

All across the United States today, American Indian youth are emerging as the next generation to carry the history, culture, and traditions of their tribes forward. How will educators equip American Indian youth with the skills to carry their communities into a proud, culturally sound, and self-sufficient future? In this chapter, we have discussed four key transition skills in which American Indian youth must become competent in order to be prepared for their future and the future of their people. These youth require positive adult cultural role models to provide the necessary supports to aid them in discovering their social supports, an understanding of their personal strengths and weaknesses, and an ability to respond to change. Indian youth today crave supportive adults who will teach them to become responsible adults who are able to set goals, self-advocate, problem-solve, organize their lives, and communicate well. These youth need exposure to a variety of postsecondary opportunities and career options, so they can find a home for their gifts and talents, and a reason to strive for excellence, in and outside of school. At no other time in our history, has it been more urgent for adults to stand up for Native youth, and help to prepare them for their future—our future.

References

Adelman, C. (2006). *The toolbox revisited: Paths to degree completion from high school through college*. Washington, DC: U.S. Department of Education. Retrieved March 30, 2010, from *http://www.ed.gov/rschstat/research/pubs/toolboxrevisit/toolbox.pdf*

Balfanz, R. & Legters, N. (2004). *Locating the Dropout Crisis* .Baltimore: Johns Hopkins University, Carnevale, A., & Desrochers, D. (2003). *Standards for what? The eco-*

nomic roots of K-16 reform. Princeton, NJ: Education Testing Service. Retrieved March 30, 2010, from http://www.transitionmathproject.org/resources/doc/ topicindex/*standards_for_what.pdf*

DeVoe, J. F., & Darling-Churchill, K. E. (2008). *Status and trends in the education of American Indians and Alaska Natives: 2008* (NCES 2008-084). Washington, DC: U.S. Department of Education, National Center for Education Statistics. Retrieved March 30, 2010, from *http://nces.ed.gov/pubsearch/pubsinfo.asp?pubid=2008084*

Gilliland, H. (1995). *Teaching the Native American.* Dubuque, Iowa: Kendall/Hunt Publishing Co.

Gambill, J., Moss, L. A., & Vescogni, C. D. (2008). *The impact of study skills and organizational methods on student achievement.* Chicago: Saint Xavier University.

Garrod, A., and Larimore, C.(1997). *First Person First Peoples.* Ithaca: Cornell University Press. Greene, J. P., & Forster, G. (2003). *Public high school graduation and college readiness rates in the United States.* Education Working Paper, 3. New York: Manhattan Institute. Retrieved March 29, 2010, from *http://www.manhattan-institute.org/html/ewp_03.htm*

Luthar, S. S., Cicchetti, D., & Becker, B. (2000). The construct of resilience: A critical evaluation and guidelines for future work. *Child Development, 71*(3), 543-562.

Masten, A. S., & Coatsworth, J. D. (1998). The development of competence in favorable and unfavorable environments. *American Psychologist, 53*(2), 205-220.

Mizelle, N. (1999) *Helping Middle School Students Make the Transition into High School.* ERIC, August 1999, (EDO-PS-99_11).

Ness & Huisken. (2002). *Expanding the Circle: Respecting the Past; Preparing for the Future.* University of Minnesota, Institute on Community Integration, Minneapolis, MN.

Peacock. R. (2001). *The Perceptions and Experiences of American Indian High School Graduates and Dropouts.* Dissertation: University of Minnesota, Minneapolis, MN

Perez, E. *Milwaukee Journal Sentinal,* Milwaukee, WI: Journal Sentinal, Inc. July 6, 2008

Schramm, J. B., & Sagawa, S. (2008). *High schools as launch pads: How college-going culture improves graduation rates in low-income high schools.* Washington, DC: College Summit. Retrieved March 30, 2010, from *http://www.collegesummit.org/ images/uploads/WhitePaper_new.pdf*

Strang, W., & von Glatz, A. (2001). *American Indian and Alaska Native education research agenda.* Washington, DC: U.S. Department of Education.

Strecher, V. J. (1995). Goal setting as a strategy for health behavior change. *Health Education & Behavior, 22*(2), 190-200.

Swisher, K. G., & Tippeconnic, J. E. (Eds). (1999). *Next steps: Research and practice to advance Indian Education.* Charleston, WV: ERIC Clearinghouse on Rural Education and Small Schools.

Closing the Mathematics Achievement Gap of Native American Students Identified as Learning Disabled

by Judith Hankes, Ph.D., Stacey Skoning, Ph.D., Gerald Fast, Ph.D., Loretta Mason-Williams, Ph.D., John Beam, Ph.D., William Mickelson, Ph.D., and Colleen Merrill, MBA

Introduction

This chapter describes the Years I and II activities and assessment findings of a three-year research study titled, *Closing the Mathematics Achievement Gap of Native American Students Identified as Learning Disabled Project* (CMAG Project). The disproportionate number of Wisconsin Native American elementary and secondary students identified as learning disabled (LD) and performing unsatisfactorily on the annual state assessment, the Wisconsin Knowledge and Concept Exam (WKCE), led to the motivation for this project (Fiedler et al, 2007; Frieberg et al, 2002; Leary, 2009). The principal investigator hypothesized that Native American students identified as LD would perform significantly better on the state's reasoning–based mathematics assessment if their teachers effectively implemented Cognitively Guided Instruction (CGI), used culturally responsive methods when teaching mathematics, and understood the alignment of the WKCE with the National Council of Teachers of Mathematics (NCTM) Content and Process Standards.

Two grants funded the project, a Wisconsin Improving Teacher Quality Grant (WITQ) and a Mathematics and Science Partnership (MSP) Grant. The combined funding provided professional development for thirty teachers from eight Wisconsin school districts serving Native American communities, twenty-two special education teachers and eight regular education inclusive classroom teachers. Though approximately three hundred students in kindergarten through tenth grade received instruction in project classrooms, each teacher was asked to report achievement data for only five target students. Teachers were instructed to choose Native American students identified as LD for the target sample. Analysis of Years I and II data found statistically significant effects on the mathematics achievement and the attitudes toward mathematics of the project students. This chapter describes how teachers were empowered to empower their students in mathematics during Years I and II of the CMAG Project.

Background Information

Failing test scores, excessive truancy, and low graduation rates provided evidence of unsatisfactory educational outcomes for Native American children and youth throughout the United States (Soldier, 2005; Starnes, 2006). Investigation into the failure of Native students to thrive educationally revealed the prevalence of under-prepared teachers, non-challenging content, and low expectations (Allexsaht-Snider & Hart, 2001; Dehyle, 1992; Donovon & Cross, 2002; Green, 2001; Haycock, 2001; Losen & Orfield, 2002; Oswald et al., 1999; Trumbull et al., 2002). Of related concern was the overrepresentation of Native students identified as LD. In fact, in parts of the U.S., no other minority culture is as overrepresented as Native American students in the category of LD (Harry & Klingner, 2006; Reschly, 2003; Turnbull et al., 2007).

Research provides a number of theories related to the disproportionate numbers of minority students, including Native students, labeled LD (Cawley & Fawley, 2000; Gould, 2007; Harry, 1994; Ladner, 2007; Losen & Orfield, 2002; Reschly, 2007). Freiberg and colleagues(2002) espoused that the lack of tests designed for students who speak non-Standard English dialects and are culturally diverse, may lead to disproportionality. This is due to the fact that during formal assessments, Native students often exhibit cultural speech patterns: not volunteering information, being quiet, and appearing not to have adequate expressive language. Such culturally-based speech patterns may increase the possibility that a Native student may be diagnosed with a language processing disorder, and identified as eligible for special education services. Harry and Klingner in their book, *Why Are So Many Minority Students in Special Education* (2006), proposed an alternative explanation to the language-related theory proposed above. They attributed disproportionate labeling and categorizing of minority students to masked social sorting and cultural stratification. They also questioned the benefits of special education, pointing out that many students identified as LD, demonstrated minimal achievement on annual state tests.

Whether Native students were misdiagnosed or accurately diagnosed, it remains important to acknowledge that students identified as LD possessed average or better reasoning ability. It was this ability that distinguished the student identified as LD, from the student identified as cognitively disabled (CD), and it was this reasoning ability that should empower the student identified as LD to achieve academically, when provided appropriate instruction (Harry & Klingner, 2006; Turnbull et al., 2007). A related fact to consider was that the accountability-driven *No Child Left Behind Act* (NCLB, 2001) mandated inclusion of all students possessing average or better reasoning ability in grade level state testing, including students identified as LD. Prior to NCLB, these students were frequently exempted.

Why do students possessing average or better reasoning ability, fail in mathematics, a content area that is reasoning-based? Analysis of mathematics instruction in special education classrooms revealed that students with LD were typically provided with less rigorous curriculum, and the educational goals identified by their special education teachers on their IEP focused on computation and procedural thinking, rather than applied problem solving and reasoning (Bottage, 2001; Bottage & Hasselbring, 1993; Wade, 2000; Ysseldyke & Thurlow, 1997). Studies also revealed that special education teachers often were unprepared to teach challenging content to students, and typically assigned low-level work or showed the student how to solve problems assigned by the regular education classroom teacher (Billingsley & McLeskey, 2004; Delvin, 1988; Maccini & Gagnon, 2002; Nolet & McLaughlin, 2000; Smith, 2004). Loucks-Horsley (2005) asserted that many elementary and special education teachers entered classrooms unprepared to teach mathematics. Billingsley and McLeskey (2004) reported that many teachers lacked up-to-date knowledge of effective teaching strategies, since very few elementary and special education teachers majored or minored in mathematics, while earning their college degrees.

Closing the Math Achievement Gap Project Intervention/Professional Development

Perhaps the most effective way to empower teachers to empower their students in mathematics is by creating opportunities for them to become actively engaged in quality professional development experiences. Half-day workshops that orient teachers to commercial curricula (typical in today's climate of the competitive textbook market) are inadequate, since no textbook can replace a content-competent teacher who understands the learner's culture and has mastered the complex art of teaching. The primary goal of the CMAG Project was to develop such teachers.

Recruitment of special education teachers for the CMAG Project was not difficult. Volunteers shared that they did not know how to prepare their students for the reasoning-based WKCE and that they were eager to participate in a project that offered extended professional development on teaching mathematics. Most were veteran special education teachers, averaging 17 years of teaching experience, with experience ranging from two years to twenty-nine years. All teachers were responsible for teaching mathematics to Native students identified as LD, and each came from a district with disproportionately high numbers of Native students in their special education programs.

Prior to the planning of the CMAG professional development experiences, goals for students and teachers were established (Tables 1 & 2). Student goal #1 specified that project students would demonstrate achievement at the *basic* level on the WKCE. The decision to identify *basic* achievement as a goal was made because, prior to Project Year I, most of the target students achieved at the *minimal* level, and many barely attempted or refused to attempt the test even when provided state-approved accommodations, such as having the test read aloud and being given extended time.

Table 1. CMAG Student Goals (achievement at grade level)

1.	Project students will achieve at the basic level on the WKCE and demonstrate problem-solving skills across all NCTM content areas (number and operations, algebra, geometry, measurement, and data analysis and probability).
2.	Project students will independently solve word problems.
3.	Project students will use numbers effectively for various purposes such as counting, measuring, estimating, and problem solving.
4.	Project students will communicate their reasoning and solution strategies verbally, with drawings, with models, and symbolically.
5.	Project students will report positive attitudes toward mathematics.

Table 2. CMAG Teacher Goals:

1.	Teachers will effectively employ Cognitively Guided Instruction (CGI) to develop mathematical reasoning and base 10 understanding.
2.	Teachers will demonstrate knowledge of culturally responsive teaching methods and apply these methods when teaching students identified as learning disabled.
3.	Teachers will demonstrate knowledge of the NCTM Content Standards and Benchmarks and will plan standards-based instruction.
4.	Teachers will authentically assess their students' mathematical thinking and plan instruction based on that thinking (formative and benchmark assessments.

The CMAG Project intervention encompassed three characteristics found in successful professional development models: (1) groups of teachers from the same school participated together; (2) workshops and reflection sessions provided high quality contact which lasted several months; and (3) teachers learned new content and pedagogy in the context of teaching (Elmore, 2002; Loucks-Horsley, et. al., 2005). A fourth important characteristic of the CMAG Project was that project personnel conducted classroom observations, and consultation sessions with project teachers several times throughout the year.

The Years I and II CMAG Project intervention activities (August 2008 to September 2009) included two 5-day workshops, two 2-day implementation reflection sessions, and at least 6 site visits per participant (lesson observations with follow-up conferences) conducted by project personnel. Face-to-face instruction during workshops and reflection sessions, totaled approximately 90 instruction hours. Additionally, project teachers were provided mathematics manipulatives and resources (i.e., published and unpublished mathematics lessons with activity packets, the Madison Metropolitan School District assessments [MMSD, 2008], and the Buckle Down Mathematics resources [Buckledown, 2008]). A website also was developed to provide teachers with online resources: http://www.uwosh.edu/coehs/mindsongmath/.

Though CMAG workshop sessions involved teachers in the exploration of many mathematics topics and experiences, those that teachers identified as most valuable will be described in the remaining sections of this chapter: Cognitively Guided Instruction (teaching through word problems and developing base 10 understanding), Culturally Responsive teaching, and use of the CMAG Benchmark Assessments. In addition, the Initial Findings from the CGI Project will be discussed.

Cognitively Guided Instruction

Teachers employing CGI in their instruction of formal mathematics concepts, utilize the knowledge that their students bring to the classroom (Carpenter et al, 1999). The approach complies with National Mathematics Reform Standards and Processes (NCTM, 2000) and is highly successful for developing mathematical reasoning and number sense with mainstream, as well as minority children, and average learners, as well as students with special learning needs (Behrend, 1994; Carey et al., 1993; Carpenter et al., 1999; Ghaleb, 1992; Hankes, 1996; Hankes, 1998; Peterson et al., 1991; Villasenor, 1991). This section describes the preparation of teachers to employ the CGI methods and describes the basic framework of CGI instruction.

Teachers participating in CGI workshops learned about relationships between the structure of primary level mathematics, and children's thinking of mathematics. The goal of this approach was that teachers would understand how their children learned mathematical concepts and use this knowledge when planning instruction (Carpenter et al., 1999). The content shared during CGI workshops was built on extensive research that identified regularities in children's solutions to different types of mathematical story problem situations, when children were allowed to solve problems intuitively, rather than following a teacher imposed procedure (Carpenter, 1985; Fuson, 1990 and 1992; Streefland, 1993). Of importance to the present study, was the fact that children from other cultural groups, including Native American (Apthorp et al., Hankes, 1998; Hankes 2007), Hispanic (Villasenor, 1991), African American (Carey, et al, 1995), and Lebanese (Ghaleb, 1992), demonstrated the same regularities in their solution strategies, as the dominant culture participants in the original study. This finding suggested that young children across cultures used similar cognitive processes when intuitively solving simple mathematics problems they encountered within their culture. Studies also document the success of CGI when teaching LD students (Bottge, 2001; Hankes, 1996; Behrend, 1994).

The problem solving regularities mentioned above became the basis for generating a complete taxonomy of addition, subtraction, multiplication, and division word problems, distinguished in terms of reasoning difficulty (Table 3). Teachers who understood this problem taxonomy were able to differentiate story problems, from easiest to most difficult, and used this knowledge to plan group or individual instruction. When used strategically, gradually increasing problem difficulty, the mathematical reasoning ability of students increased significantly. Table 1 provides examples of CGI one-step story problem situations with related number sentences. The location of the unknown quantity, whether at the end, middle, or beginning, influences the difficulty of the problem. The problems were coded for reasoning difficulty: easiest with a shamrock ♣, slightly more difficult with a shamrock and diamond ♣ ♦, more difficult   with a diamond ♦, and most difficult with a heart) ♥. The story problems in Table 3 are based on the story *How the Bear Lost His Tail.* This story is included in the section titled, A CGI Culture-based Lesson.

Table 3. CGI Story Problem Situations

JOINING PROBLEMS		
Join: Result Unknown (JRU) ♦	Join: Change Unknown (JCU) ♥	*Join: Start Unknown (JSU) ♣*
Bear had 5 fish. Otter gave him 8 more fish. How many fish does Otter have now? $5 + 8 = \square$	Bear had 5 fish. Otter gave him some more. Then Bear had 13 fish. How many fish did Bear give Otter? $5 + \square = 13$	Bear had some fish. Otter gave him 8 more. Then he had 13 fish. How many fish did Bear have before Otter gave him any? $\square + 8 = 13$
SEPARATING PROBLEMS		
Separate: Result Unknown (SRU) ♦	Separate: Change Unknown (SCU) ♥	Separate: Start Unknown (SSU) ♣
Otter had 13 fish. He	Otter had 13 fish. He	Otter had some fish. He

gave 5 fish to Bear. How many fish does Otter have left?	gave some to Bear. Now he has 5 fish left. How many fish did Otter give Bear?	gave 5 to Bear. Now he has 8 fish left. How many fish did Otter have before he gave any to Bear?
13 - 5 = ☐	13 - ☐ = 5	☐ - 5 = 8

PART -PART -WHOLE PROBLEMS

Part-Part-Whole: Whole Unknown (PPW:WU) ♦	Part-Part-Whole: Part Unknown (PPW:PU) ♥
Otter has 5 big fish and 8 small fish. How many fish does Otter have altogether?	Otter has 13 fish. Five are big and the rest are small. How many small fish does Otter have?
5 + 8 = ☐	13 - 5 = ☐ or 5 + ☐ = 13

COMPARE PROBLEMS

Compare: Difference Unknown (CDU) ♦♥	Compare: Quantity Unknown (CQU) ♣	Compare Referent Unknown (CRU) ♣
Otter has 8 fish. Bear has 5 fish. How many more fish does Otter have than Bear?	Bear has 5 fish. Otter has 3 more fish than Bear. How many fish does Bear Otter have?	Bear has 5 fish. He has 3 fewer fish than Otter. How many fish does Otter have?
8 - 5 = ☐ or 5 + ☐ = 8	5 + 3 = ☐	☐ - 3 = 5 or 5 + 3 = ☐ 8 - 3 = ☐ or ☐ + 3 = 8

MULTIPLICATION & DIVISION PROBLEMS

Multiplication (M) ♦	Measurement Division (MD) ♦	Partitive Division (PD) ♦♥
Otter has 4 piles of fish. There are 3 fish in each pile. How many fish does Otter have?	Otter had 12 fish. He gave them to some crows. He gave each crow 3 fish. How many crows were given fish?	Otter has 12 fish. He wants to give them to 3 crows. If he gives the same number of fish to each crow, how many fish will each crow get?
4 x 3 = ☐	12 ÷ 3 = ☐	12 ÷ 3 = ☐

Problem chart based on Cognitively Guided Instruction Problem Types (Carpenter et al., 1999

Extensive research documented that the taxonomy of CGI story problems (Table 3), provided a framework for identifying the intuitive cognitive processes that children use when solving word problems. After conducting interviews with hundreds of primary-age children, during which the children were encouraged to intuitively solve word problems without assistance, researchers found that when children first begin to solve problems, they concretely represent the number relationship within the problem. They also found that, over time, concrete strategies were abstracted to counting strategies and then to derived fact strategies. These reasoning strategies were categorized into three developmental stages: direct modeling, counting on/back and derived facts (Carpenter et al, 1999). An explanation and example of the type of solution that a child would use at each stage are given in Table 4.

Table 4. Children's Solution Strategies for Solving Word Problems

Word Problem (Join Result Unknown) Grace had 4 cookies. Bryce gave Grace 8 more cookies. How many cookies does Grace have now?		
Direct Modeling	Counting On/Back Strategies	Derived Facts
The child uses concrete objects or tally marks to represent each whole number in the problem type. The child uses the objects to "act out" the problem when solving.	The child generally begins by counting on from the first number given in the problem. A child who is at a slightly more advanced level will count on from the larger number.	The student uses known facts and understands relation-ships between numbers.
The child counts out 4 cubes and puts them in a pile. Then the child counts out 8 cubes and puts them in a pile. Finally, the child pushes the two piles together and counts all cubes to reach the answer.	The child holds 4 in his/her mind and counts on the additional quantity of 8 saying, "Five, six, seven, eight, nine, ten, eleven, twelve." The child thinks to begin with the larger number, 8, and counts on saying, "Nine, ten, eleven, twelve."	The child splits the 4 into 2 + 2, adds one of the 2s to the 8 to make 10 and then adds the other 2 to make 12.

Knowledge of CGI word problem situations (Table 3) and stages of children's mathematical thinking (Table 4), provides a coherent analysis of the structure of single-step word problems, as well as the developmental strategies that children use when acquiring the ability to solve such problems.

Working with the CGI problem-solving taxonomy had a cumulative effect: experience solving single-step problems built toward the ability to solve multi-step problems; place value concepts and multi-digit operations became natural extensions of the processes children used when frequently solving problems; when solving partitive division problems, children's understanding of fraction concepts also emerged (Emspon, 1995; Streefland, 1993); and posing frequent problems to students and attending to their solutions enabled teachers to explore other mathematics content (telling time, geometry, measurement) through the eyes of their students (Carpenter et al., 1999; Hankes, 1998).

Developing mastery of CGI (teaching mathematics content through problem solving, basing instruction on student thinking, and developing number sense in the context of problem situations) takes time. However, providing frequent problem-solving experiences develops competence and confidence, within both students and the teachers. Students become independent problem solvers, and teachers learn to base instruction on their students' reasoning abilities. Understanding their students' thinking was especially important for teachers in special education, and in inclusive general education classrooms, since possessing the taxonomical knowledge of CGI allowed the teacher to differentiate instruction.

During the CGI workshop, emphasis also was placed on developing student understanding of base ten, in the domains of addition and subtraction, multiplication and division, multi-digit operations, algebra, geometry, and fractions. Typically, in regular education and special education classrooms, students had not been expected to do story problems, until they mastered their number facts and routine arithmetic procedures. However, this was not the case in the CGI classroom. In contrast, students developed number sense by solving story problems, gradually progressing from manipulating with counters, to deriving quantities using non-routine procedures.

One CMAG Project expectation was that teachers would provide whole class or small group story problem instruction daily. Teachers also were asked to organize a classroom Word Problem Center, placing story problems in coded folders (based on the difficulty taxonomy coded in Table 3: shamrock, shamrock/diamond, diamond, heart, and multi-step problems). Numbers were not included in some problems to allow students the opportunity to develop more independence by choosing their own numbers. Students were to be given time each day to self-select and independently solve, at least one problem from the Word Problem Center, pasting the self-selected problem in a Math Journal (a spiral notebook) and drawing or writing the solution beneath the problem.

Culturally Responsive Teaching

Along with CGI, the principal investigator focused on culturally responsive teaching during the CMAG Project workshops, making clear to the teachers how intrinsically linked the two were as CGI teaching methods, aligned to a great extent with traditional Native American teaching methods. This section describes the alignment and presents an example of a CGI culture-based lesson.

The comparison of methods, presented in Table 5, was developed during a three-year research study analyzing the compatibility of CGI with Oneida Indian teaching practices (Hankes, 2008). The study investigated how CGI influenced the mathematics achievement of seventeen Oneida kindergartners. Findings of the study demonstrated that Oneida children's achievement was as good as, even slightly better than, the comparison group of non-Native students. As part of the Oneida study, Hankes conducted interviews with Oneida elder educators and identified practices commonly recognized as traditional Oneida ways of teaching. Briefly summarized, these practices are: 1) lessons are time generous; 2) lesson concepts are completely relational, with emphasis on solving real life problems; 3) manipulatives and models are present and used; 4) students work in cooperative groups and discuss tasks with each other; and 5) classroom discussion is mostly conversational, with the teacher facilitating lesson study. Native American educators throughout the United States have identified these same practices as being culturally responsive (Bradley & Taylor, 2002; Davison, 1994; Davison, 2002; Hankes & Fast, 2002; Nelson-Barber & Estrin, 1995; Hillibrandt et al., 1992; Trumbell et al, 2002).

Table 5. A Comparison of Principles across Instructional Approaches

Instruction Focus Area	Dominant Culture Pedagogy	CGI/Constructivist Pedagogy	Native American Pedagogy
Role of the Teacher	The teacher generally behaves in a didactic manner, disseminating information to students.	The teacher facilitates student learning by selecting developmentally appropriate lessons. The teacher is a "guide on the side" rather than "sage on the stage" during these lessons.	The teacher guides the student to learn age appropriate tasks. Conversational topics are not controlled by individual speakers.
View of Learner	Students are viewed as blank slates onto which information is etched by the teacher.	Students are capable of complex problem solving. Learning is a natural and motivational experience.	Each student possesses Creator-given strengths and is born a thinker with a life mission.
Curriculum	Curriculum activities rely heavily on textbooks and workbooks.	Curriculum blends content with meaningful real life situations. In this way, content becomes relevant and helps the learner link	Lessons relate to real problems that will likely confront the student.

		knowledge to many kinds of situations.	
Time	The day is partitioned into blocks of time and content coverage. "Time on task" is considered important.	Content is taught through problem solving that may take hours, days, and even weeks.	Instruction/learning is time-generous rather than time-driven. When an activity should begin is determined by when the activity that precedes it is completed.
Concept Formation	Concepts are presented part to whole with emphasis on basic skills.	Concepts, procedures, and intellectual processes are interrelated. In a significant sense, "the whole is greater than the sum of its parts."	All knowledge is relational, presented whole to part not part to whole. Just as the circle produces harmony, holistic thinking promotes sense making.
Student to Student Interaction	Students primarily work alone.	Student to student interaction is encouraged. Interacting with classmates helps students construct knowledge, learn other ways to think about ideas, and clarify thinking.	Care-taking patterns of extended families and bonded community interactions are replicated in-group learning experiences.
Assessment	Student assessment is viewed as separate from teaching and occurs almost entirely through testing. Testing often stratifies students and promotes competition.	Decisions regarding students' achievement are made on the basis of balanced and equitable sources that authentically document performance.	Age and ability determine task appropriateness. Learning mastery is demonstrated through performance. Creator ordained mission determines one's role in life, and no one mission is bet-ter than another. Com-petition, situating one as better than another, is discouraged.

(Hankes, 1998; Hankes & Fast, 2002)

Like the climate in a culturally responsive classroom, the climate of a CGI classroom is one in which each person's thinking is important and respected by the group. In this type of classroom, children approach problem solving willingly. Each child is perceived to be in charge of his or her own learning, as individual knowledge of mathematics is used to solve problems that are realistic and relevant. The critical elements in classrooms implementing culturally responsive teaching/CGI are:

1. Children spend most of their time solving problems related to something going on in their lives: a family or community event, a theme or unit being studied outside of mathematics class, a book or story shared by the teacher;
2. Various physical materials are available to children to assist them in solving problems. Each child decides how to solve a problem, which may include using materials, such as manipulatives and/or paper and pencils, or solving a problem mentally;
3. Children work in groups solving problems and sharing their solution strategies. Collaborative rather than competitive problem solving is encouraged;
4. To assess their students, these teachers do not rely on written tests or formal assessment procedures. Instead, assessment is an ongoing part of instruction. Teachers continually ask their students to show and describe how they solved a given problem;
5. Teachers assess what their students are accomplishing so that they continue to expand the students' knowledge by giving increasingly challenging problems that are not beyond their students' capabilities. They do not simply give increasingly more difficult problems; they are able to match the problems to each individual student's abilities; and;
6. When a student's solution process is in error, teachers ask the student to explain her/his thinking. During this explanation, teachers guide the student to discover and understand the error. Teachers do not directly point out the error.

A CGI Culture-based Lesson

The following story with related word problems is as an example of how mathematics can be integrated into a culture lesson. The story, written by a team of students studying CGI during a summer pre-college program, is available with other stories on the CMAG website at *http://www.uwosh.edu/coehs/mindsongmath/ethnomath/legend/legend1.htm*.

How Bear Lost His Tail. A legend told by Jerry Smith, an Ojibwe Elder, to Marian, Doreen, and Leonard Belille:

> Long, long ago there were only creatures on the earth. There were birds, bears, deer, mice, everything but people. In this long time ago, all the animals spoke the same language. And just like some people nowadays, they played tricks on one another and made each other laugh. They also helped each other. So it was with all the animals.

One day in the winter, when the lakes had frozen, but before the winter sleep, Bear was walking along the lakeshore. As he was walking, he came upon Otter sitting near a hole on the ice with a pile of fish. "You've got a mighty big pile of fish there," Bear said. "How did you get them fish?" Instead of telling how he dove down into the water and caught the fish, Otter decided to trick Bear. You see, back then Bear had a very long bushy tail. He was very proud of his tail and all the animals knew it.

"The way I catch my fish is by putting my tail in this ice hole," Otter explained. "I wiggle it around once in a while so the fish see it. When a fish bites onto my tail, I quickly pull it up and out of the water."

"That sure is an easy way to catch fish," Bear said. "Do you mind if I use your fishing hole?" Otter, laughing behind Bear's back, said, "I have enough fish. Use my fishing hole as long as you like." Then Otter picked up his fish and walked away. Bear carefully poked his tail into the ice hole and waited. He waited and waited. Once in a while he'd wiggle his tail so the fish could see it. Bear waited until the sun began to set, but not one fish even nibbled at his tail. At last, he decided to go home, but when he tried to stand up, his tail had frozen into the ice! He couldn't move! He pulled and pulled at his tail, but it was stuck tight. Finally, he pulled with all of his strength and ripped off half his tail!

Now you know why the Bear has a short tail, and remember, don't always believe what people tell you.

Instructions: Choose numbers that you want to work with and solve the problems. Show how you solved them using a drawing or with words in your Math Journal.

1. Otter went fishing. He caught ____ big fish and ____ little fish. How many fish did Otter catch?   ♦ (PPW:WU)
2. Otter caught ____ fish. He gave ____ fish to a friend. Now how many fish does Otter have? ♦ (SRU)
3. Otter has ____ fish. Bear has ____ fish. How many more fish does Otter have than Bear? ♦♥ (CDU)
4. ____ fish were swimming in the pond. Some swam away. Then there were ____ fish swimming. How many fish swam away? ♥ (SCU)   5. Otter caught 12 fish. He put them into 3 piles. How many fish did he put in each pile? ♦♥ (PD)

Teaching suggestions: After reading the story aloud, project or write the problems on the chalk/white board, or copy and give them to the student/s. Read all problems aloud (re-read as needed), and have students solve independently or in small groups. After solving the problems, have the student/s explain their solution strategies by demonstrating and using words.

Initial Findings from the CMAG Project

Following completion of Project Years I and II, analysis of coded lesson observation data, teacher interview transcriptions and email surveys, teacher content knowledge assessments, and analysis of target student attitudes and achievement data was completed. This section describes findings of this analysis. Similar data collection and analysis will continue throughout Project Year III.

Results from an Email Survey

An email survey sent to project teachers in September 2009, posed two questions:

> Since beginning the CMAG Project, have you observed noticeable improvements in your students' mathematics performance and achievement?
> If so, what are the three main reasons for this improvement? Please begin with the one that you feel had the greatest influence.

Response analysis revealed that all of the teachers believed their students' mathematics achievement had improved.

The 10 commonly shared reasons were:
1. Students were solving and writing their own word problems, and this improved comprehension;
2. Students were solving problems in different ways, trying new ways to solve;
3. Students were thinking about what the problem was asking, not just adding numbers;
4. Instruction was not textbook and worksheet driven;
5. Students could use manipulatives when solving problems;
6. The chalkboard and whiteboards were used more often;
7. The teacher asked more "Why?" questions;
8. Students worked in groups, and more students were teaching students;
9. Students were thinking through math more; and
10. Students were writing number sentences and understanding what they meant.

One teacher responded, "The largest improvements have come in the area of self-confidence. The kids are not afraid to share or make mistakes. They can also solve more problems, because they can do it any way they know how to, instead of relying on the one procedure they had been taught in the past. More specifically:
1. They have been given permission to use their own thinking;
2. The students are learning from each other; and
3. They actually understand what they are doing and can explain it!"

These anecdotal remarks provided evidence suggesting the effectiveness of using CGI instructions with students. The next section documents some of the emerging statistical evidence related to the Project.

CGI Assessment Findings

During the first introductory workshop in Fall 2008, teachers were trained to pre and post-assess target students, grades K–10, with three informal ability-adaptable protocols: 1) the CGI Word Problem Interview; 2) the Base 10 Interview; and 3) the Student Attitude Assessment. Due to confusion over expectations and procedures, many teachers did not properly administer these assessments. Consequently, there were fewer complete data sets than anticipated.

Forty-three target students, grades 3–8 were assessed Fall 2008 and again spring 2009, with the CGI Word Problem Interview (14 test items). This assessment could be adjusted by the teacher to meet the instructional level of the student. For instance, depending on a student's number sense, the teacher could choose to use single digit numbers in the word problem, or double- and triple-digit numbers. The mean score in the fall was 6.58, with a standard deviation of 3.92. In the spring, the mean score increased to 9.23, with a standard deviation of 3.70. A paired t-test indicated a statistically significant improvement in problem solving performance from the fall to the spring of the same academic year (t= 4.24, α < .01).

Thirty-six target students (grades 3 through 8) were assessed in Fall 2008, and again Spring 2009, with the Base Ten Assessment (10 test items). This assessed student understanding of quantity and place value. The mean score in the fall was 3.51, with a standard deviation of 2.42. In the spring, the mean score increased to 5.76, with a standard deviation of 2.76. A paired t-test indicated a significant improvement in Base Ten understanding from the fall to the Spring ($t = 6.10$, α < .01).

Thirty target students (grades 3 through 8) were assessed Fall 2008, and again Spring 2009, with a 50-point Student Attitude Assessment. On this assessment, the student's mean score in the Fall was 30.7, with a standard deviation of 10.3. In the spring, the mean score increased to 34.7, with a standard deviation of 8.50. A paired t-test indicated a significant improvement in attitude toward mathematics from the fall to the Spring, at the .05 level of significance (t= 2.60, α = .014).

Reports from Teachers on Student Preparation for the State Test

Analysis of pre and post CMAG Project mathematics scores on the state test, the Wisconsin Knowledge and Concept Exam (WKCE), documented significant mathematics achievement gains. Project teachers attributed this improvement not only to their implementation of Cognitively Guided Instruction but also because, as participants in the CMAG Project, they had come to understand how test items aligned with state mathematics content standards, and they learned how to prepare their students for solving the types of problems likely to be encountered on the WKCE. One special education teacher explained: "Before working with this project, I didn't know anything about the state math standards and how the test related to them. To me, the math section of the WKCE seemed to be a bunch of disjointed test questions. I objected to being required to give the test to my students because, well, I didn't think they could do it."

The NCLB accountability-driven mandate to include students with LD in state testing created a unique dilemma for special education teachers. The basis for this dilemma was that the assessment of mathematics knowledge changed significantly, following the 1989 National Council of Teachers of Mathematics (NCTM) reform, a constructivist-based reform (Brooks & Brooks, 1999) that called for mathematics instruction in the United States to focus on reasoning and problem solving, rather than basic skills (NCTM, 1994). In spite of three decades of opposition from proponents of the "Back to Basics" movement (Delvin, 1998), the NCTM "thinking math" reform became established in regular education classrooms (NCTM, 2000). However, this reform did not impact special education, until the NCLB mandate (Brownell, Hirsch, and Seo, 2004; Sherman, 2008).

Not unlike special education teachers across the nation, the CMAG Project teachers were frustrated by the NCLB mandate, that required students identified as learning disabled to be included in state testing. The primary cause for their concern was the fact that their pre-service preparation, most predating the NCTM reform, had prepared them to focus on basic skill development, and they realized that this form of instruction did not prepare their students for the state reasoning–based assessment.

Some teachers attempted to use sample test items that were posted online by the Wisconsin Department of Education but found these to be developmentally inappropriate. During a discussion regarding the use of released items, several teachers commented that they believed prepping with them was counter-productive. One special education teacher said, "Working with them [released items] created more anxiety, and they [her students] gave up before they started. They didn't even try." Another teacher wrote, "Because of failing over and over again, my students give up when they are expected to do something that they find difficult. Instead of trying them [released items], they just give up. So, I end up showing them how to solve, but it doesn't help." What teachers described was the phenomenon of learned-helplessness, the tendency to give up when confronted with a task considered too challenging (Abrahamson & Seligman, 1978; Roth, 1980; Young & Allin, 1986).

When preparing students who exhibit learned helplessness for a problem-based test like the WKCE, it is important to make the experience safe, not insultingly simple and not overwhelmingly difficult. To achieve this balance, a leveled assessment for grades K–7th was developed, the CMAG Benchmark Assessment. This multi-grade assessment included WKCE aligned assessments developed by the Madison Metropolitan School District, assessments for grades K–2nd (MMSD, 2008) and by the Buckle Down Publishing Company, assessments for grades 3–7th (Buckledown, 2008). At the beginning of Project Year I, teachers were asked to use these benchmark assessments strategically: to begin with one that they felt was at the student's confidence level and to progress on toward the student's instructional level. If a student achieved 75% on one level, the student was to be assessed with the next level.

The CMAG Benchmark Assessments were coded with grade-associated symbols, rather than identified by grade level numbers. Because of the wide range of students in inclusive classrooms or pullout special education classrooms, this manner of coding was especially important because it allowed teachers to begin assessing at each student's comfort level, and to progress to the instruction level without using a test the student could identify as indicating that he/she was below grade level.

Additionally, teachers were instructed to have the student/s solve no more than five items at a time, and then to discuss these items before progressing to the next five items. When discussing test items with the students, teachers were advised to probe for understanding and to guide students with questions, rather than show how to solve the problem. In this way, teachers developed the ability to teach through questioning, the teaching approach used during Cognitively Guided Instruction, and recommended by the National Council of Teachers of Mathematics (NCTM, 2000).

To determine views about using the CMAG Benchmark Assessments, teachers were asked, "What impact did the CMAG Assessments have on your teaching and student learning?"

They reported that:
1. Students were more willing to attempt WKCE test items;
2. They became knowledgeable about what mathematics content they needed to teach to prepare their students for the WKCE. One high school teacher wrote, "Now I know what to teach, and I can explain to parents that we are covering number operations, algebra, measurement and data and stuff like that. I didn't know what to say before;"
3. Processing the CMAG Benchmark Assessments with their students changed how they taught; they began to ask questions rather than showing how to solve;
4. They were surprised that their students were able to reason and problem

solve and were impressed with their students' unique solution strategies;

5. Their students enjoyed math discussions; and
6. They were surprised that their students did not know basic skills or possess base 10 understanding—this lack of basic skills knowledge was especially surprising since basic skills had been the focus of instruction in previous years.

These comments suggest that working with the CMAG Benchmark Assessments accomplished far more than preparing students to write the state test. Of special importance, is the fact that teachers reported that their students enjoyed the mathematics discussions that the CMAG assessments stimulated.

Target student achievement gains on the state test also suggested that preparation with the CMAG assessments contributed to student learning. The mathematics results of 56 target students in grades four to eight who completed the standardized state test, the Wisconsin Knowledge and Concept Exam (WKCE), in both 2008 and 2009 were analyzed and compared. Students on this test are rated as having achieved minimal, basic, proficient, or advanced competency. These competencies are also scored numerically as 1, 2, 3, or 4 respectively. The 2008 test resulted in a mean score of 1.68 with a .88 standard deviation. The 2009 test resulted in a mean score of 2.02 with a .96 standard deviation. A t-test comparing these results indicated a significant improvement ($\alpha = .001$) in the 2009 test results over the 2008 results. The average increase in scores of the 2009 results compared to the 2008 results was .34 with 18 students advancing in their rated competency category, and of the 56 students, 18 rated proficient or advanced.

Furthermore, the WKCE mathematics results of 26 students in grades four to eight who completed this test in both 2007 and 2009 were analyzed and compared. As described above, students were rated as having achieved minimal, basic, proficient, or advanced competency scored as 1, 2, 3, or 4 respectively. The 2007 test resulted in a mean score of 1.15 with a .46 standard deviation, and the 2009 test resulted in a mean score of 1.62 with a .85 standard deviation. A t-test comparing these results indicated a significant improvement ($\alpha = .001$) in the 2009 test results over the 2007 results. The average increase in scores of the 2009 results compared to the 2008 results was .46 with 10 of the 26 students advancing in their rated competency category.

It should be noted that the minimum raw score for a particular competency category increases as the grade level increases. Consequently, even though a student remains at a certain competency level, it does not mean that the student has not obtained a higher raw score or has not learned anything. For a student to advance in competency level indicates that that the student is doing better with the more advanced content in the higher grade than they did with the more basic content in the lower grade. This is indeed a noteworthy achievement. The fact that the achievement scores of minority students typically decline significantly in middle and high school (Boyer, 2000; Hannah-Jones, 2009; Toppo, 2009), suggests that the CMAG Project positively influenced the achievement of the target students. This effect will be further explored as the study progresses.

Target Students' Ability to self-select and Solve Word Problems

At the end of Year II, target students' Math Journals were collected and 58 journals were randomly selected for analysis to determine whether 1) the level of difficulty of the problems students were self-selecting at the beginning of the year compared to the level of difficulty of the problems they were selecting at the end of the year; and 2) the success students were experiencing with the self-selected problems at the beginning of the year compared to the success they were experiencing at the end of the year.

The difficulty level of each problem attempted was rated as 1 (easiest), 2 (moderate), and 3 (challenging). Two problems were selected at random from those attempted at the beginning of the year. They were rated according to the preceding scale. The mean of these ratings was then computed and used to represent the student's problem difficulty level attempted. The same procedure was used to determine the rating for the students' problem difficulty level attempted at the end of the year.

The mean attempted problem difficulty level at the beginning of the year for the 58 students selected was 1.74 with a standard deviation of 0.69. The mean attempted problem difficulty level at the end of the year was 2.42 with a standard deviation of 0.58. A paired sample two-tailed t-test showed that the attempted problem difficulty level at the end of the year was significantly greater than the attempted problem difficulty level at the beginning of the year with $\propto < .001$.

The success level in solving each of these problems attempted and randomly selected for analysis, as described above, was also rated. A rating of 0 to 3 was utilized with 0 indicating no success to 3 indicating complete success. The mean of these ratings was then computed and used to represent the student's level of problem solving success at the beginning of they year and at the end of the year.

The mean attempted problem success level at the beginning of the year for the 58 students selected was 1.49 with a standard deviation of 0.84. The mean attempted problem success level at the end of the year was 2.04 with a standard deviation of 0.76. A paired sample two-tailed t-test showed that the attempted problem success level at the end of the year was significantly greater that the attempted problem success level at the beginning of the year with $\propto < .001$.

Conclusion

The fact that disproportional numbers of Native students identified as learning disabled fail to achieve academic success is a concern for Wisconsin tribes (Fiedler et al, 2007; Leary, 2007). However, this problem is not unique to Wisconsin, it is a problem facing tribes across the nation (Deloria & Wildcat, 2001; Demmert, 2001; Soldier, 2005). This is a problem that impacts the self-sufficiency of tribal nations, since success in today's society, on and off the reservation, requires mathematical competence. However, empowering teachers to empower students is more than an economic driven goal. When failure results in underdeveloped potential, learned helplessness, and discouragement, *empowering teachers to empower students with mathematical competence* becomes a sacred mission. Efforts of the CMAG Project to embrace this mission have proven to be positive. During the writing of this chapter, Year III of the study was being conducted, and project teachers continued to report positive student achievement, as well as positive student attitudes. The following teacher comments regarding student attitudes toward math have been and continue to be typical:

1. They are coming up with a solution that makes sense to them, and this makes them feel good.
2. There is not somebody saying, "That is not right. Do it this way." So they are feeling better about themselves.
3. It's not a matter of them seeing that they get F's on their paper, or their work is marked wrong. They just explore, and they have fun doing it.
4. They love story problems, and graphing.
5. I see the kids enjoying more, so much more. They love it.

****

The CMAG Project was funded by two grant sources awarded to mathematics and special education faculty at the University of Wisconsin Oshkosh, a Mathematics and Science Partnership Grant (Grant# 09M-3434-MSP) and a Wisconsin Improving Teacher Quality Grant (Grant #08-0532 -WITQ). The instructional practices and assessments discussed or shown in this paper are not intended as an endorsement by the U. S. Department of Education.

References

Abrahamson, L. Y., Seligman, M. E. P., & Teasdale, J. D. (1978). Learned helplessness in humans: Critique and reformulation. *Journal of Abnormal Psychology*, 87(00), 49–74.

Allexsaht-Snider, M., & Hart, L. E. (2001). Mathematics for all: How do we get there? *Theory Into Practice, 40*(2).

Apthorp, H., Hankes, J., Livingston, R., Woempner, C., Barley, Z., Enriquez-Olmos,

M., & Fast, G. (2005). Mathematics lesson interactions and contexts for American Indian students in Plains region schools: An exploratory study. Aurora, CO: Regional Education Laboratory. *http://www.mcrel.org/pdf/ Diversity/5051RR_AmericanIndianMathInstruction.pdf*

Behrend, J. L. (1994). *Mathematical problem solving processes of primary grade students identified as learning disabled.* Ph.D. Unpublished Dissertation, University of Wisconsin Madison.

Billingsley, B., & McLeskey, A. (2004). Special Education teacher retention and attrition: a critical analysis of the research literature. *The Journal of Special Education,* 38 (1), 39-55.

Billingsly, B. (2004). Promoting teacher quality and retention in special education, *Journal of Learning Disabilities,* 37 (5), 370-376.

Bottge, B. A. (2001). Reconceptualizing mathematics problem solving for low-achieving students. *Remedial and Special Education,* 22, (2), 102-112.

Bottge, B. A., & Hasselbring, T.S. (1993). A comparison of two approaches for teaching complex, authentic mathematics problems to adolescents with learning disabilities. *Exceptional Children, 59(00),* 556-566.

Boyer, E. E. (2000). *High school: A report on secondary education in America.* NY: Harper and Row.

Bradley, C., & Taylor, L. (2002). Exploring American Indian and Alaskan Native cultures and mathematics learning. In J. E. Hankes & G. R. Fast (Eds.), *Changing the faces of mathematics: Perspective on indigenous people of North America.* Reston, VA: National Council of Teachers of Mathematics.

Brooks, J. G., & Brooks, G.M. (1999). *In search of understanding: The case for the constructivist classroom.* Portsmouth, NH: Heinemann.

Brownell, M. T., Hirsch, E., & Seo, S. (2004). Meeting the demand for highly qualified special education teachers during severe shortages. *Journal of Special Education,* 38 (1), 56-61.

Buckle Down Publishing. (2008). What is the title of this book? Littleton, MA.

Carey, D. A., Fennema, E., Carpenter, T. P., & Franke, M. L. (1995). Equity and mathematics education. In W. Secada, E. Fennema, & L. Byrd (Eds.), *New directions in equity for mathematics education.* New York: Teachers College Press.

Carpenter, T. P. (1985). Learning to add and subtract: An exercise in problem solving. In E. A. Silver (Ed.), *Teaching and learning mathematical problem solving: Multiple research perspectives.* Hillsdale, NJ: Lawrence Erlbaum.

Carpenter, T. P., & Fennema, E. (1992). Cognitively guided instruction: Building on the knowledge of students and teachers. In W. Secada (Ed.), *Curriculum reform: The case of mathematics in the United States. Special Issue of the International Journal of Educational Research* (pp. 457–470). Elmswood, NY: Pergamon Press, Inc.

Carpenter, T. P., Ansell, E., Franke, M., Fennema, E., & Weisbeck, L. (1993). Models of problem solving: A study of kindergarten children's problem–solving processes. *Journal for Research in Mathematics Education,* 24 (5), 427–440.

Carpenter, T. P., Fennema, E., Franke, M. L., Levi, L, & Empson, S. B. (1999). *Children's mathematics: Cognitively guided instruction.* Portsmouth, NH: Heinemann.

Cawley, J. F., & Foley, T. E. (2000). Connecting math and science for all students. *Teaching Exceptional Children*, Missing issue and volume 14-19.

Chinn, P. C., & Hughes, S. (1987). Representation of minority students in special education classes. *Remedial and Special Education, 8* (4), 41-46.

Davison, D. (1994). Mathematics. In J. Reyhner (Ed.), *Teaching American Indian students mathematics*. Norman, OK: University of Oklahoma Press.

Davison, D. (2002). Teaching mathematics to American Indian students: A cultural approach. In J. E. Hankes & G. R. Fast (Eds.), *Changing the faces of mathematics: Perspective on indigenous people of North America*. Reston, VA: National Council of Teachers of Mathematics.

Deloria, V., & Wildcat, D. (2001). *Power and place: Indian Education in America*. Golden, CO: American Indian Graduate Center and Fulcrum Resources.

Demmert, W. (2001). *Improving academic performance among Native American students*. Charleston, WV: ERIC Clearinghouse on Rural Education and Small Schools. Washington, DC: U.S. Government Printing Office.

Devlin, K. (1998). Forget "back to basics." It's time for "forward to (the new) basics."

Retrieved from http://www.maa.org/devlin/devlin_3_98.html.

Dehyle, D., & Swisher, K. (1997). Research in American Indian and Alaska Native Education: From assimilation to self-determination. *Review of Research in Education*, 22(00), 113-194.

Donovan, M. S., & Cross, C. T. (2002). *Minority Students in special and gifted education*. Washington, DC: National Academy Press.

Elmore, R. F. (2002). Bridging the gap between standards and achievement: The imperative for professional development in education. Eric Document Reproduction Service No. ED475 871.

Empson, S. (1995). Using sharing situations to help children learn fractions. *Teaching Children Mathematics. NCTM:* Reston, VA: National Council of Teachers of Mathematics. 2(00), 156-161.

Frieberg. C. & School Consortium Members. (2002). *Linguistically and culturally diverse populations: American Indian and Spanish speaking*. Cooperative Educational Service Agency (CESA) No. 9. Tomahawk, WI.

Fiedler, C. R., Chiang, B., Van Haren, B., Halberg, S., & Boreson, L. (2008). Culturally Responsive Practices in Schools: A Checklist to Address Disproportionality in Special Education, *Teaching Exceptional Children*, 40 (5), 52-59.

Fuson, K. (1990). Issues in place value and multi-digit addition and subtraction learning and teaching. *Journal for Research in Mathematics Education*, 21 (4), 273-280.

Fuson, K. C. (1992). Research on whole number addition and subtraction. In D. Grouws (Ed.), *Handbook of research on mathematics teaching and learning*, New York: McMillan.

Ghaleb, M. S. (1992). *Performance and solution strategies of Arabic–speaking second graders in simple addition and subtraction word problems and relation of their performance to their degree of bilingualism*. Unpublished doctoral dissertation, University of Wisconsin Madison.

Gould, M. (2007). *Minorities in Special Education: A Briefing Before The United States Commission on Civil Rights* (Briefing Report). Retrieved from http://www.usccr.gov/pubs/MinoritiesinSpecialEducation.pdf.

Green, R. S. (2001). Closing the achievement gap: Lessons learned and challenges ahead. *Teaching and Change, 8* (2), 3-13.

Haycock, K. (2001). Closing the achievement gap. *Educational Leadership, 58* (6). 6-11.

Hankes, J. E. (1996). An alternative to basic skills remediation. *Teaching Children Mathematics*, 2 (6), 452-58.

Hankes, J. E. (1998). *Native American pedagogy and cognitive-based mathematics instruction.* New York, NY: Garland Press.

Hankes, J. E., & Fast, R. G. (2002). *Using Native American legends to teach mathematics.* Omro, WI: Honor Press.

Hankes, J. E., & Fast, R. G. (2002). Investigating the correspondence between Native American pedagogy and constructivist–based instruction. In J. E. Hankes & G. R. Fast (Eds.), *Changing the faces of mathematics: Perspective of indigenous people of North America.* Reston, VA: National Council of Teachers of Mathematics.

Hankes, J. E., Fast, G. R., Mahkimetas, M., LaTender, K., & Arndt, J. (2007). *Using action research to assess the effectiveness of cognitively guided instruction in a school district serving Native American students.* Manuscript submitted for publication.

Hannah-Jones, N. (2009). Improving minority education. *Washington Times.* Retrieved from http://www.washingtontimes.com/news/2009/dec/28/citizen-journalism-improving-minority-education//print/.

Harry, B. (1994). *The disproportionate representation of minority students in special education: Theories and recommendations.* Alexandria, VA: National Association of State Directors of Special Education

Harry, B., & Klingner, J. (2006). Why are so many minority students in special education? Understanding race and disability in schools. NY, NY: Teachers College Press.

Haycock, K. (2001). Closing the achievement gap. *Educational Leadership, 58* (6), 6-11.

Heller, K. A., Holtzman, W. H., & Messick, S. (1982). *Placing children in special education: A strategy for equity.* Washington, DC: National Academic Press.

Hillabrant, W., Romano, M., Stang, D., & Charleston, M. (1992). American Indianeducation at a turning point: Current demographics and trends [Summary]. In P. Cahape & C. B. Howley (Eds.), *Indian nations at risk: Listening to the people* (pp. 6–9). Charleston, WV: ERIC Clearing House on Rural Education and Small Schools.

Hosp, J., & Reschly, D. J. (2003). Referral rates for intervention or assessment: A meta-analysis of racial differences. *The Journal of Special Education*, 37 (2), 67-80.

Howley (Eds.), *Indian nations at risk: Listening to the people* (pp. 6–9). Charleston, WV: ERIC Clearing House on Rural Education and Small Schools

Ladner, M. (2007). *Minorities in special education: A briefing before the United States commission on civil rights,* Retrieved from: http://www.usccr.gov/pubs/MinoritiesinSpecialEducation.pdf.

Leary, J. P. (2009). What we know. What they need. Critical reflections on professional education and professional development. Power point slides retrieved from *http://www.docstoc.com/docs/18180972/What-We-Know-What-*They-Need.

Losen, D. J., & Orfield, G. (2002). *Racial inequity in special education.* Cambridge, MA: The Civil Rights Project at Harvard University, Harvard Education Press.

Loucks-Horsley, S., Stiles, K., & Hewson, P. (2005). Principles of effective professional development for mathematics and science education: A synthesis of standards. *National Institute for Science Education (NISE) Brief,* 1(1), page nbrs.

MMSD Mathematics Task Force. (2008). Primary level assessments. Madison Metropolitan School District, Madison, WI.

MindSong Math (2009). CMAG web site: *http://www.uwosh.edu/coehs/ mindsongmath/.*

Maccin, P. and Gagnon, J. C. (2002). Perceptions and Application of NCTM

Standards by Special and General Education Teachers, *Exceptional Children,* 68(00) 43-57.

National Council of Teachers of Mathematics. (1994). *Professional standards for teaching.* Reston, VA: National Council of Teachers of Mathematics.

National Council of Teachers of Mathematics. (2000). *Professional standards for teaching.* Reston, VA: National Council of Teachers of Mathematics.

Nelson-Barber, S., & Estrin, E. (1995). *Culturally responsive mathematics and science education for American Indian students.* San Francisco: Far West Laboratories for Educational Research and Development.

No Child Left Behind. (2001). Retrieved from http://www2.ed.gov/policy/ elsec /leg/esea02/index.html.

Peterson, P. L., Fennema, E., & Carpenter, T. P. (1991). Using children's mathematical knowledge. In B. Means (Ed.) *Teaching advanced skills to educationally disadvantaged students.* Menlo Park, CA: SRI Internationals.

Oswald, D. P., Coutinho, M. J., Best, A. M., & Singh, N. N. (1999). Ethnic representation in special education: The influences of school-related and demographic variables. *The Journal of Special Education, 32*(4), 194-206.

Reschly. (2007). Disproportionality and minority students. In S. Jimmerson, M. Burns, & A. VanDerHeyden (Eds.) *Addressing disproportionality with response to intervention.* NY:Springer.

Ross, J. A., Xu, Y. M., & Ford, J. (2008). The effects of a teacher in-service on low-achieving grade 7 and 8 mathematics students. *School Science and Mathematics.* Retrieved from *http://www.thefreelibrary.com/The+effects+ of+a+teacher+in-service+on+low-achieving+grade+7+and+8-a0191854790*

Roth, S. (1980). A revised model of learned helplessness in humans. *Journal of Personality,* 48(00), 103–133.

Sherman, W. H. (2008). No child left behind: A legislative catalyst for superintendent action to eliminate test-score aaps? *Educational Policy,* 22(5), 675–704.

Smith, T. (2004). Curricular reform in mathematics and science since a nation at risk. *Peabody Journal of Education, 79* (1), 105-129.

Soldier, L. W. (2005). *Indian Education Today,* New York, NY: Oneida Nation.

Starnes, Bobby. (2006). What we don't know can hurt them: White teachers, Indian children. *Phi Delta Kappan.* 87 (5).

Streefland, L. (1993). Fractions: A realistic approach. In T. Carpenter, E. Fennema, and T. Romberg (Eds.), *Rational numbers: An integration of research.* Hillsdale, NJ: Lawrence Erlbaum Associates.

Theobald, J. R. & Livingston, R. (2005). *Determining the effectiveness of collaboratively designed and implemented cultural curriculum on classroom pedagogy.* Unpublished master's thesis, University of Minnesota Duluth, MN.

Toppo, G. (2009, July 14). Young students improve, but later minority achievement gap remains. *USATODAY.com.* Retrieved from   *http://www.usatoday.com/news/education/2009-07-14-naep-minorities-achievement_N.htm.*

Trumbull, E., Nelson-Barber, S., & Mitchell, J. (2002). Enhancing mathematics instruction for Indigenous American students. In J. E. Hankes and G. R. Fast (Eds.), *Changing the faces of mathematics: Perspective on indigenous people of North America perspectives.* Reston, VA: National Council of Teachers of Mathematics.

Turnbull, A., Turnbull, R. , & Weymeyer, M. L. (2007). *Exceptional lives: Special education in today's schools* (5th ed). Upper Saddle River, NJ: Pearson Merrill Prentice Hall.

Villasenor, A. (1991). *Teaching the first grade mathematics curriculum from a problem–solving perspective.* Unpublished doctoral dissertation, University of Wisconsin Milwaukee, WI.

Wade, S. E. (ED) (2000). *Inclusive education: a casebook and readings for prospective and practicing teachers.* Lawrence Erlbaum Associates, Inc. Mahwa, NJ. Published in the Taylor & Francis e-library 2009.

Young, L. D., & Allin, J. M. (1986). Persistence of learned helplessness in humans. *Journal of General Psychology,* 113(00), 81–88.

Ysseldyke & Thurlow. (1997). *Assessment for effective intervention.* The National Center on Educational Outcomes.

Subject Index

About the Editor

Dr. Sheila T. Gregory is a mentoring faculty with Fielding Graduate University. In addition, she is the founder and managing partner of Dissertation Coaching Services. Dr. Gregory received her B.A. degree in Communications and Journalism from Oakland University, an M.P.A. degree in Health Care Administration from Wayne State University, and a Ph.D. in Higher Education Administration from the University of Pennsylvania, where she graduated with highest distinction.

In 2005, Sheila Gregory's sixth book, *Daring to Educate: The Legacy of the Early Spelman College Presidents*, was nominated for an NAACP Image Award. Also in 2005, she received the prestigious national award of *Teacher and Scholar of the Year*. Dr. Gregory has received numerous other awards beginning with her dissertation award in 1995 from the Black Caucus of the American Association for Higher Education (AAHE). Dr. Gregory has been the recipient of numerous scholarships, honors, awards and grants.

Dr. Gregory has served as a tenure-track faculty member at six institutions over the past 16 years, including Kingsborough Community College (CUNY) in Brooklyn, NY, Kennesaw State University in Atlanta, GA, the University of Nevada, Las Vegas, the University of Memphis, TN, Wayne State University, Detroit, MI, Fielding Graduate University, Santa Barbara, CA and Clark Atlanta University, Atlanta, GA. Dr. Gregory continues to work with several P-12 school districts on community service projects, curriculum development, mentoring programs, Small Learning Communities (SLC) and School Improvement Plans, including a two-year collaboration with the New Schools for New Orleans (NSNO) and the New Orleans Public School District (NOPSD) which provides opportunities for doctoral students to also serve as mentor and visiting teachers in the NOPSD.

Dr. Gregory is the author of six scholarly books, four dozen articles, book chapters, and other scholarly publications. In the past few years, she has been awarded and completed three Indigenous Visiting Research Scholar Appointments at the American University in Cairo, Egypt, the University of South Australia, Adelaide, and the University of the West Indies System in Jamaica, Barbados, and Trinidad-Tobago. Dr. Gregory has also consulted with the Shoshone-Bannock Tribal Association in Pocatello, Idaho, and the Las Vegas Piautes, in Nevada, where she trained and evaluated Non-Native American Indian teachers on the ways of knowing and learning within the Native American Indian culture. She continues to consult with numerous universities, community colleges, P-12 school districts, and tribal associations around the country and abroad.

Dr. Gregory's major research interests are in the areas of faculty and student recruitment and retention, professional and educational leadership, urban education, the development of women and girls, and student academic achievement with a special emphasis on race, ethnicity, class, and gender.

About the Contributors

Jim Barta, Ph.D. is an Associate Professor in the Regional Campus and Distance Education Program at Utah State University and has taught for over 30 years. He consults with teachers and districts in the state and throughout the region. Dr. Barta has taught students from Kindergarten to those completing their doctorate. He has taught in Alaska, Colorado, Oregon, Georgia, and Utah, as well as, in Canada, Great Britain, and Norway. He has been involved in multicultural mathematical educational research and curricular development for over 17 years, with a particular emphasis in Native American mathematics education. His current research involves working with Mayan teachers in the rural highlands of Guatemala in developing culturally responsive, mathematical professional development.

John Beam, Ph.D. is an associate professor of mathematics at the University of Wisconsin, Oshkosh and is a specialist in probability theory. His research interests include mathematics education and how culture influences student learning. His primary teaching responsibilities are in mathematics courses for pre-service elementary, middle, and high school teachers.

Fred Beauvais, Ph.D. is a Senior Research Scientist at the Tri-Ethnic Center (TEC) for Prevention Research at Colorado State University, in Fort Collins, Colorado. His doctoral degree is in clinical/counseling psychology. He has been with the TEC for 33 years, with most of his time devoted to the study of social problems among American Indian youth, with an emphasis on substance abuse issues. He has also maintained an interest in inhalant abuse, school dropout and suicide. He has been funded by the National Institute on Alcoholism and Alcohol Abuse, the National Institute on Drug Abuse and the National Science Foundation and has served on 10 grant review sections for these organizations. Dr. Beauvais has an adjunct faculty position in the psychology department at Colorado State. Dr. Beauvais has authored or co-authored over 130 book chapters and articles and served as a member of the NIAAA national advisory board. Over the years he has overseen the collection of data from over 75,000 Indian youth, whose data has been used by local communities to raise awareness of substance abuse problems, to evaluate intervention, to apply for prevention funding, and to inform policy decisions regarding allocation of resources for substance abuse prevention and treatment.

Stephan Carlson, Ph.D. is an Extension Educator/Professor at the University of Minnesota in Environmental Science Education.

Marilyn Cuch, M.S. is a Hunkpapa Lakota and a lecturer in secondary education for Utah State University, Uintah Basin. She has served most recently as the Education Director for the Northern Ute Indian Tribe in Northeastern Utah. With her bachelor's and master's degrees from Kansas State University, Marilyn's professional and academic background includes experience in secondary science education, curriculum development and instruction, public health, cultural awareness education and Tribal College teacher preparation. Her rich professional experience with the Native American populations in the United States and in Utah, will better enable Utah State University to meet critical education needs in the Uintah Basin and across the state.

Mia Dubosarsky, Ph.D. is a recent doctoral graduate from the science education department at the University of Minnesota's Department of Curriculum and Instruction. Mia has over 10 years of experience in designing, implementing and teaching science curricula to young children.

Virginia (Vini) Norris Exton, Ed.D. is an assistant professor in the School of Teacher Education and Leadership at Utah State University. She has been involved in literacy instruction and teacher education at the postsecondary level for 15 years, with an emphasis in Native American teacher education and recruitment. She has worked collaboratively with the Ute and Navajo Tribes to increase the numbers of Native American teachers in schools on or near indigenous communities. Her current research involves recruitment and program development for Native para-professionals in rural Utah who wish to become certified teachers.

Mary Farley, is the Interim Director of the White Earth Head Start program.

Gerald Fast, Ph.D. is a professor of mathematics education at the University of Wisconsin, Oshkosh. He has extensive experience investigating how culture influences mathematical thinking. In addition, in his articles related to this topic, he has co-authored with Dr. Hankes, the National Science Foundation volume, *Changing Faces of Mathematics: Perspectives of Indigenous Peoples of the Americas and Using Native American Legends to Teach Mathematics.* Dr. Fast also conducted research in Zimbabwe investigating the intuitive problem solving strategies of Zimbabwean children and mathematical misconceptions of Zimbabwean college students.

Henry H Fowler, Ed.D. is a Navajo. Dr. Fowler is a math teacher on the Navajo Reservation. He has been teaching for over 14 years. Dr. Fowler is of the "Bitter-Water" clan, born for the "Zuni-Edgewater" clan. His maternal grandfather is "Many Goats" and his paternal grandfather is "Red-running-into-the-Water." He is from Tonalea, Arizona. Dr. Fowler started his formal education at age four at Kaibeto Boarding School in Kaibeto, Arizona. He received his mathematics education degree from Northern Arizona University, and recently received his Ed. D in Educational Leadership and Change from Fielding Graduate University. His passion is promoting math literacy. He advocates social justice through mathematics. Dr. Fowler supports cultural relevant materials to guide math instruction and he creates instructional math materials based on the Navajo perspective. Dr. Fowler is also a math consultant and his research interest is in ethnomathematics.

Kay Fukuda, Ph.D. is an Associate Specialist and the Project Director for the Program for Afterschool Literacy Support (PALS) at the University of Hawai'I, at Manoa. Her interests include education for social justice, place-based education, and multicultural education. She does not hold a tribal affiliation.

Freda B. Garnanez, Ed. D. has spent 30 years working with Native American students, predominately Navajos, in the undergraduate and postgraduate education systems. She has made a career in higher education to work with young and elderly adults. During the 30 years, she served 10 years as an instructor and 13 years and an administrator in the community college system, including 7 years as an adjunct faculty in a doctoral program. Freda is a Navajo who was born into the "Redhouse" maternal clan and born for the "Water's Edge" paternal clan. She lives in Shiprock, NM with her husband and son. Having earned a Bachelor of Arts and Master of Science degrees, Freda received her Ed.D. in 2001, in the Department of Educational Leadership and Change from Fielding Graduate Institute in Santa Barbara, CA.

Judith Hankes, Ph.D. is a professor and teaches mathematics methods and classroom research courses. She is the author of numerous articles dealing with multi-cultural education issues and mathematics. Dr. Hankes' teaching career spans thirty years and includes primary level classroom teaching, counseling of at-risk high school students, coordinating gifted and talented programs, and mathematics in-service education for public and tribal schools nationally. She is also the founder and co-director of the University of Wisconsin's Oshkosh Intertribal Pre-College Program. Dr. Hankes is also the co-editor of two books entitled, *Changing Faces of Mathematics: Perspectives of Indigenous People of North America* (National Council of Teachers of Mathematics) and *Using Native American Legends to Teach Mathematics* (Honor Press). She is also the co-author of *Lost and Found and Found Again* (Whales Library), a primary level mathematics curriculum resource text and game.

Susan Devan Harness, M.A., works as a field director with the Tri-Ethnic Center for Prevention Research at Colorado State University in Fort Collins, Colorado. She received her Master's Degree in 2006 from Colorado State University in Cultural Anthropology. Ms. Harness is a member of the Confederated Salish Kootenai Tribes and has worked with Native communities for many years. Her work at the Tri-Ethnic Center has revolved around issues of substance and alcohol use, as well as issues of partner violence. Funded by the National Institute of Drug Abuse in the National Institutes of Health, Ms. Harness currently recruits rural schools with a significant number of Native students 7th through 12th grade to participate in the American Drug and Alcohol Survey. The survey is used to follow trends in drug and alcohol use over time, and correlate those trends with student's attitudes, beliefs and behaviors about drug and alcohol use within their social environments, such as school, friends and family. Ms. Harness's interest in American Indian trans-racial adoption has resulted in her book, *Mixing Cultural Identities Through Transracial Adoption: Outcomes of the Indian Adoption Project (1958-1967)*, released by Edwin Mellen Press.

ku`ualoha ho`omanawanui, Ph.D. is an Assistant Professor of Hawaiian literature, specializing in Hawaiian folklore, mythology, Oceanic literature, and indigenous perspectives on literacy. A key interest is place-based literature, literacy and learning. She is Native Hawaiian and also is the founding and current Chief Editor of *'Ōiwi: A Native Hawaiian Journal*.

Sandy L. Kewanhaptewa-Dixon, Ed.D. is Hopi and she received her doctorate in Educational Leadership and Change, from Fielding Graduate University in 2006. She is currently an assistant professor at California Polytechnic University, Pomona in the Ethnic & Women's Studies Department in the College of Education and Integrated Studies. Before teaching in higher education, Sandy taught special education in Los Angeles Unified School District, Los Angeles County Office of Education. She also worked at the Bureau of Indian Affairs for sixteen years and Sherman Indian High School. At Sherman, she served as the Special Education Coordinator and Curriculum & Instruction Coordinator and was a former Principal at Noli Indian School in San Jacinto, California. She is the CEO of *SKD Consulting* which provides educational consulting for Native American schools, school boards, teachers and parents. She has served on many educational school boards and commissions. She is the mother of two children

Ann Mogush Mason, M.Ed is a doctoral student in Culture and Teaching at the University of Minnesota's Department of Curriculum and Instruction. Annie has been an early childhood and elementary school teacher and is interested in using anthropological theory and methods to address issues related to justice in education.

Loretta Mason-Williams, Ph.D. is an assistant professor in the special education department at the University of Wisconsin, Oshkosh. She completed her bachelor's degrees in general and special education from the University of Dayton and her master's degree as a Reading Specialist at Loyola College in Baltimore, Maryland and earned her doctorate from the University of Maryland in Special Education. Prior to entering her doctoral program, she worked as a middle school special education teacher in Maryland, working collaboratively with general education teachers to provide the appropriate accommodations and supports to include students with a variety of strengths and needs. Her areas of research and expertise include teaching students with high incidence disabilities, the economics of education, and special education teacher

Colleen Merrill, M.B.A. brings a wealth of experience in sales, operations and project management to her role of data collection/analysis for the project, *Closing the Mathematics Achievement Gap of Native American Students Identified as Learning Disabled.* As a non-traditional graduate earning both her bachelor's degree and her MBA from UW, Oshkosh, she understands the value of education, and helping others achieve the goals they set for themselves. Colleen believes all children have the right to culturally responsive material that is effectively integrated through cognitively guided and differentiated instruction.

William Mickleson, Ph.D. is an assistant professor in the Department of Mathematics and Computer Science at the University of Wisconsin, Whitewater. He has had extensive experience working with schools serving Native American reservation communities, with a focus on the culturally relevant constructivist approach to American Indian learning of mathematics, science, and statistics. Titles of his national conference presentations include *Jumping Frogs and Gummy Bears* at the Coeur D'Alene Tribal School and *A Culturally Relevant Constructivist Approach to American Indian Learning of Mathematics, Science, and Statistics.*

Kimberly Miller, Ph.D. is am Alabama Cherokee and is a Research Associate at the Tri-Ethnic Center for Prevention Research, within the Department of Psychology. at Colorado State University. Dr. Miller has degrees in Psychology from Auburn University (BA), Ball State University (MA), and Colorado State University (Ph.D.). She is also an alumnus of the American Psychological Association Minority Fellowship Program. Clinically, Dr. Miller has worked with diverse clients in both inpatient and outpatient settings. Her areas of expertise include: assessment, substance abuse, eating disorders, meaning in life, and depression. She has received several grants for her research and is currently funded by the National Institutes on Drug Abuse for the grant: *Drug use among young Indians: Epidemiology and Prediction* and the Administration for Children and Families for the grant: *Health Care Literacy for Head Start Families. PROJECT HOME: Healthcare Options Made Easy.* Dr. Miller's responsibilities include serving as a cultural liaison between the project team and the tribes, data collection and analysis and the development of presentations and publications.

Barbara Murphy, M.A. is the Coordinator of the Early Childhood Programs and Director of the Shirley G. Moore Laboratory School in the Institute of Child Development at the University of Minnesota. She has been an early childhood teacher and teacher educator for 30 years. Barbara is a past president of the Minnesota Association for the Education of Young Children and one of the founders of the Minnesota Reggio Network; a grassroots organization of early childhood teachers who are interested in learning about the world-renowned early childhood programs of Reggio Emilia, Italy and improving their teaching. In her work as an early childhood professional she has been committed to investigating and exploring the best ways to support the growth and development of young children. Her special areas of interest are the development of cognitive abilities, creativity and the integral nature of the arts to human development as well as key issues in environmental design for early childhood programs. Barbara Murphy has no Tribal affiliation, but is collaborating with other contributors that are Native American Indian educators.

Jean E. Ness, Ed.D. is a Principal Investigator and Project Director at the Institute on Community Integration at the University of Minnesota. Dr. Ness holds a bachelor's degree in elementary education and special education, a Masters' in Learning Disabilities and Emotional Disturbances, and an Ed.D. in Educational Policy and Administration. The focus of her work is in developing programs for and with American Indian high school and tribal college students to support the retention and completion of their goals. She also has extensive experience in dropout prevention strategy development. She is the co-author of a transition curriculum for American Indians that addresses key skill areas to prepare students for higher education and work, which was published in 2002, and is currently being implemented in BIA schools, school districts, and tribal and community colleges throughout the country. In addition, Dr. Ness is the co-author of a curriculum (2010) entitled, "The Young American Indian Entrepreneur" designed to prepare high school American Indian students to become small business-entrepreneurs.

Dennis W. Olson Jr., M.S. was appointed Mille Lacs Band Commissioner of Education in May 2009. In this role, Olson oversees the Band's educational programs and services, including the Nay Ah Shing Schools, early education, higher education, and the Boys and Girls Clubs of Mille Lacs. Prior to joining the Band, Olson served as project coordinator at the University of Minnesota's Institute on Community Integration and has worked with American Indian high school students in their transition to higher education, coordinated federal grant projects, and worked with students with disabilities. A member of the Fond du Lac Band of Ojibwe, Olson holds a BA degree from the University of Minnesota in American Indian studies, sociology, and communications. He also holds a, MA degree in liberal studies and MA degree in education from the University of Minnesota, Duluth.

Carl Rempp, M.S. began her teaching career in 1989 as a sixth grade teacher. Since 1997, she has been working directly with Indian Education serving as a classroom & special education teacher, assessment coordinator and principal at St. Francis Indian School and Todd County School Districts on the Rosebud Reservation in south central South Dakota. She has also served as adjunct faculty and student teaching supervisor in the education department with Sinte Gleska University in Mission, South Dakota. She is a member of the Ogalala Lakota Tribe of Pine Ridge. She holds a BA degree from the University of Nebraska, Kearney, with endorsements in elementary education and special education and an MA from Chadron State College in elementary administration. She began her doctoral studies program at the University of Nebraska, Lincoln in the area of Teaching, Learning and Curriculum, with an emphasis in Multicultural Education. She is a member of the Carnegie Program for the Educational Doctorate (CPED) Cohort and was named as the Program Coordinator for Multicultural/Diversity Education. The *Fortitude, Generosity, Bravery, Wisdom: Using Popular Culture to Teach Traditional Culture* began as a research project for a class at the University of Nebraska—Lincoln on using popular culture to teach literacy.

Gillian Roehrig, Ph.D. is an associate professor of science education in the department of Curriculum and Instruction at the University of Minnesota. Dr. Roehrig brings an existing collaborative relationship with the White Earth reservation and expertise in culturally responsive STEM education.

Stacey Skoning, Ph.D. is an assistant professor of special education at the University of Wisconsin - Oshkosh. Her B.S. Ed and M.S. ED were both in special education, while her doctorate is in curriculum and Instruction. As a K-12 teacher, she taught in many environments including elementary, middle, and high schools. Her teaching experience began in segregated special educational settings, before moving to a resource model and eventually, an inclusive teaching model. In these settings, she has taught students with Learning Disabilities, Emotional Disorders, Cognitive Disabilities, and Autism. Her current research focuses on developing new teaching methods and strategies that better support all students within the general education setting, whether they have disabilities or gifts and talents. She also is the editor of IN (Inclusion News).

Vincent Whipple, M.A. is a Navajo/Oglala Sioux educator with extensive work in Southern California tribal communities. He received a Master of Arts degree in American Indian Studies, with a specialization in Expressive Arts, from the University of California, Los Angeles. Vincent is the former Coordinator of the Native American Student Center at California State Polytechnic University, Pomona as well as a former Associate Instructor in the Dance Department at the University of California, Riverside where he taught American Indian dance utilizing Native artistic methodologies and traditional performance techniques. He served as Indian Education Director for Los Angeles and Orange Counties, California, administering K-12 student support services and programs on behalf of the American Indian Education Office within the California Department of Education. Vincent was also the Social Services Administrator and Cultural Heritage Director for the Morongo Band of Mission Indians, overseeing human services program delivery in a complex tribal government operation in Southern California. He spent several years on tour as a Principal Dancer and Performer with Hanay Geiogamah and the critically acclaimed American Indian Dance Theatre and also with Rosalie Jones and the Daystar Native American Modern Dance Theatre. Vincent currently serves as Artistic Director of the Wichozani Dance Theatre, a Native theater company concerned with the interdisciplinary creation, performance, and preservation of American Indian expressive art forms and cultural traditions.